THE ARC OF THE PENDULUM

A *Philosophy for Government in the 21st Century*

Charles Stewart Goodwin

University Press of America, Inc.
Lanham • New York • London

Copyright © 1996 by
University Press of America, ® Inc.
4720 Boston Way
Lanham, Maryland 20706

3 Henrietta Street
London, WC2E 8LU England

Library of Congress Cataloging-in-Publication Data

Goodwin, Charles Stewart.
The arc of the pendulum : a philosophy for government in the 21st
century / Charles Stewart Goodwin.
p.   cm.
Includes bibliographical references.
l. Federal government--United States. 2. Decentralization in
government--United States. 3. Political science--United States--
Philosophy.   I. Title.
JK325.G66   1996   320.473--dc20   96-29299 CIP

ISBN 07618-0481-1 (cloth: alk. ppr.)
ISBN 0-7618-0482-X (pbk: alk. ppr.)

O let America be America again—
The land that has never been ...
O, Yes,
I say it plain,
America never was America to me, And yet I swear this oath ——
America will be!

Langston Hughes

ALSO BY CHARLES STEWART GOODWIN

The Third World Century

A Resurrection of the Republican Ideal

This book is dedicated to Joe Hinkle, whose vision of government broadened my own.

Contents

Preface

A main theme of this book is derived from the persistence of several strains of our governmental philosophy and their varying applications at different periods in our history. This collective philosophy has transcribed an arc etching a path reaching from the supremacy of states, as exhibited under the Articles of Confederation of the 1780s, to active centrism, as exemplified by the Great Society of the 1960s. The position of the pendulum on the arc at any given time can be determined by the needs of the country and the mood of its people. I contend in this book that the needs of this country cry out for a transposition of American antifederalism along the pendulum's arc to the twenty-first century. I further contend that this transposition can realistically be accomplished, and describe several enabling methodologies.

Of the many primary and secondary sources I have consulted none has captured my imagination as did Charles L. Mee Jr.'s *The Genius of the People*.[1] The lessons I carried away from this book and its close inspection of the events during 1787 and 1788 remain fresh, are relevant to our current political challenges and provide hope for the future.

One especially important lesson emerges from the process that took place over the hot Philadelphia summer of 1787. Mee highlights its applicability despite the many years that have passed.

> What one sees, indeed, is a group of men forced by their differences into a succession of vexing or detestable compromises. A group of men forced, in one argument after another, to fall back to general principles in order to buttress their positions—to embrace general principles that finally, by the sheer force of logic, would have to promise liberty and justice for all.
>
> To be sure, these compromises did not at once eliminate slavery, or give the vote to women, or embrace the destitute. But the principles to which the delegates forced one another to resort placed the country on a course from which—so long as it adhered to the Constitution—there could never be a turning back: a course to an increasingly open form of government, open to both sexes, to all races, to the poor and the politically oppressed of other countries; to the free exercise of speech and press and religion (including the freedom to believe in no God); to the guarantee of due process equally to all; to ensuring that the system not be distorted by too great concentrations of power in large business concerns, or in the military, or in the office of president.[2]

Sometimes in the heat of debate and under the pressure of repeated crises each of us can forget these simple truths and basic principles. We shouldn't. They shine forth from post-revolutionary Philadelphia and are ready to guide us into the next century.

Another valuable lesson is the meaning of liberty, as it appeared to our founders.

Liberty in the eighteenth century meant not simply liberty from some intrusive outside power; it meant the active exercise of control over one's life, the possession of power in one's own hands. It meant government small enough and close enough to home to be directly accountable and responsive; it meant self-government; not government handed over to some remote lot of rulers. Strictly understood, the principle of local self-government meant a share of power more or less equal in wealth and status, not one dominated by one small group or another; that is to say, it meant democracy.[3]

Our recent record of voting and of governing indicates that we may have forgotten these principles. They wouldn't be bad ideals for us to strive toward or at the very least, to keep in mind.

Although they became somewhat unfairly known as antifederalists, and were only later rescued by Jefferson's talent for public relations to be called Republicans, those who most strongly favored local government advocated specific tenets which are positive in nature. Mee's summary of these tenets illustrates why I contend that the philosophy of antifederalism will be even more applicable to the twenty-first century than it was to the nineteenth.

A central government might best ensure order and even uniform standards of justice by way of uniform laws. But local governments were best able to see to it that individuals actually participated in their own government; controlled their own affairs; had the direct experience of governing themselves and so knew best from their own experience how to govern and what they could reasonably expect and demand from their representatives; and had the power, because their government was so close to them, to insist that the government do their bidding. Local government actually bred better citizens than did a central government which sent down its rules from on high to a distant, uninvolved, and even apathetic population. Local governments were indisputably the best guardians of the genius of self-government.[4]

In a previous book I argued for an accelerating reliance on localism for our governmental power.[5] In this book I intend to pursue the matter further by delving into the philosophy of antifederalism, not as some esoteric academic exercise, but as a practical rationale for grappling with the particular challenges this country faces.

These days our nation often seems to be stumbling about in a governmental wilderness. We appear rootless with no current philosophy to guide us toward logic and rationality. Our existing philosophies, conservatism and liberalism, are perched on extremes and most commonly attached as litmus tests to specific issues. Our national financial condition is so precarious as to severely restrict our freedom of action, proving an impediment to philosophical integrity.

Antifederalism expressed as localism is suited to adapt to the massive socio-economic changes likely over the next 50 years. These changes, coupled with our financial situation, indicate that the political, the social, and the economic restructuring that must come in the next decade or two will have to be significant. We are fortunate that such a philosophy as antifederalism exists in our heritage. Its precepts can be studied, its concepts applied.

Although the antifederalists lost the battle over the Constitution's ratification, they won important victories, such as the inclusion of the Bill of Rights and the conversion of important thinkers, among whom was Thomas Jefferson. In point of fact they were more *pro* than *anti*. They were *for* extensive citizen involvement in government. They were *for* citizen obligations. They were *for* preservation of the strength of state and local governments. They were *for* fiscal conservatism. They did express opposition to a large and powerful executive branch. They were fearful of an intrusive federal judiciary. In short, these antifederalist men and women espoused principles that have had value at many moments in our history. They have never been more relevant than they are today.

In the 1780s men did wear powdered wigs, tricorn hats and knee britches. Women wore elaborate hoop skirts. Transportation and communication were time consuming. Cities were small and settlements were scattered. We may now tend to sneer at these characteristics as evidence of a society that was horribly old-fashioned. However, eighteenth-century political thought was not primitive. It sparkled with classical knowledge and Enlightenment idealism. Dialogue radiated both common sense and hope for the future.

In the 1990s we can use a healthy dose of these qualities. In the following pages I will uncover many of them and illustrate how they may be applied to our version of democracy, and the continuation of our republican experiment. As I have railed against one or another of our government's failings over the years, I have from time to time been asked a pertinent question: "What would you do?" Sometimes I was able to reply, sometimes not. This book is my answer. It lays out a system. It is accompanied by a philosophy, mechanics, and specific solutions to specific problems. I recognize that there may be other valid paths to a feasible future for our government. For example, in a well reasoned recent book Michael Lind, editor of *The New Republic*, arrives at conclusions and solutions diametrically different from mine.[6] Nevertheless, this book espouses my ideas. It contains my opinions on the best course of action, given prevalent conditions. This book constitutes my path to optimism. It contains ingredients from my own experience in local government. It represents my hopes for the future.

---

[1] Charles L. Mee, Jr., *The Genius of the People* (New York: Harper & Row Publishers, Inc., 1987).

[2] Ibid., 4.

[3] Ibid., 52.

[4] Ibid., 183.

5 Charles Stewart Goodwin, *A Resurrection of the Republican Ideal* (Lanham, MD: University Press of America, 1995).

6 Michael Lind, *The Next American Nation* (New York: The Free Press, 1995).

Part I

Hope and Despair in the 1780s

CHAPTER 1

Inception Rhythms

In that year of 1783, the efforts of the United States to establish a republican government were unique in the world. Modern history presented no evidence that people could rule themselves. Even political philosophers who thought that the people might under some circumstances be able to do so, commonly believed that republican forms could only survive on a small scale.[1]

Parameters of the New Nation

If we are to transpose pre-constitutional antifederalism to the next century we first have to perceive its applicability. With this in mind, this chapter will inspect a few characteristics of our nation as it emerged from the revolution against Britain.

In 1787 the United States was composed of thirteen entities situated along a ribbon of territory bordering the Atlantic Ocean. Over 80 percent of its 3.8 to 3.9 million inhabitants lived within two days travel of the coast.[2] Most of the people were clustered around communities, farms, and small businesses, loosely bound by ties of extended family or national origin or religious similarity. Professor Gordon S. Wood of Brown University succinctly sketched this social fabric.

The family remained the primary institution for teaching the young, disciplining the wayward, and caring for the poor and insane. No wonder that the colonists believed that society was little more than a collection of family households, to which all isolated and helpless individuals necessarily had to be attached. Everywhere families reached out and blended almost imperceptibly into the larger community. Sometimes colonial communities seemed to be only enlarged families.[3]

These strings of cohesive communities were, among other things, ideal territory for the creation of a series of little republics. That is what pre-constitutional America most closely resembled—skeins of little republics.

More than 90 percent of the American population was rural. The largest city was Philadelphia with 40,000 inhabitants. Next in order of size came New York with 33,000, Boston with 18,000, Charleston with 16,000 and Baltimore with 13,000 residents. These cities were minuscule compared to the metropoli of Europe. In 1787 London contained 950,000 people amidst a nation of 10 million. Paris had 600,000 residents surrounded by 25 million French. Even the 19 million living in Latin America with cities such as Mexico City, Lima and Bogota, dwarfed their northern neighbors. The rural ambiance and small urban centers of the United States were critical to the development of our particular blend of political philosophies.

As might be expected, the population of the United States was largely white—3.2 million of them in fact. African-Americans fell into two categories. There were 60,000 who were free. There were 700,000 of them who were slaves. For the purposes of calculating population to determine the number of elected representatives, slaves, as a concession to the South, were deemed three-fifths of a person by the Constitution. For these purposes the figure of 420,000 was added to the population of the several slave states. By 1787 New England had relatively few slaves. Massachusetts reported none in a population of 475,189 and New Hampshire had 157 in a population of 144, 885. By contrast, the South had large numbers. Virginia reported 293,000 slaves out of 747,610 people. South Carolina had a mixture of 140,178 white persons and 107,000 African-American slaves. In addition, it may be worth noting that by 1790 between two-thirds and three-quarters of all immigrants to this country who were not slaves had been bound or indentured laborers, with an average term of service of four years.[4] In an important sense, then, this country had been founded upon bondage— for both white and black. This contributed to and sustained its lust for freedom.

The white population of the new United States was virtually all Euro-sourced. About 60 percent came from England, 10 percent from Ireland, 8 percent from Scotland, 7 percent from various German states and 3 percent from France. The majority religion was Protestantism. There were 575,000 Congregationalists, 500,000 Anglicans, 400,000 Presbyterians and 300,000 were either Quakers, Dunkers, Mennonites, Lutherans or Dutch Reform. Less than 25,000 Americans were Catholic in 1790.[5] This is significant in one philosophical aspect: both the Enlightenment and Protestantism were deeply entwined in the thoughts and beliefs of most American citizens.

When our ancestors traveled in the late 1780s it was an arduous process. There were no railroads. There were turnpikes, but none were paved. There were only a handful of small canals. The first great one, the Erie Canal, wasn't completed until 1822. Steamboats were just being tested. John Fitch tried his out in 1786 and James Rumsey introduced his for trial runs the following year.

Most people clattered over the cobblestones of cities and squelched through the mud or dust of highways on horseback, in wagons and in carriages. Road travel was possible along most of our seaboard. There was a continuous system of highways that stretched from Boston to Savannah. There were stagecoaches on the most well-traveled routes. The first regular service had been established in New Jersey in 1732 to go from Burlington to Amboy. Progress by coach was slow and often uncomfortable. It took three days of traveling 18 hours per day to go from New York to Philadelphia. More rapid movement was done by horseback. In 1774 Paul Revere made five separate journeys of 6 days each between Boston and Philadelphia. This was considered breathtakingly fast even in 1790.

Perhaps the easiest travel was by sail, between those areas lucky enough to have a major port nearby. Of course, weather played an important part in the speed, and the comfort, of any particular passage. There was a network of regularly scheduled sailing packets between major American ports as well as between those ports and Europe.

Although the states were oriented on a north-south axis, there were a number of routes to the frontiers, which were relatively close. The frontier at this time was found in the western sectors of New York, Pennsylvania, Virginia, North Carolina, and Georgia. These areas abutted sparsely settled territories largely out of United States' control. Some bordered Native American nations such as the Iroquois, the Cherokee, and the Creek. Some touched Spanish or French possessions. All trans-frontier areas were viewed as a potential land of opportunity by our citizens who began to flow West with the slightest urging, regardless of whether land title was legally possible. The real westward tide of expansion began after 1790, a scant fifteen years following Daniel Boone's blazing of his famous trail through the Cumberland Gap from Virginia into Kentucky.

Westerners in general tended to be the most independent of our citizens. They were of necessity skilled in the use of firearms, and could protect themselves. They were also opposed to government interference in their lives. Most of our radical politics were sited in these areas, as were those armed uprisings that occurred.

Health care in the young United States was extremely basic. While there were some centers of relatively advanced practices, and two medical schools (in Philadelphia and New York) most citizens had to make do with primitive care and home remedies. There were inoculations in existence to guard against some diseases. Smallpox was one of these. But reception of these preventatives was actually illegal in many locations. At the very least they were looked upon with superstition. For example, Thomas Jefferson obtained a smallpox inoculation surreptitiously in 1767 for himself, but the rest of his family refused to undergo the procedure. Thus, epidemics flourished from the absence of preventatives and from poor sanitation. Hospitals were few, primitive and often filthy. The ravages of diet and disease produced an average life span in 1790 of 34.5 years for men and 36.5 for women. The average married woman produced six offspring during her lifetime, of which two usually survived to be teenagers.

Overall health was not aided by the high-fat consumption and by the enormous amounts of alcohol imbibed. The average American adult of over fourteen had an absolute alcohol content intake of 5.8 gallons annually derived generally from fermented cider and home-made whiskey. This was an enormous amount, nearly twice the levels seen in Europe. Foreign observers of our new nation repeatedly commented upon the amount of alcohol consumed. Consumption was to continue upward to a peak level of 7.1 gallons per adult in 1833, before plunging to 1.8 gallons by 1845 as temperance societies flourished and habits changed.

Another characteristic of the new United States that was universally noted was its industriousness. Our early citizens were a hard working, profit-oriented people. One of the main reasons they or their ancestors had come here in the first place was to have the opportunity to make something of themselves. Commerce abounded and was respected, unlike the situation in Europe where it was often held in contempt. Farms were lush and prolific and the country was largely self-sufficient agriculturally. Rice and indigo were the major crops of the deep South (cotton had yet to spread). The mid-Atlantic and New England states grew large quantities of wheat and corn. Vegetables and meat of various types were found everywhere.

Industrial prosperity existed as well. The United States produced one-seventh of the world's iron supply in 1790 and was dotted with small mills and factories. Our most productive early inventor, Oliver Evans, created a machine for carding wool (in 1777), an automatic flour mill (in 1785) and a steam engine (in 1787). Seth Thomas began to manufacture clocks in Plymouth Hollow, Connecticut in 1785. By 1790 the United States had the capacity to produce 25,000 deadweight tons per year of shipping. American ship owners possessed 127,000 deadweight tons for their own account. Most ships were used in trade with Europe and the Caribbean as well as for whaling.

Small businesses popped up everywhere, especially in the Northeast. Quite naturally these were accompanied by combinations of laborers that today we would call unions. The largest of these organized labor entities was the Federal Society of Cordwainers, which conducted strikes and protests as early as 1774.

The financial wherewithal that ran the engines of government and industry (which were often combined in joint associations) was in many cases funneled through domestic banks. The first private commercial bank, the Bank of North America, was chartered by Congress in 1781. Alexander Hamilton's Bank of New York was also born that year. On December 12, 1791 the First Bank of the United States, the ancestor of the Federal Reserve System, opened its first office in Philadelphia. Thus an indigenous financial network, to supplement capital from Europe, had developed by the time our Constitution was ratified. In 1787 the total public debt was $77.1 million of foreign debt and $18.2 million of assumed state debt. Most of the debt was left over from the war and awaited the remedial actions of the new Secretary of the Treasury, Alexander Hamilton. He had at his command a burgeoning economy with its growing manufacturing sector, millions of acres of public lands to sell and, most of all, a population that was willing to work. The population was also willing to speculate, largely in land. Many of our great figures, such as George Washington, were lifelong land speculators. Although ideological purists, such as Jefferson and Madison, often professed distaste for financial speculators—particularly those engaged in buying government bonds at a discount—both of them bought and sold land. So endemic was the rise and fall of speculators (who often ended up in debtors' prison) that it rarely caused comment or drew criticism. Even as our Constitution was being written, two of its major contributors, Robert Morris and James Wilson, were experiencing severe financial setbacks. Both died bankrupt, Wilson as a sitting Associate Justice of the Supreme Court in flight from his creditors.

The people of the United States were at least as well informed and as well educated as their European contemporaries. Taken together and compared to other nations, they were more so. Most communities had elementary schools. Many had the equivalent of high schools, which often overlapped the functions of college. There were ten institutions of higher learning in this country at the time of the Constitution.[6] In addition, there were specialty schools, such as the law school run in Williamsburg by George Wythe or the one in Litchfield, Connecticut conducted by Tapping Reeve.

Our ancestors were especially interested in, involved with and informed about politics. America possessed 37 newspapers in 1775, which promulgated information and opinion. By 1790 the young nation had 92 newspapers. Of these eight were daily, 70 were weekly and 14 were bi-weekly. Finally, a national postal service had functioned since colonial days under the aegis of Benjamin Franklin and it facilitated the rapid (for the times) transmission of correspondence.

The young United States was thus a small but prosperous nation. It was basically a vast middle class with very little abject poverty and only a minor sprinkling of great wealth. The people were often contentious. They favored individual freedom. They respected law, but demanded explanations for any directives. They were adventuresome, constantly probing frontiers, new businesses and different lifestyles.

This prolific, hardy, intrepid, industrious population generally agreed with the philosophy of Cato the Elder, Censor of Rome. "Our republic was not made by the services of one man, but of many, not in a single lifetime, but through many centuries and generations."[7] They lived in the present but thought of the community and built for the future.

Propinquity to Revolution

Perhaps the most significant aspect of the collective psyche in 1787 was that this country was only a few years removed from a bitter six-year war of independence with Great Britain. Stanley Elkins and Eric McKittrick, writing in *The Age of Federalism,* understood this factor. "What sets the men of this generation apart from those of any other in American history is that their every response to virtually every question of a public nature was conditioned by their having just been through a revolution."[8] Let us take a moment to inspect a few of the ways in which the revolution impacted policy and activity in the 1770s, 1780s, and 1790s.

Most families and communities had seen the ravages and divisiveness of war first hand. Many people had a loved one who was under arms, even wounded. Strife between loyalist Tories and revolutionist Whigs had split neighborhoods, fractured families and separated friends. Economic and political chaos had left citizens bruised and fearing a reprise of conflict. The fruits of liberty seemed sweet and had been hard won. Few wanted to risk having to try again.

Another factor left over from the war era loomed over the Constitution's creation and ratification. In the years prior to 1776 most of those colonists opposed to Great Britain had come to believe that there had been a giant conspiracy conducted against their rights and their welfare. They believed that a coterie of powerful ministers and royal favorites, led by the shadowy figure of the Earl of Bute, were conspiring to deprive Americans of their liberty. The newspapers and pamphlets of the time commented extensively on conspiracy. Historian Bernard Bailyn stresses that the well-known corruption of British and colonial officials was behind these fears. "In the end I was convinced that the fear of a comprehensive conspiracy against liberty throughout the English-speaking world—a conspiracy believed to have been nourished in corruption, and of which, it was felt, opposition in America was only the most immediately visible part—lay at the heart of the Revolutionary movement."[9] No less a figure than John Adams wrote on this subject as early as 1765. "There seems to be a direct and formal design on foot to enslave all America. This, however, must be done by degrees. The first step that is intended seems to be an entire subversion of the whole system of our fathers by the introduction of the canon and feudal laws into America."[10]

As intimated by Adams, the initial aim of this perceived conspiracy was to be the proliferation of the Anglican Church, using the influence of the state. The next imagined aim was to be the dilution of the colonial judiciary, an issue which heated up in the 1760s as the British denied life tenure to judges in their American colonies. Life tenure had existed in England since 1701. Furthermore, the British government attempted to control judicial appointments, setting off legislative rows in Pennsylvania, New York, North Carolina and Massachusetts in turn. Colonials saw their judiciary destined to become just one more cog in the ministerial patronage machine rather than what it had been—a respected group of independent arbiters acting as the guardians of liberty.

The Sugar Act (1764), The Stamp Act (1765), The Townshend Duties (1768), The Tea Act (1773) and finally, The Quartering Act (1774) served to heighten these conspiracy fears. The Quartering Act arose from the arrival of substantial bodies of regular troops, ostensibly to maintain order. Thus the disestablishment of religion, maintenance of an independent judiciary and absence of standing armies became associated with liberty in the minds of most new United States citizens. Any attempt to tamper with them revived the spectre of conspiracy and of domination by an overbearing center.

Any measure suspected of being a threat to liberty was fiercely resisted. It was this attitude, replete with memories and fears from revolutionary days not so long past, that prevailed in the minds in many quarters as the new nation prepared to debate the merits of a constitution. The antifederalists were especially alarmed by any accrual of power at the center of government, which could be regarded as a precursor to oppression. Bernard Bailyn described the nature of their reaction and the resulting confrontation.

> Because the antifederalists saw corruption and lust for power everywhere, they argued that the weaker the power available, the less harm the manipulation of power could do. The federalists argued that the problem in the American situation had been exaggerated. Yes, people were innately evil and self-seeking, and, yes, no one could be trusted with unconfined power. That was as true in America as anywhere else. But under the Constitution's checks and balances power would be far from unconfined, and for such a self-limiting system there would be virtue enough for success.[11]

Thus the ideological battle lines came to be drawn. The compromise that eventually convinced the antifederalist moderates, by allaying their worst fears, and eventually won the day for the Constitution, was an agreement to adopt a Bill of Rights. Its necessity arose directly from the experiences of pre-revolutionary colonials, and the propinquity of these trials to the Constitutional Convention.

Mileposts on the Road to a Constitution

The Constitutional Convention of 1787 didn't just happen spontaneously. There were several defining events which transformed the malaise developing under the infirm rule of the Articles of Confederation into a movement actively desiring to change the mode of government.

Perhaps the most pervasive was the 41 months of depression lasting from 1784 through 1788. During that period the crushing impact of debts left over from the war was exacerbated by the inability of government at all levels to generate adequate revenue. Compounding the difficulties posed by persistently large debt levels were the high rates of inflation that raged in the years preceding the economic collapse. A symptom of these times was the widespread speculation in real estate, especially on the frontier. Most delegates to the Convention were engaged in such speculation and several were heading rapidly towards bankruptcy as the proceedings unfolded. They symbolized the distress that raged throughout the nation whose economy lay in tatters.

The economic distress which left thousands destitute heightened the push for reform. Procedurally the momentum of governmental reform developed from a rather unlikely source. For decades there had been discussions to determine the navigational and commercial rules that would apply to the Potomac River. In 1785 a meeting of the Potomac River Commission was held at Mt. Vernon. It involved delegates from Virginia and Maryland. At that meeting, instead of discussing canals and oyster harvests, it was decided to hold a convention at Annapolis in September of 1786 to discuss broader economic topics. That convention was attended by the delegates from only five states (Virginia, New York, Pennsylvania, New Jersey and Delaware). Despite the sparse attendance, the efforts of Alexander Hamilton and James Madison produced a resolve to convene an even more comprehensive convention in Philadelphia in May of 1787. The purpose of this convention would be to revise the Articles of Confederation under which the nation was being governed. Significantly, in the minds of many who attended and those who supported them, this gathering became a Constitutional Convention, and delegates eventually straggled in from 12 of the 13 states (all except Rhode Island). The almost unconscious transformation of a revision of the Articles of Confederation into a Constitutional Convention was to have important consequences for the ratification process. Most importantly, one of those delegates in attendance was the only man who could unify the country, General George Washington of Virginia. His very presence, even if not accompanied by oration, served to sanction the proceedings in the eyes of the disparate factions at large in the nation.

Catalyst for a Constitution

One event more than any other jolted moderates into action and made potential founders who, like Washington, were wary of conventions and massive changes in government, realize that something had to be done. That event was Shays' Rebellion.

Captain Daniel Shays was a 39 year old war veteran who had served with distinction. He was a farmer in western Massachusetts. Like many frontier veteran-farmers, he was in debt and in serious financial difficulties. In those days the remedy for debt was debtors prison, a fate to which thousands had been consigned.

Shays and his compatriots felt they had not fought an eight-year struggle for national existence just to live in an environment dominated by wealthy conservative elites, in this case epitomized by Massachusetts Governor James Bowdoin. In October of 1786 Shays and his followers began to seize courthouses in the western part of the state to prevent the courts from sitting and throwing farmers into prison. They hoped to suspend legal activities until the legislative elections in the spring of 1787, in which they were confident of a victory. That would change the system to their advantage.

Governor Bowdoin reacted quickly and decisively. He dispatched General Benjamin Lincoln with 4,400 troops to put down the uprising. After a couple of skirmishes in the snow, the rebels were dispersed and order was superficially restored. The repercussions were dramatic. Those leaders, such as Washington, who realized the plight of these poor frontier farmers was not unique, feared the outbreak of another revolution. They were galvanized to support a Constitutional Convention that would strengthen the ability of their government to deal with its socio-economic problems and stave off further unrest.

In Massachusetts itself the political ends advocated by Shays and his followers were largely achieved. In the spring elections the conservatives lost their legislative control to a pro-Shaysite majority. Governor Bowdoin was turned out of office in favor of John Hancock, who ran on a moderate, amnesty for the rebels, platform. Measures were passed that reduced the financial and legal burdens on the poor.

The stage was thus set for the Constitutional Convention. Federalists and antifederalists marshaled their philosophical principles. Delegates were elected. The new nation prepared for another beginning.

---

1 James Thomas Flexner, *Washington: The Indispensable Man* (New York: Penguin Books, 1984), 174.

2 Closeness to the littoral is still true. In 1994 the Census Bureau reported that 54% of all Americans lived within 50 miles of the shore.

3 Gordon S. Wood, *The Radicalism of the American Revolution* (New York: Vintage Books division of Random House, 1991), 44.

4 Richard B. Morris, *Forging of the Union 1781–1789* (New York: Harper & Row Publishers, 1987), 175.

[5] Page Smith, *The Shaping of America* (New York: Penguin, 1980), 3:313.

[6] They were or became: Harvard; Yale; Princeton; William & Mary; Columbia; Rutgers; Dartmouth; Pennsylvania; Brown; Virginia, and Rhode Island.

[7] Donald R. Dudley, *The Civilization of Rome* (New York: Penguin Books, 1960), 38.

[8] Stanley Elkins and Eric McKittrick, *Age of Federalism: The Early American Republic 1788 -1800* (New York: Oxford University Press, NY 1993), 78.

[9] Bernard Bailyn, *The Ideological Origins of the American Revolution* (Cambridge, MA: Belknap Press of Harvard University Press, 1992), XIII.

[10] John Adams, *The Works of John Adams*, ed. Charles Francis Adams (Boston 1850-1856), 3:464.

[11] Bernard Bailyn, *The Ideological Origins of the American Revolution* (Cambridge, MA: Belknap Press of Harvard University Press, 1992), 368-9.

CHAPTER 2

The Crucible of Antifederalism

I have but one lamp by which my feet are guided, and that is the lamp of experience. I know no way of judging the future but by the past.

Patrick Henry
23 March 1775

Preamble to Antifederalism

The term *antifederalism* appears in several different forms in various literary works. I have seen the following: antifederalism (with and without capitals); Anti-Federalism (also with and without capitals); Anti Federalism (again, both capitalized and not) and anti-Federalism. I have chosen to use the non capitalized, non hyphenated, one word form, mainly because it is simpler. Quotes, of course, are cited as written. Federalist, in its several incarnations, is capitalized when it refers to the political party of that name and not capitalized when it refers to a system of beliefs. There was no specific antifederalist party. It was a term of collective referral until Jefferson began his overt opposition in 1798.

The *Oxford English Dictionary* defines *Federal*: "Of or pertaining to, or the nature of, that form of government in which two or more states constitute a political unity while remaining independent as to their internal affairs."

It has an alternate definition listed under *United States History*: "Favoring a strong federal, i.e. central government."

Antifederalists in the late 1780s would likely have concurred with the first definition as a reasonable description of government but vigorously disagreed with the second. The word *federal* itself is derived from the Latin *foederal*, which in turn came from both *foedus*, meaning treaty or compact, and *fidere* meaning to trust. Antifederalists considered themselves proponents of a compact republic (comprised of a confederation linked by mutual treaties among a group of commonly associated republics) and believers in the value of personal trust. They were fiercely independent, and reacted very negatively when any government outside their state, or even their locality, tried to tell them what to do.

The connotation of the word *antifederalism* is negative. This resulted from an astute act of political imagery on the part of those favoring a stronger central government who called themselves Federalists. Essayists, pamphleteers, and other publicists built on the initial coining of the terms *foederal* and *antifoederal* by Noah Webster, who was describing the two opposing factions in 1786. One of these pamphleteering politicians was James Madison. When he later came to espouse certain antifederalist tenets, under the influence of Thomas Jefferson, he helped popularize new names for their opposition party. First the party was called Republican, and then Democratic-Republican.

Antifederalists were not really *anti*. As noted earlier, they were for many principles. They helped mold some of our great concepts. We will outline their achievements in the next two chapters.

Along with many other *antis*, such as the Anti-Masonic Party, antifederalism as a label slipped into an historical void. In a political sense it was reborn as Democratic-Republicanism and the Jacksonian Democratic party, both ancestors of the current Democrats. Philosophically, however, the antifederalists of the 1780s were closer to the populists of the late nineteenth century and the libertarians of the 1990s.

Philosophical Antecedents

The cornerstone of antifederalist philosophy was contained in Montesquieu's *The Spirit of the Laws* published in 1748. This work advocated separation of powers among a legislature, a judiciary, and an executive. "Montesquieu identified liberty with a life lived under the rule of law."[1] He favored taxes on consumption, international free trade and an important socio-political role for women. His "little republic" theory used Greek city states, as well as the United Netherlands and Swiss Cantons from his era, as examples of confederational governing bodies to be emulated. He favored a political entity of small enough size so that people could know each other and could take turns temporarily serving in official positions. Montesquieu was a frequent correspondent of Scottish Enlightenment figures David Hume and

Adam Smith, with whom he debated issues and with whom he often disagreed. His work was essential reading for every educated colonial American.

Machiavelli, particularly in his *Discourses* displayed an appreciation of the Roman Republic. The Roman system of government fit the natural inclination of Americans better than did the Greek city states, and therefore served as their model. Thus inspired, Americans admired citizen heroes such as Cincinnatus, Cicero, and Cato the Elder who served as reference points for their own leaders. Little republics emulating Rome gathered together in confederations and founded upon Montesquieu's principles formed the basis for the antifederalist theory of government. Acceptance of Montesquieu, tempered with philosophers of the Enlightenment, assisted Americans in adapting some of the concepts conveyed along the philosophical chain from Aristotle and Aquinas. Specifically, the philosophical view that deference to authority was natural, and consent of the governed need not always be obtained, was modified into a form of democracy more familiar to us today.

The philosophers of the Scottish Enlightenment, especially John Locke and David Hume, influenced the thinking of most politically aware Americans, particularly those destined to support federalism. Locke's *The Second Treatise of Government* and Hume's *Political Discourses of 1752* helped form the governmental thinking of many great American statesmen. Hume had advanced the idea, antithetical to Montesquieu, that a large republic could be an ideal seat for the practice of democracy. Students at the several colonial colleges came under the direct tutelage of noted Enlightenment scholars. One such scholar destined for greatness was James Madison, who attended the College of New Jersey (later Princeton). Princeton's president was John Witherspoon, who took office in 1768. He was a Scot who had studied at Edinburgh University under several of the Enlightenment's leading figures and then had become a Presbyterian minister. Witherspoon was a dynamic and inspirational teacher who taught nine of the signers of our Constitution.[2] Fifty-six of his students became state legislators. Thirty-three of them became judges, three of whom sat on the United States Supreme Court. Twelve students became state governors. Twenty-nine were elected to the House of Representatives. Twenty-one became United States Senators. One would become vice president—Aaron Burr. Madison was elected president. During the immediate pre-revolutionary years Witherspoon was an academic with considerable political impact. He was also an American patriot, serving in the Continental Congress and signing the Declaration of Independence. He epitomized the theoretical and practical philosophical impact transmitted at our institutions of higher learning.

Along with Montesquieu and the philosophers of the Scottish Enlightenment, American political intellectuals spiced their thoughts with French writers, led by Jean Jaques Rousseau and Michel Montaigne, who enlarged the idea of social contract. Englishmen John

Milton and James Harrington contributed as well. Milton discussed how a society could develop truth from below. Harrington elaborated on how government by discussion could flourish in the extended republic. What emerged was a cadre of educated, literate, and articulate individuals deeply committed to putting into practice a self-governing nation featuring active political debate. They were well-versed in the several theories of government and their philosophical articulations were well-researched and supported. Moreover, their written and oral expositions of these theories were widely comprehended.

republican Concepts

Those incipient federalists and antifederalists within whom the yearnings for self-rule were stirring were imbued with a conceptual core that inspired their thoughts and actions. Before we move on to uncover their activities, we should take a closer look at a few of these concepts.

James Madison gave his basic definition of a republic in *Federalist 39*, first published in the New York *Independent Journal* on January 16, 1788. "We may define a republic to be, or at least may bestow that name on, a government which derives all its powers directly or indirectly from the great body of the people; and is administered by persons holding their offices during pleasure for a limited period, or during good behavior."

The early political activists understood that there were two types of republics. One was called a *compact* republic. Its entities (cantons in Switzerland, states in the United Netherlands) assumed the role of independent individuals and voluntarily agreed, via a written compact, to associate in a confederation to achieve certain ends (common defense or economic advantage).

The second was called a *compound* republic. When the Constitution was ratified, this country became a compound republic despite the frequent attempts of states' rights advocates to define our nation otherwise. Our compound republic was defined by Professor Samuel Beer. "The core of the idea is that the sovereign American people, who did ordain the Constitution, far from having been constituted by the various state people at the time of ratification, had already existed for a generation and indeed was the sovereign power which had created the states in the first place and had given them such authority as they did or ever would possess."[3] The locus of legitimacy in a compound republic was the nation as a whole, and it has since remained so.

The Articles of Confederation which governed from 1776 to 1787 described a compact republic. The new Constitution created a compact republic, which has existed from 1787 onwards. As we look forward into the coming century, portions of both of these conceptual republics can be applicable. Specifically, the overall compound republic can contain confederations of small republics, which can exercise considerable autonomy.

Back in the late 1780s, the emerging republic, or republics, depending upon the particular definition, professed an overriding sentiment—a desire for liberty. Madison in *Federalist 37*, which was first published on January 11, 1788, concisely defined the American version of liberty. "The genius of republican liberty demands not only that all power should be derived from the people, but that those entrusted with it should be kept in dependence upon the people." In the political sense then, liberty meant participation to these nascent United States citizens. It meant the ability to have a personal say in the governing of their lives, an ability that had been denied them as colonials. This liberty would be important, and be exercised, regardless of the type of republic.

Jeremiah Atwater, later the first president of Middlebury College, delivered a sermon in the year 1801 when he was 28 years old. In it he gave a another summary of how liberty was generally regarded during our early national period. "Liberty, if considered as a blessing, must be taken in a qualified sense. The freedom which it implies, must be limited, not absolute freedom; unless we will pronounce government itself a curse; for the very idea of government always supposes some restraint." The people of the constitutional era generally had Atwater's idea of liberty, once their revolt and its immediate aftermath had passed. They accepted the conceptual fact of restraint. What they did argue about was the precise nature of the government and its attendant restrictions on their activities. Federalists and antifederalists primarily fell into conflict over the location of power. Secondarily they argued over the size of their governmental entities. Federalists wanted the locus in the center and have government backed by the authority and wherewithal to act. Antifederalists wanted power cited in the states and localities. They also wanted executive and legislative or judicial power to carry less weight.

Another concept that permeated early American society and has continued to be vital throughout our history, was equality. It has assumed many forms. We have stressed equality of opportunity. We have often seen egalitarians pitted against elitists. We repeatedly see flashes of envy or conflict between those who lack some particular quality or benefit, and those who might be fortunate or able enough to possess it. Equality, along with liberty, was critical to our independence and to the foundation of our nation.

Equality was a relatively new idea at the time of our revolution, as Hannah Arendt explained. "The very idea of equality as we understand it, namely that every person is born as an equal by the very fact of being born and that equality is a birthright, was utterly unknown prior to the modern age."[4] The United States served as a testing ground for the development and practice of equality in government. Its formative period was extensive. In fact, the concept is still being delineated in this country.

In 1787, Europe, as well as the rest of the world, was largely controlled by monarchies supported by aristocracies. Equality as a concept had just begun to poke through the philosophical surface in scattered locations. In this country the concept became more acceptable and more persistent. The way we were settled and the type of people who became our settlers had a lot to do with this. Equality may have been new to the world but in the United States it was ingrained. It was even taken for granted by all but a few in the most conservative faction of the Federalist party. "Equality became so potent for Americans because it came to mean that everyone was really the same as everyone else, not just at birth, not in talent or property or wealth, and not just in some transcendental religious sense of the equality of all souls. Ordinary Americans came to believe that no one in a basic down-to-earth and day-in-day-out manner was really better than anyone else."[5] Equality became a cornerstone of our philosophical formulation. However, its definition and its application became one of our ongoing national debates.

These concepts of liberty and equality were revolutionary because they weren't found anywhere else. Virtually no nation was free of highly structured classism. Nowhere else did citizens enjoy the type of liberty Americans cherished. For virtually all of our early citizens, federalists and antifederalists alike, these constituted cornerstone beliefs, with only the shadings to be debated.

We have seen that as the United States struggled through its first decade of existence, it did so bolstered by a phalanx of firmly imbedded and generally accepted concepts. What it did not have, however, was a clear idea of how to practically interpret these concepts, or how to make government work. That is not too hard to understand. No nation of any size had tried to operate a government like ours before. We were the laboratory where theory was transformed into practice. Thus, the nature and weight of government became the primary field of ideological clash, the center of political debate. It remains so to this day as our democratic experiment continues to evolve.

Pre-Constitutional Expressions

In the opinion of many, the Declaration of Independence was our premier founding document. Gary Wills echoed that sentiment. "According to Lincoln and Webster...the Declaration of Independence was closer to being the founding document of the United States than was the Constitution."[6] The importance of this statement to our discussion is that the Declaration was largely composed by men, led by Thomas Jefferson, who expressed beliefs that later generally came to be identified with antifederalism. This contrasts with the Constitution, which was essentially an expression of federalism and federalists.

Some of the philosophical differences between the two documents and their creators can be attributed to political evolution and to the unfortunate experiences of governing under the Articles of Confederation. Nevertheless, a substantial portion of the difference was due to fundamental beliefs. These differences became more sharply etched in subsequent debate. They would later emerge in the policies advocated by presidents such as Thomas Jefferson and Andrew Jackson. By the time the Constitution was written the cast of characters present in Philadelphia was substantially different than it had been 11 years earlier. Only five individuals signed both of our founding documents, the Declaration of Independence and the Constitution. Only one man signed these two plus the Articles of Confederation.[7] During the lapse of time between 1776 and 1787 there was a distinct shift of popular political sentiment. It moved the majority from an advocacy of the several states as the loci of power to a realization that the center had to be at least somewhat strengthened. What brought this about was the cumulative impact of general ineptitude, especially financial ineptitude, displayed by the Continental Congress both during and after the war. Even so, when the Constitution was first published the initial reaction was widespread shock at the degree of power allocated to the central government and the extent of the alterations made to the Articles of Confederation. This shock gradually wore off under the scrutiny of our operational weaknesses and our future needs, but it did overhang the ratification debate and helped bring about the Bill of Rights.

It was chaotic finances more than anything else which prompted convocation of the Constitutional Convention. If there was an immediate catalyst that can be identified, it was Shays' Rebellion. As described in the previous chapter, this uprising in western Massachusetts during the winter of 1786-7 pitted poor farmers, all Revolutionary War veterans, led by Captain Daniel Shays, against the Boston establishment. These farmers, who served as a proxy for impecunious veterans in many states, were striving to keep from being jailed for debt and having their possessions seized. The Shaysites' distress and reaction was our first national reminder that violent class conflict could erupt if the gap between the wealthy elite and the lower economic regions of the populace grew too wide.

The turmoil that reverberated from Shays' Rebellion alarmed and energized many leaders, including George Washington, James Madison, and Alexander Hamilton. The efforts of Washington, Madison, and Hamilton transformed the Potomac River Commission, which had existed unobtrusively for over a century, into the Philadelphia Convention. which convened in May of 1787. The cast of characters was almost entirely changed from those who had gathered in the same State House 11 years earlier. By the time the delegates had gathered in the heat of summer, most of the signers of the Declaration of

Independence's were either out of the country (John Adams, Robert Paine, Thomas Jefferson), dead (John Hurt, Lyman Hull, Joseph Hewes) or remaining at home (John Hancock, Patrick Henry, Samuel Adams). If the financial situation hadn't been so serious none of these events would have likely occurred or produced such a great reaction. Thus, there was a perceptible psychological shift that could be detected on the floor of the State House from the atmosphere prevailing at the event in that building when the Declaration was signed under the looming shadow of Britain.

The tenor of the nation's philosophy had changed. Federalism was in the air, ranged against it the tenets of antifederalism were beginning to coalesce into a philosophical system, itself distinct from the one that had governed, and in fact was still governing, under the Articles. But, as Samuel Beer tells us, antifederalism as a coherent philosophy arose mainly in opposition, well after its main principles had been employed for over a decade in government. "It was not, however, deployed by Americans until well after independence, when the Anti-Federalists made the case for the small polity as the forum where republican virtue could best be cultivated."[8] The beginning of antifederalism's articulation was in response to the Constitution. Its governing philosophy actually arrived even later, as Jefferson reacted to the federalism of John Adams as president and Alexander Hamilton as his chief ideologue.

When the conventioneers gathered in 1787 there were a few articulate spokesmen, such as George Mason of Virginia, for what became known as antifederalist views. After the convention concluded and the ratification battle heated up, spokesmen began to proliferate, and the rudiments of a doctrine became defined. The nuances of the ratification process will be covered in the next chapter. Our main concern at the moment is to realize that even as the tide built in support of a constitution outlining a stronger central government, the elements which were to constitute the heart of antifederalism remained deeply ingrained in our political thinking and gradually began to emerge in the form of articles and speeches. An antifederalist philosophical system arose from the voices raised during the convention's oratory. It strengthened and solidified as scrutiny of our Constitution created a crucible for antifederalist beliefs. This incipient system, both articulated and rejected during the ratification debate, awaited a leader to turn it into a political force to be reckoned with.

Jeffersonian Extension

Throughout the late colonial period the foremost issue that divided Americans was whether to support continued union with England or to demand independence. As the ensuing war was being fought the mechanics of its sustenance both overwhelmed and unified those in rebellion. There was an earnest striving for legitimacy and a formalizing of social contracts reflected by the many state constitutions written between the years 1776 and 1780. These accompanied the publishing of the Declaration of Independence and the Articles of Confederation. But our existence was so precarious that ideological dissent, and even contemplation of differing philosophies of government, remained subterranean. As the country began to sort itself out in the early 1780s, stress fractures traced their network through our various levels of government. The lack of executive power was the largest crack, and was most keenly observed as the Continental Congress displayed an inability to enforce any revenue generating tax policy or to regulate commerce. Concerned citizens struggled to gain control over the deteriorating situation. "The mood in 1787—not merely among Federalists but even among many who for highly particular reasons chose briefly to be Anti-Federalists—might be described as 'restorationalist,' meaning that the recovery and firm establishment of authority became at least as important as unqualified assertions of individualistic liberty."[9] Philosophy had taken a back seat to necessity. It wasn't until the Constitutional Convention actually assembled that the views subsequently to be classified as federalist and antifederalist really began to take shape.

After the triumph of the Constitution's ratification, the Federalist party's ascendancy was relatively brief. It officially lasted for Washington's two terms and John Adams' single four-year term. In reality it didn't last that long. Before Adams' term was over, Vice-President Thomas Jefferson, who had been enticed back from Paris to serve as Washington's Secretary of State, was in open opposition and antifederalism as a political expression had been revived, consolidated, and promulgated.

Jefferson had always radiated the philosophy of agrarian simplicity and individual independence cherished by the antifederalists. Although in Paris when the Constitution was written, Jefferson's correspondence, particularly to Madison, left the distinct impression that were he present ,he would have disapproved of much that had transpired. He was appalled that the convention had vastly exceeded its original mandate, which was merely to improve the Articles of Confederation. He trusted in majority rule, temporary office holders, and the independence of the individual states. He distrusted enhanced power in the hands of a federal executive and judiciary. He, like many of "the founders had assumed an involved citizenry; and the governmental system they created functions best when that assumption is validated."[10] Jefferson felt that the Constitution de-emphasized this involvement and removed government from the citizens. He especially objected to the absence of a Bill of Rights.

Jefferson had been disturbed by the fact that "the Constitution challenged every dimension of the theory that had guided the Revolution. It offered a new conception of the people, their representatives, the link between them, and the role of administrators within a republican regime."[11] As he began to organize opposition to President Adams, assisted by his protégé but not always his ideological soul mate, Madison, these sentiments, which had been expressed by antifederalists during the ratification battle, resurfaced. Jefferson saw his worst fears being realized. Rights were being trampled. Power was accruing to the few. The Supreme Court was exerting its influence.

Hannah Arendt described Jefferson's affinity for local government, which was the essence of his antifederalism.

> According to Jefferson, it was the very principle of republican government to demand "the subdivision of the counties into wards,'" namely, the creation of "small republics" through which "every man in the State" could become an "acting member of the Common Government transacting in person a great portion of its rights and duties, subordinate indeed, yet important, and entirely within its competence." It was these "little republics that would be the main strength of the great one," for inasmuch as the republican government of the Union was based on the assumption that the seat of power was in the people, the very condition for its proper functioning lay in a scheme "to divide government among the many, distributing to everyone exactly the functions he was competent to." Without this, the very principle of republican government could never be actualized, and the government of the United States would be republican in name only.[12]

Prompted by an increasing disenchantment with the Federalists' policies culminating in the undeclared war with France; the Alien Act of June 25, 1798 (which authorized the President to expel any non-naturalized individual born abroad who he determined to be "dangerous to the peace and safety of the United States"); and the Sedition Act of July 14, 1798 (which made it a crime to utter or publish "any false, scandalous, and malicious writing or writings against the Government of the United States, or either House of the Congress of the United States), Jefferson sought to form a political party which would reclaim sovereignty for the people.

Jefferson disagreed with the theories soon to be identified with Willem Fredrich Hegel and to become a staple of nineteenth century academicians. Federalists almost simultaneously with the pen of Hegel claimed the prerogatives of elitism.

> The prevalent idea that the people itself best understood what would promote the common weal, and that they have indubitably the good will to promote it is fallacious. The people stands precisely for the part that does not know what it wills. To know what one wills, and, what is more difficult to know what the absolute will, viz, reason, is the fruit of deep knowledge and insight; and that is obviously not a possession of the people.[13]

Jefferson was a lifelong champion of majority rule and a foe of elitism.

Jefferson believed in the supremacy of the national will, but was not really comfortable when this will was expressed through a compound republic, particularly one with a strong center. He was even less comfortable when he perceived the center to be acting contrary to the will of the majority and in violation of the Bill of Rights whose adoption he had urged so fervently. Furthermore, Jefferson was distrustful of professional politicians and office holders, expressing these sentiments in a letter to Richard Henry Lee on June 17, 1779. "Public offices are what they should be—burdens to those appointed to them which would be wrong to decline, though foreseen to bring them intense labor and great private loss." This was his version of term limits, the burdens of temporary office, eagerly escaped. The burgeoning opponents to Adams' policies looked longingly toward such service, which would seem like a breath of fresh air compared to the entrenched Federalist bureaucrats they perceived as controlling the government in the late 1790s.

In 1797 Jefferson and Madison formed a party (initially called Republican, it later became Democratic-Republican) which was designed to uphold the agrarian principle of the Revolution and to combat the British influence seen to be creeping into both politics and finance under Federalist rule. The principles of the new party hoped to revive the republican ideal and return the misappropriated government to its rightful place—with the people. It is remarkable that Jefferson launched this effort as a sitting Vice President, but he deemed the manifestation of a new political philosophy a necessity. It represented a resurrection of antifederalism and included many original antifederalists in the ranks of its supporters.

There was an important and sinister implication hidden in the new Jeffersonian doctrine which was to plague it as it mushroomed throughout the first half of the nineteenth century. This influence was contained in the twin concepts of *nullification* and *secession*. *Nullification* came to mean that a government entity, usually a state, which disapproved of a law passed by a higher government, usually at the federal level, could declare this objectionable law null and void within its borders. The doctrine of *secession* meant that any entity, usually a state, which could no longer abide by the rules of the nation as interpreted by the federal government could choose to leave the union. These concepts had been inherent in the theories of Montesquieu and remained largely unexpressed in the philosophy of pre-constitutional antifederalism. They had not been explicitly articulated as part of the core of beliefs. For example, the battle over ratification of the Constitution had been hotly contested in many states. However, there was no serious thought given to a portion of the states operating under its governance and some outside. The Constitution was to either be voted up or be voted down, and the pressure for unanimous consent was considerable. This attitude eventually brought all 13 states into the national fold. Now a new interpretation was introduced that added a malignant nuance to antifederalism. This interpretation is why I take such pains to distinguish between pre-constitutional and post-Jeffersonian antifederalism. The schism divided antifederalism's next governmental expression during the Jacksonian era. It is why I have selected the pre-constitutional variety with its greater degree of ideological purity as a model for transposition to the future.

The opening salvo of Jefferson's and Madison's campaign against the Alien and Sedition Acts, which was designed to place Jefferson in the White House, was fired late in 1798. Two resolutions were passed by the legislatures of Kentucky (November 13) and Virginia (December 24), which protested the abuses of an overtly powerful central government and extolled the virtues of states' rights. Although the resolutions were introduced by John Breckenridge in Kentucky and John Taylor in Virginia, they had in reality been authored by Jefferson (Kentucky) and Madison (Virginia), a fact that came to light only many years later. Aside from their value as a political platform, the resolutions formed the basis for the extreme states' rights policies advocated by militant Southerners for decades to come.

This interpretation was primarily due to the florid language of Jefferson, which left room for inference in interpretation of the resolutions.

> Their theoretical side proved more a liability than an asset, both then and later on. The doctrinal implications are anything but clear-cut, owing, in large measure to the part Jefferson played, even with Madison's moderating influence, in the movement that produced them, and to the ambiguities and fluctuations of Jefferson's own mind during the period of their formation. Actually, neither Jefferson's nor Madison's version was acceptable to any of the states that replied to them [fourteen in all], and in the case of all who gave their reasons the principle objection was everywhere the same. "It belongs not to state legislatures [as the Vermont reply to Virginia phrased it] to decide on the constitutionality of laws made by the general government; this power being exclusively vested in the judiciary courts of the Union." Madison, whose mind, as usual worked with greater precision than Jefferson's, had couched his version in language decidedly less prolix and less menacing than that of the Kentucky Resolutions. Not that this mattered much for immediate purposes; the responding states saw little or no difference between them. Yet Jefferson, to a far greater degree than Madison, had left some ill-omened hostages to an unforeseen future.[14]

In fact, Jefferson's first draft of the Kentucky Resolution, which was finally published in 1832, actually used the word *nullification*, excised in later versions. Thus, the implications of his ideas at that time became a threat to the union, which antifederalists had theretofore always revered. This factor permanently tainted the rebirth of antifederalism under its guise of Jeffersonian republicanism. While antifederalism attained greater political success in this form than in pre-constitutional days, it contained a cancer whose metastasizing would in time nearly destroy the union . The power of Jefferson's governmental thoughts and the philosophical impact of his political revival were limited in this one key area (the permanence of the union) by the looseness of his phrasing, if not his actual intent. His legacy, and that of antifederalism as well, carries the stain of secession that periodically has almost overwhelmed the validity of its other tenets.

Jacksonian Culmination

Andrew Jackson rose to national prominence as the victorious commander of the melange of United States forces who defeated the cream of the British regular army in the Battle of New Orleans on January 8, 1815. He continued to serve as an occasional military officer, a sometime territorial governor and a significant player on the Tennessee political scene. He was thrust into the presidential arena in 1824 by a confluence of events.

The country was enduring a major depression which lasted from 1819 until 1829. It remained in the grip on an increasingly ingrown group of politicians and bureaucrats presided over by a succession of four Virginians and two Adamses. Apathy for national politics was growing, with less than one-quarter of those eligible (who in turn amounted to less than one-half of our adult population) voting in presidential elections. Pessimism and cynicism abounded. These sentiments were reinforced by the election of 1824 in which Jackson won the popular vote with 43 percent to 31 percent for his closest rival, John Quincy Adams. He also won the electoral vote 99 to 84 but since there was no majority, the election was thrown to the House of Representatives. The ensuing Adams victory was achieved with the support of Henry Clay, and invoked suspicions of a deal when Clay was appointed Secretary of State, then the traditional stepping stone to the presidency. This set the stage for a populist eruption.

Jackson swept into the White House four years later with a clear majority and with 56 percent of the electorate voting. He offered the alternative of an outsider. He was a strong advocate of states' rights but equally adamant about keeping them within the framework of the union. He was a westerner in a country which, thus far, had been run by easterners. These qualities not only refreshed the presidency but they also helped to usher in a final incarnation of antifederalism.

This incarnation included a struggle spawned by Jefferson's possibly intemperate, possibly deliberate wording of the Kentucky Resolution in 1798. The struggle first flared in the nullification crisis of 1832-1833, and eventually in 1860 came within a whisker of destroying the nation.[15]

It was between proponents of different kinds of states' rights thought. It was between the advocates of *states' rights* who believed in perpetual union and decentralization of power as the best way to fulfill the democratic promise of the American Revolution and keep government responsible to the wishes of the people and those who advocated that a state had a constitutional right to withdraw from the Union and believed the doctrine of *states' rights* provided the best way to protect the rights of the minority from the tyranny of the majority. An important result of the nullification crisis was that the doctrine of states' rights became fatefully entwined with the concepts of slavery and secession.[16]

Jackson was firmly for preservation of the union. His actions during the crisis, those actions of his chief rival, South Carolina's John C. Calhoun, and the subsequent compromise engineered by Henry Clay, served only to make the final confrontation inevitable and violent.

Jackson came to office as a populist, a fighter for the rights of the common man. As Governor of Florida he wrote to then Secretary of State John Quincy Adams on August 26, 1821 expressing this view. "I did believe, and ever will believe, that the laws can make no distinction of privilege between the rich and poor; and that when men of high standing attempt to trample upon the rights of the weak they are the fittest objects for example and punishment." Eleven years later on July 10, 1832 when, as president, he vetoed the bill rechartering the Second Bank of the United States he re-iterated these sentiments, combining them with his version of states' rights and localism. This statement made him sound like an orthodox, pre-constitutional antifederalist.

It is to be regretted that the rich and powerful too often bend the acts of government to their selfish purposes. Distinctions in society will always exist under every just government. Equality of talents, of education, or of wealth cannot be produced by human institutions. In the full enjoyment of the gifts of Heaven and the fruits of superior industry, economy and virtue, every man is equally entitled to protection by the law; but when the laws undertake to add to these natural and just advantages artificial distinctions, to grant titles, gratuities, and exclusive privileges, to make the rich richer and the potent more powerful, the humble members of society—the farmers, the mechanics and laborers—who have neither the time nor the means of securing like favors to themselves, have the right to complain of the injustice of their government. There are no necessary evils in government. Its evils exist only in its abuses. If it would confine itself to equal protection, and, as Heaven does its rains, shower its favors alike on the high and low, rich and poor, it would be an unqualified blessing. In the act before me there seems to be a wide and unnecessary departure from these just principles.

Nor is our government to be maintained or our Union preserved by invasions of the rights and powers of the several states. In thus attempting to make our General Government strong we make it weak. Its true strength consists in leaving individuals and states as much as possible to themselves—in making itself felt, not in its power, but in its beneficence; not in its control but in its protection; not in its binding the states more closely to the center, but leaving each to move unobstructed in its proper orbit.

There are those, myself among them, who believe that in these two paragraphs Andrew Jackson eloquently stated a social and political philosophy that could be profitably transposed to the twenty-first century.

Jackson's First Inaugural Address and First State of the Union Message (then called Annual Address) outline a policy of fiscal conservatism, federal minimalism, and social responsibility that would fit our era like a glove.

Jackson proposed paying off the national debt in his First Inaugural Address. "It would appear that advantage must result from the observance of a strict and faithful economy. This I shall aim at the more anxiously, both because it will facilitate the extinguishment of the national debt, the unnecessary duration of which is incompatible with real independence, and because it will counteract that tendency to public and private profligacy which a profuse expenditure of money by government is but too apt to engender." Paying off the national debt was accomplished in his second term, the only time in its history that the United States has been debt-free. Also, as promised, the surplus in the treasury was distributed to the states.

In this climate of financial austerity the new president proposed cutting defense spending but increasing funding for education and for the alleviation of poverty.

He proposed an amendment to the Constitution that would eliminate the Electoral College system of electing a president in favor of direct selection by a majority of the people, although he did agree that some relative weighting of states might be incorporated. "I would therefore recommend such an amendment of the Constitution as may remove all intermediate agency in the election of the President and Vice President. The mode may be so regulated as to preserve to each state its present relative weight in the election."

Jackson also favored term limits. His First Annual Message outlined both philosophy and specifics.

> I cannot but believe that more is lost by the long continuance of men in office than is generally to be gained by their experience. I submit therefore to your consideration whether the efficiency of the government would not be promoted, and official industry and integrity better secured by a general extension of the law which limits appointments to four years. In a country where offices are created solely for the benefit of the people, no one man has any more intrinsic right to official station than another. Offices were not established to give support to particular men at the public expense.

Specifically he averred that "it would seem advisable to limit the service of the chief magistrate to a single term of either four or six years." In this address he reiterated his philosophy on holding office. "The proposed limitation would destroy the idea of property, now so generally connected with official station; and although individual distress may be sometimes produced, it would by promoting that rotation which constitutes a leading principle in the republican creed, give healthful action to the system."

Jackson did favor a strict interpretation of the Constitution, particularly its Tenth Amendment, which emphasized states' rights. He also supported reduction in the high protective tariffs that had been enacted in previous administrations, although not their elimination which was called for by the South Carolina nullifiers.

This agenda constituted an antifederalist expression as comprehensive as any ever promulgated in our country. While antifederalist principles bubbled to the surface from time to time (such as in the populism of the 1890s or in the two Coolidge administrations) they never again scaled the heights layed out in Jackson's initial messages to his people. Financial conservatism, direct election of the President, term limits, enhanced local power together make a political agenda worthy of study.

If the spirit of pre-constitutional antifederalism combined with Jacksonian principles could be transposed along the pendulum's arc to ..the twenty-first century and be accompanied by a program of compassion for the disadvantaged as well as a restructured tax code, our society and our prospects would be the richer.

---

[1] Thomas L. Pangle, *Montesquieu's Philosophy of Liberalism* (Chicago: University of Chicago Press, 1973), 109.

[2] Those delegates to the Constitutional Convention who attended Princeton were: James Madison of Virginia; Luther Martin of Maryland; Gunning Bedford of Delaware; William Davie of North Carolina; Jonathan Dayton of New Jersey; Oliver Ellsworth of Connecticut; William Houston of New Jersey; Alexander Martin of North Carolina; William Patterson of New Jersey.

[3] Samuel Beer, *To Make a Nation: The Rediscovery of Federalism,* (Boston: Belknap Press of Harvard University Press, 1993), 322.

[4] Hannah Arendt, *On Revolution* (New York: Penguin Books, 1963), 40.

[5] Gordon S. Wood, *The Radicalism of the American Revolution* (New York: Vintage Books division of Random House, 1991), 234.

[6] Gary Wills, *Lincoln at Gettysburg*, Simon & Schuster, NY 1992),130.

[7] Future Vice President Elbridge Gerry signed the Declaration and was a delegate to the Constitutional Convention from Massachusetts but didn't sign it. George Clymer of Delaware signed the two documents. Benjamin Franklin, Robert Morris, and James Wilson of Pennsylvania also signed both. The only signer of these two documents plus the Article of Confederation was Roger Sherman of Connecticut.

[8] Samuel Beer, *To Make a Nation: The Rediscovery of Federalism* (Boston: Belknap Press of Harvard University Press, 1993), 180.

[9] Michael Kammen, editor, *The Origins of the American Constitution* (New York: Penguin Books, 1986), xv.

[10] Ibid., xxi.

[11] James A. Morone, *The Democratic Wish* (New York: Basic Books, 1990), 63.

[12] Hannah Arendt, *On Revolution* (New York: Penguin Books, 1963), 253.

[13] Jacob Lowenberg, editor, *Hegel: Selections* (New York: Random House, 1963), 456.

[14] Stanley Elkins and Eric McKittrick, *The Age of Federalism: The Early American Republic, 1788-1800* (New York: Oxford University Press, 1993), 720.

[15] South Carolina attempted to nullify the tariff laws of 1828 and 1832, claiming they unduly benefited the Northeast and harmed the Southern states.

[16] Richard E. Ellis., *The Union at Risk: Jacksonian Democracy, States' Rights and the Nullification Crisis* (New York: Oxford University Press, 1987), ix.

CHAPTER 3

The Ratification Battle

The Constitution of the United States is "a charter of power
granted by liberty rather than a charter of liberty granted by power."

James Madison

The Constitutional Convention exceeded its original mandate, which
was merely to revise the Articles of Confederation. This produced some
resentment and some alarm. It consolidated the opposition to a stronger
central government, which initially was nearly as great as the support.
The battle over the ratification of the Constitution, which raged for
twelve months starting in the fall of 1787, was impassioned. It also was
a model both for contests over the philosophy of government and for
the resolution of differences through compromise. While the *Federalist
Papers* of Madison, Hamilton, and Jay are by far the most well-known
examples of writing that emerged from the period, they are by no means
the only well-constructed, cogently reasoned and logically persuasive
documents produced. The Federalists were not the only ones to
distinguish themselves in debate. Antifederalists rallied around their
principles, presented them effectively, and were able to stamp their
imprint upon the final product.

Crystallized Positions

The ratification process brought about statements of competing
governmental philosophies. It etched them in the minds of the populace

more sharply than had occurred previously. In that regard it was a benefit to the nation, both then and for many years thereafter.

The antifederalists were largely agrarian, populist, and wary of government. They were products of an environment that was typical of the early United States of America.

> The representative community of that age was the hamlet or village, an entity so small and self-contained that it could not afford any appreciable degree of conflict or contention. All its social values emphasized peace, and its rudimentary institutional structure—the church and town meeting in particular—was organized not so much to 'manage' conflict as simply to absorb and perhaps even to evade it. The urge was toward settling potentially divisive issues informally before they became matters of open contention; the town meeting was seen not primarily as a forum for debating issues but rather as a device for exacting consent. Nor was majority consent enough. The ideal was unanimity; the town could not afford disaffected minorities.[1]

It was this basic mind set, replicated in thousands of communities, which the antifederalists brought to the debate. As much as any other factor it may have pointed them not only towards a solution in which some of their views could be reflected, but also towards positions from which unanimity could be achieved. Although the rhetoric was often fierce, the antifederalists generally were probing for compromise. In this they were successful, and the nation profited. The lessons gleaned therefrom can be valuable.

Charles Mee effectively summarized the way antifederalists of the 1780s viewed the several layers of government.

> A central government might best ensure order and even uniform standards of justice by way of uniform laws. But local governments were best able to see to it that individuals actually participated in their own government; controlled their own affairs; had the direct experience of governing themselves and so knew best from their own experience how to govern and what they could reasonably expect and demand from their representatives; and had the power, because their government was so close to them, to insist that the government do their bidding. Local government actually bred better citizens than did a central government which sent down its rules from on high to a distant uninvolved, and even apathetic population. Local governments were indisputably the best guardians of the genius of self-government; and localists would not ever give up such a treasure.[2]

This is what committed antifederalists, who made up somewhere between one-quarter and one-third of the 1787 population, venerated and hoped to preserve. They had fears to be sure, and we will cover them in a subsequent section. What predominated in their ranks, however, was a desire to preserve a form of government that they loved and trusted. It was their version of democracy—localism.

Antifederalists envisioned an optimum government emerging from an improved Articles of Confederation. They did not expect radical surgery. They still favored a loose organization of small republics in some sort of confederation. "To make these small republics the basic constitutional units of polity also shapes the political process of its central government. The representatives of the member states at the center will be like ambassadors of independent nations, and their discussion and decision-making will have the nature of diplomatic bargaining among the interests of their constituencies."[3] States, not the central government, would be the premier entities.

This collection of small republics would each be governed by majority rule, as Tenche Coxe writing as *An American* in the Philadelphia *Gazette* on May 21, 1788 pointed out. "In a *free* government, the *voice of the people*, expressed by the votes of a *majority*, must be *the rule*, or we shall be left without any *certain* rule to determine what is politically right. To depart from it is establishing *tyranny by law*. It would be a *solemn renunciation* of the forms and substance of liberty; and our affairs, on this *dangerous principle*, must rapidly hasten to an *oligarchy* —the most dreadful of all government." Coxe was expressing a major difference between federalists and antifederalists. The former were concerned with tyranny of the majority. The latter viewed the prospect of minorities imposing their wishes upon majorities, who would thus be unable to exercise their will, as the chief republican evil. Jefferson was concerned about this influence of minorities and frequently argued the point with his friend Madison who had great fear of majority domination. The debate continues to this day.

An advantage of small republics, both then and now, is that they operate under unrestrained majority rule and homogeneity permits a sense of fairness with a minimum of discrimination. In the opinion of most antifederalists of the 1780s, extended republics contain too many minorities whose interests have to be accommodated. As our nation has grown it has run up against the problem of minority accommodation, and there is as yet no adequate remedy. This contrast in views, power, and responsibility constituted a fundamental philosophical difference between the two factions. It would affect debate over the size and role of their government. It would affect their opinions on equality, liberty, and basic human rights.

Another point of difference was the issue of egalitarianism versus elitism. Only the right wing of the Federalist party, led by Alexander Hamilton, were outspoken elitists. But the Federalist party in general looked to a small cadre to provide their leadership. The antifederalists were more ecumenical. "In short, the Anti-Federalists were saying that liberally educated gentlemen were no more capable than ordinary people of classical republican disinterestedness and virtue and that consequently there was no one in the society equipped to promote an exclusive public interest that was distinguishable from the private interests of people."[4] This fit in with their views on citizen-governors and temporary government service. The administration of both Jefferson and Jackson radiated this populist outlook.

David Brinkley captured one aspect of antipathy towards elites, which was essentially antifederalist in nature. A similar attitude surfaced virulently in Jeffersonian rhetoric. It also has been expressed at many other times in our history.

> Beneath the surface of the income tax debate could be seen one of the less sensible features of the emerging American character, envy and resentment of wealth. It came to these shores with the cold and unforgiving Puritans who began arriving in the new world in the seventeenth century. They were English Protestants, so furious they were willing to cross the Atlantic and abandon their homes and their country because they thought the churches of England were too lenient, even going to the intolerable extreme of allowing their members to accumulate more money than the church thought they should have. In their Presbyterian and Episcopalian Sunday sermons the message every week and every day was that money was evil and it was evil to pursue it. Their spoor is still with us.[5]

This destructive form of egalitarianism has rarely resulted in sensible policy. It lies beneath the surface in discussions on many issues. This malignant egalitarianism poisons rational debate and deepens difficult problems as severely as does rampant elitism.

As mentioned previously, along with their belief in local government, antifederalists idealized the republican citizen-governor. They, as well as many federalists, advocated universal, but temporary, service in some form of government. James Kent, a law professor who happened to be a Federalist, outlined this belief in a New York lecture in 1794 illustrating that it spread far beyond the antifederalist segment of society.

> There is no individual in any station, art, or occupation, who may not entertain a reasonable expectation in some period of his life, and in some capacity, to be summoned into public employment. If it be his lot however to be confined to private life, he still retains the equal and undeniable Rights of a Citizen, and is deeply interested in the knowledge of his social duties; and especially in the great duty of wisely selecting and attentively observing those who may be entrusted with the guardianship of his Rights; and the business of the Nation.

There was general agreement that this new United States, whatever its form of government, could not operate effectively without the participation of its citizens. This was not uniquely an antifederalist principle, but it was accepted by most citizens who took their civil obligations seriously. A principle that was able to transcend the political differences that separated our founders deserves to be taken seriously by us as well.

The location of power was a cause of dispute. Antifederalists wanted it sited in localities, or at the highest states. Federalists saw the need for a stronger center. The still anonymous writer *Brutus* framed the antifederalist position in the *New York Journal* of March 6, 1788. In this particular article, *Brutus XIV*, he was discussing the Supreme Court but his observations on power were generic. "For to answer objections made to a power given to a government, by saying it will never be exercised, is really admitting that the power ought not to be exercised, and therefore ought not to be granted." *Brutus* and other antifederalists felt very strongly that power should not be ceded to the center, except in rare, and ephemeral, instances. They feared that such a siting would ultimately disenfranchise the ordinary citizen and lead to tyranny of the elite.

In their cogitations on the subject of power the two sides were not in total disagreement. Federalists were not immune to the teachings of Montesquieu. Hannah Arendt has captured their adaptation of his theories.

> For Montesquieu's discovery actually concerned the nature of power, and this discovery stands in so flagrant a contradiction to all conventional notions on the matter that it has almost been forgotten, despite the fact that the foundation of the republic in America was largely inspired by it. The discovery, contained in one sentence, spells out the forgotten principle underlying the whole structure of separated powers: that only "power arrests power," that is, we must add, without destroying it, without putting impotence in the place of power.[6]

This discovery has characterized political discussions and disputes throughout our history. It has also characterized the construction of our governmental institutions and, as Robert J. Samuelson so ably described, the creation of our Age of Entitlement.[7]

Federalists looked at a United States under the Articles of Confederation and saw economic chaos. They decried the absence of an effective foreign policy. They were abashed by the lack of respect we received from abroad. They felt their country had a questionable ability to defend itself. They were convinced that the key to all these problems was the fact that the nation had no real executive to be responsible for its operation. In order to rectify this deficiency, federalists perceived a clear need for more power at the center. In the context of the times they were correct. However, the more extreme federalists viewed power as did Benjamin Rush. He cynically observed that "although all power is derived from the people, they possess it only on the days of their elections. After that it is the property of their rulers."[8]

Rush's version was a far cry from the participatory local government idealized by the antifederalists, and in actuality represented the thinking of only the most conservative and elitist of the Federalist party. The vast majority of the middle, encompassing all persuasions, realized that some further assignment of power to the center was a practical necessity. The ratification debate swirled around the issues of exactly what power would be located where. The debate also involved implications for the future in the event that central power became too concentrated, too oppressive. The perception by moderate antifederalists that a somewhat stronger center was indeed necessary is what brought about ratification. The perception by moderate federalists that individuals needed more protection brought about the Bill of Rights. Together they gave us a government.

Media Organs

In the United States of 1787 the idea of a free press was cherished. However, the idea of an impartial, objective press didn't exist. Newspapers, pamphlets, and magazines were created to engage in advocacy. Each important faction in each geographical area had its own outlets. The *Federalist Papers*, for example, were conceived and organized by Alexander Hamilton in New York and published in the capital's leading Federalist papers. Antifederalist tracts in the same city came out in rival publications.

New York was typical. It had one major antifederalist newspaper, the *New York Journal* which published authors like *Brutus* and *Cato*. The *Federalist Papers*, as well as other Federalist essays, were published in three New York newspapers: the *Packet*, the *Daily Advertiser*, and the *Independent Journal*. Other major population centers were similarly split with the number of outlets often depending upon the relative strength of sentiment, although the antifederalists continued to assert, with some justification, that in most areas the Federalists controlled the lion's share of the media.

The country was well-informed, despite the partiality. Impassioned, often eloquent and well reasoned dissertations emerged from both sides in the ratification debate. In fact, a perusal of the literature that was generated in the 12 months from September 1787 to August 1788 reveals some of the most comprehensive writing on the philosophy and practice of government that this country has ever seen.

It was a fashion of that era to write under pseudonyms. Most often they had some Roman origin or implication such as *Publius*, *Brutus*, and *Cato*. Other pseudonyms, such as *An American Farmer* and *Giles Hickory*, sought to protect simplicity and wholesomeness. The reason for disguise was, as might be expected, protection from libel lawsuits, preservation of public positions from compromise, or simply a search for the peace of anonymity. In some cases the veils were easily pierced. For instance, most people knew immediately that the *Publius* of the *Federalist Papers* referred to Hamilton, Madison, and Jay. Sometimes the deception persisted for many years. The true authors of the Kentucky and Virginia Resolutions, for example, were concealed for decades. Sometimes the author's identity has never been discovered, as is the case with the antifederalist *Brutus*.

Articulated Fears

The reader may remember from the previous chapter that prior to the American Revolution there was a widely-held conspiracy theory involving the British Government's subterranean designs on the government of its colonies. The anger resulting from the Constitutional Convention's production of an extraordinary, and some thought extralegal, document revived some of these fears in certain antifederalist quarters. Our people no longer acutely feared the British government (although the anglophile leanings of some Federalists produced increasing anxiety). Antifederalists were wary of an aristocratic, elitist group who they perceived as anxious to impose oligarchial rule.

The fears centered on four basic concerns: 1. The lack of a Bill of Rights; 2. The supremacy of a federal judiciary over state courts; 3. The danger of standing armies; and 4. The ability of the central government to levy taxes.

Absence of a Bill of Rights was the most frequently cited failing of the Constitution as presented for ratification. As soon as he received a copy of the proposed Constitution (the copy sent by Elbridge Gerry was the first to reach him), Thomas Jefferson wrote from Paris that a Bill of Rights was absolutely necessary. Antifederalists were by no means the only proponents of a Bill of Rights. Many Americans felt unprotected without specifically enumerated rights attached to the Constitution of their nation as they had been attached to several state constitutions.[9]

Those who argued that a Bill of Rights was not necessary were represented by Madison in *Federalist* 45, which appeared in the New York *Independent Journal* on January 26, 1788.

> The powers delegated by the proposed Constitution, to the Federal Government are few and defined. Those which are to remain in the State Governments are numerous and indefinite. The former will be exercised principally on external objects, as war, peace, negotiation and foreign commerce; with which last the power of taxation will for the most part be connected. The powers reserved to the several states will extend to all objects, which, in the ordinary course of affairs, concern the lives, liberties and properties of the people.

It is worth noting that the eventual Tenth Amendment, the last article in the Bill of Rights, was written by Madison and read similarly. "The powers not delegated to the United States by the Constitution, nor prohibited by it to the States, are reserved to the States respectively, or to the people." Since that time strict constructionists have used the Tenth Amendment to justify states' rights.

A argument similar to Madison's against the need for a Bill of Rights was given by Noah Webster writing as *Giles Hickory* in New York's *American Magazine* for December 1787. "In our government, there is no power of legislation, independent of the people; no power that has an interest detached from that of the public; consequently there is no power existing against which it is necessary to guard. While our Legislatures therefore remain elective, and the rulers have the same interest in the laws, as the subjects have, the rights of the people will be perfectly secure without any declaration in their favor." The majority of the electorate found these arguments disingenuous and continued to demand specific enumeration contained in a Bill of Rights as the price for ratification. Even George Washington saw the need to pacify an uneasy public. In his First Inaugural Address he recommended that a Bill of Rights be enacted. This was the only specific legislative request that he ever made as president.

The issue of the federal judiciary was less straightforward, and the antifederalists had less support for their position. Antifederalists understood very well that "for the framers of the Constitution and all orthodox Federalists, the Supreme Court was the linchpin of the Constitution."[10] They feared that the federal judiciary system would transform state courts and even Congress into irrelevancies. They agreed with the comments of Benjamin Hoadly, Bishop of Bangor, made in 1717. "Whoever hath an absolute authority to interpret any written or spoken laws, it is he who is truly the lawgiver, to all intents and purposes, and not the person who first wrote or spoke them."[11] Antifederalists saw the Supreme Court in a unique interpretive position and didn't wish to bestow such power upon it. There have been many throughout our history who agreed with this assertion and wished the antifederalists had emerged triumphant on this issue. However, they were not able to whip up a groundswell of support, and the federal judiciary survived. In 1803 when Chief Justice John Marshall delivered a strongly Federalist opinion asserting the power of the Court over Congress in *Marbury* vs. *Madison*, many Jeffersonians regretted this development, but the verdict stood and the Court's power was established.

A third point of conspiracy fear revival was the objection to standing armies controlled by the central government. Agrarian localists felt local militia was sufficient for defense. They were deeply suspicious of a regular army and the uses to which it might be put. This view was particularly prevalent along the western frontiers, which were strong antifederalist areas. These frontier areas were peopled by men skilled in fighting and men who had felt the sting of regular troops during Shays' Rebellion (western Pennsylvanians were also to face regulars in the Whiskey Rebellion of 1794).

The majority felt enough potential threats from abroad, from Indians and also from the westerners themselves to want a standing regular force, albeit of small size. Those that felt that standing armies were not expressly prohibited in the Constitution and should be specifically forbidden, found themselves not widely supported. The effort to curtail standing armies by amendment was dropped for the moment. The first electoral manifestation of anti-military sentiments on a national scale was at the time of Andrew Jackson's ascendancy to the presidency in 1828 with heavy support from the West. He immediately recommended a reduction in defense expenditures, primarily by cutting the regular military. But a professional army had been a feature of our society, with periodic fluctuations in size and consistent bolstering by a militia (later called the National Guard), and a standing army remained a feature of our society.

What did emerge as a result of this discussion was the Second Amendment as a part of the Bill of Rights. Those who supported a militia defense wanted the right to own their weapons specified. "A well regulated militia being necessary to the security of a free state, the right of the people to keep and bear arms shall not be impinged." The repercussions from this amendment are being felt to this day.

The final fear involved taxation and is another one that has never been settled and is still being debated. "The Congress is to have the power to lay and collect taxes, duties, imposts and excises...but all duties, imposts and excises, shall be uniform throughout the United States." So read Article I, Section 8, paragraph (1) of the Constitution. Readers should realize that in 1787 taxes generally meant excise taxes and customs duties. There was no income tax. For the states to lose the right to levy import duties would severely change the balance of power. Tariff policy was a key to regional prosperity. The South Carolinians made everyone aware of this in 1832. Regardless of how badly the country needed a central source of financing, antifederalists bridled at so drastic and so ominous an alteration of current practice.

The decision ultimately turned upon who would control import levies, and with them de facto foreign policy. In the Adams and Jefferson administrations tariffs, and their expected impact upon England and France, became a matter of policy debate.[12] In fact, in every administration up through the nullification crisis of 1832-33 tariffs created intensive debate, dividing parties and regions.

In 1787 and 1788 voters responded to the financial impotence of the central government by assenting to its taxation authority. As intimated above, although included in the ratified document, the federal taxation powers remained an item of sensitivity for generations. Throughout our history many American have remained unconvinced that the correct decision on this matter was made in 1788. This became a more acute issue for debate after the federal income tax was permanently established by Constitutional Amendment in 1913.

Keystones of Compromise

As the ratification conventions began to meet in the states, approval of the Constitution was far from certain. Both sides cranked up their public relations machines. Hamilton's organization of the *Federalist Papers* was one such effort, designed to persuade the voters of New York and dissipate their misgivings.

The closeness of the contest can be seen in the final tally, even after compromise had been reached on the Bill of Rights. It was by no means a certainty that the Constitution would be ratified by the requisite nine states, much less all 13. Rhode Island had not even sent a delegate to the convention. In other instances (New York was one) a majority of the delegates sent had not signed the final document. In some cases an important delegate (future Vice President Elbridge Gerry of Massachusetts and future Chief Justice of the Supreme Court Oliver Ellsworth of Connecticut were two) were non-signatories. The following table shows the progress and the numbers of the Constitution's ratification.

STATE	DATE RATIFIED	VOTE
Delaware	December 7, 1787	unanimous
Pennsylvania	December 12, 1787	46 - 23
New Jersey	December 18, 1787	unanimous
Georgia	January 2, 1788	unanimous
Connecticut	January 9, 1788	128 - 40
Massachusetts	February 6, 1788	187 - 168
Maryland	April 28, 1788	63 - 11
South Carolina	May 23, 1788	149 - 73
New Hampshire	June 21, 1788	57 - 47
Virginia	June 25, 1788	89 - 79
New York	July 26, 1788	30 - 27
North Carolina	November 21, 1789	194 - 77
Rhode Island	May 29, 1790	34 - 32

If the three unanimous results are eliminated, the tally of delegates was 828 for ratification and 504 against. Thus, the antifederalist position captured 38 percent of all the contested delegates. It was actually even closer than that.

Pennsylvania's convention was raucous, with physical force eventually being used against antifederalists from the western part of the state. The final vote was close, and the victorious Federalists had badly tarnished their image with their strong arm tactics.

This did not set an auspicious tone, and Massachusetts was the next important state to convene. As its convention opened, antifederalists actually held a majority of delegates by a margin of 192 to 144. The debate proved civilized, a great improvement from the days of Shays' Rebellion. Samuel Adams and John Hancock, both of whom started out skeptical about the Constitution, helped engineer an ingenious and pivotal compromise. Although the issue presented to the state conventions had been to vote either for or against the Constitution, Massachusetts refused to accept that limitation. Its convention decided to attach a series of "suggestions" for subsequent amendments, which primarily involved the addition of a Bill of Rights. An antifederalist lawyer from Andover, William Semmes, was swayed by this tactic and switched sides, bringing with him enough other supporters to ensure a close positive vote. While the nation may be grateful to Semmes, his constituents weren't. They angrily hounded him until he eventually left town.

Virginia was in position to provide the key ninth ratification. The antifederalist side was stacked with luminaries led by Patrick Henry. It also included Benjamin Harrison and John Tyler (both fathers of future presidents), George Mason, James Monroe and Richard Henry Lee. The keystone of compromise was Governor Edmund Randolph. He had been a delegate in Philadelphia (in fact he had presented Madison's original Virginia Plan), but had not signed the final document. Acting upon the Massachusetts formula, Randolph advocated approving ratification with suggested amendments. He convinced enough antifederalists who were concerned for the preservation of the union to vote in favor of a Constitution with "suggestions" (20 of them) and thus ensure a narrow victory in the state that provided legal ratification.

Although the Constitution was legally accepted, agreement by all states was crucial to the integrity of the nation. That made New York's convention important. Despite the persuasiveness of the *Federalist Papers* and other articles, antifederalist sentiment was very strong. The keystone of compromise turned out to be a wealthy lawyer and business-man named Melancton Smith. He proved to be more important to this convention than the two antifederalist Constitutional Convention delegates, John Lansing and Robert Yates, who accompanied Hamilton to Philadelphia but did not sign the Constitution. Smith was firmly opposed to ratification without prior amendments and fiercely debated Hamilton both on the Albany convention floor and in print. When he saw Virginia approve without prior conditions (but with suggestions) he agreed to cease his opposition. His request was that Federalist John Jay should circulate a letter to other states asking for a second Constitutional Convention where key elements could be added. Smith's support brought with it enough adherents to put New York narrowly in the ratification column and confirmed the general sentiment for a Bill of Rights. Jay wrote the letters, but no second convention was seriously considered.

Rhode Island was the last state in the union to ratify the Constitution. It had been so strongly antifederal that it never sent any delegates to Philadelphia. It had conducted a popular referendum on March 24, 1788, which rejected the very idea of a ratification convention. Ratification was eventually, but barely, achieved in mid-1790.

Thus, after an often stimulating, sometimes acrimonious process, the union was preserved and the central government was strengthened. The outpouring of popular sentiment produced a Bill of Rights consisting of ten amendments that were ratified by December 5, 1791.

Not only did the ratification battle place the pendulum of governmental power in a new place upon its arc of emphasis, it also set an example for articulate and responsible debate. It showed us how controversial issues could be decided and resolved in the best interests of the country. It established compromise as an American political art form which would serve us well in many future crises. Finally, and possibly most significantly, it provided us with a treasure trove of governmental philosophy. By reading the literature and correspondence of that electric year we can learn much about what might work in the century ahead. Rather than underlining the differences between that society and this, they highlight the similarities. I believe the words of the ratification battle offer us reasons for optimism, if we will but heed them.

---

[1] Stanley Elkins and Eric McKittrick, *The Age of Federalism: The Early American Republic, 1788-1800* (New York: Oxford University Press, 1993), 452.

[2] Charles L. Mee, Jr, *The Genius of the People* (New York: Harper & Row Publishers, 1987), 183.

[3] Samuel H. Beer, *To Make a Nation: The Rediscovery of American Federalism* (Boston: The Belknap Press of Harvard University Press, 1993), 224.

[4] Gordon S. Wood, *The Radicalism of the American Revolution* (New York: Vintage Books Division of Random House, 1991), 256.

[5] David Brinkley, *David Brinkley: A Memoir* (New York: Alfred A. Knopf, 1995) 261.

[6] Hannah Arendt, *On Revolution* (New York: Penguin Books, 1963), 151.

[7] Robert J. Samuelson, *The Good Life and its Discontents: The American Dream in the Age of Entitlement 1945–1995* (New York: Times Books, 1995).

[8] William S. Carpenter, *The Development of American Political Thought,* (Princeton: Princeton University Press, 1930), 103.

[9] Virginia, Massachusetts, Connecticut, Maryland, and New Jersey.

[10] Page Smith, *The Shaping of America: A People's History of the Young Republic* (New York: Penguin Books, 1989), 3:479.

[11] James Bradley Thayer, "The Origin and Scope of the American Doctrine of Constitutional Law," *Harvard Law Review* 7 (1893), 152.

[12] John Adams and his Federalist supporters favored trade with England. Thomas Jefferson hoped to change the balance of trade to favor France. He eventually obtained passage of the Embargo and Non-Importation Acts in 1809 in an attempt to put pressure on both the English and the French who were harassing our ships and impressing our seamen. Rather than forcing these nations to change their policies, the acts caused a depression in this country and were disastrous failures.

CHAPTER 4

The Accommodation of Moral Inconsistency

He who would distinguish the true from the false must have an adequate idea of what is true and false.

Spinoza
Ethics, Part II, Prop. XLII

Moral inconsistency is not unique to our country's founding era. It has been present in all societies at every historical juncture. However, just because they are not unusual doesn't mean that moral dilemmas don't raise relevant questions.

How can it be that a group of white males who condoned slavery, denied the vote to women, and imposed property qualifications upon their fellow men before they could cast a ballot, produced the shining principles that have provided the foundation for our philosophy of government? Should we discount the wisdom of these and other individuals who persecuted Native Americans and refused to distribute their cherished rights equally throughout the population? Should hypocrisy, intellectual dishonesty, or even moral turpitude tarnish the wisdom of our founding fathers? Many in our present society would answer the question in the affirmative. They seek different principles and models for our society. They would diminish the accolades for those found wanting when judged by the criteria of the present.

What really are the alternatives? Can we find greater purity in diversity? We can assuredly benefit from an exploration of the inner workings of the many cultures that have sourced our melting pot. In so doing, however, we may not be able to avoid blemishes similar to those that tainted the founding fathers.

One example is the collection of great civilizations comprising the heritage of our African-American citizens. As broadly accomplished as they undeniably were, they contained most of the evils that we now disdain. There was inherent slavery, autocracy, oppression of women as well as abundant cruelty. That is not an indictment. The result is similar if we trace other physical and philosophical lineages back to Meso-America, to ancient Greece, to Egypt or to China. Female rulers, such as Queen Victoria, Catherine the Great and Hatshepsut, rank among the greatest the world has ever known, but their reigns contained abuses similar to those in the reigns of outstanding males.

What are those of us seeking principles and ideals to do? Are we bound to sanitize historical events or philosophical dialogue? Can we strive for utopia? Will we be able to adequately and responsibly separate "good" from "bad?" These are age old questions. No definitive answers have yet been found. Breadth, skepticism, impartiality of historical examples, a healthy dose of skepticism, and an effort to retain impartiality offer some antidotes. There are some methods we can employ to avail ourselves of our founders' wisdom and the wisdom of others with a minimum of guilt and inconsistency.

One method is to add a dash of realism. It helps to place ideas into the context of their times, to provide perspective before they are extracted into the limbo of immortality. Bernard Bailyn adds a jolt of reality to our conception of life in the 1770s and 1780s.

> While Americans of the Revolutionary generation struggled for freedom and equality in public life, they remained remarkably insensitive to the human consequences of deprivation. In such a world—where the blatant humiliation of inferiors by social superiors was a matter of common experience and where degrading physical punishment for civil and criminal offenses was routine – the utter debasement of chattel slavery needed little justification, and lesser forms of servitude were regarded as normal.[1]

This neither makes the founding generation better nor worse that we are today. It makes us both different. This difference in no way should dilute the value of pre-constitutional ideals. These ideals were a product of human beings, as flawed as we are ourselves, but worth heeding nonetheless.

Slavery is a good place to begin a comprehensive inspection. It was, we can all agree, an unspeakable evil. We recognize that as a fact, and so did many of the founders—even those who were slave owners. Two men who were prominent politicians provide samples of the era's convoluted reasoning.

"We have the wolf [slavery] by the ears, and we can neither hold him, nor simply let him go. Justice is in one scale and self-preservation in the other."—Thomas Jefferson

"Slavery was a nefarious institution. It was the curse of heaven on the states where it prevailed."—Gouverneur Morris

Those perceptive and sensitive enough to understand both sides of the issue realized that the problem contained economic contradictions that were difficult to reconcile. Jefferson, Madison, Washington, and John Rutledge all owned slaves, acknowledged slavery's inherent evil and could not come up with a viable alternative. Southern agriculture was wedded to slave labor to raise tobacco, cotton, and rice at competitive prices. Whether the economic problem was analyzed accurately is another matter. Dependence was believed. I have never seen an analysis that compared the amortized fixed cost of slaves plus the variable cost of their maintenance with the cost of free labor, if it could be attracted and used. If such analysis existed, it did nothing to convince agricultural Southerners, especially those from the lowlands, that they could survive economically without slavery. Hence, the practice was sustained even as it gnawed at the consciences of its more sensitive practitioners.

By 1787 the slave trade had been abolished by the constitutions of six states.[2] The Constitution of the United States declared that importation of slaves would become illegal by the year 1808.[3] Massachusetts had abolished slavery entirely in its constitution, largely written by John Adams in 1780.[4] Nevertheless, when the 55 delegates met in Philadelphia in May of 1787 16 of them owned working slaves (field hands). Nine more owned domestic slaves.

This is a disgraceful record. It jeopardizes the ideals we have ardently and continuously avowed. Many of our most eloquent statesmen, such as Jefferson and Madison, comprehended and acknowledged their own hypocrisy. What does this imply about their lofty sentiments? Should they be expunged from our annals and our precedents for being stained with the blood of thousands of innocent slaves? Can we accept them despite their accompanying injustices?

My own conclusion is that the words of our founders should be taken at face value for what they say about society in general. Their context can be evaluated and understood, even condemned, but it doesn't change the universal value of what was spoken or written. The personalities, the evils, the contradictions, the hypocrisies that lurked behind the words are grist for biographers or historians. They do not diminish the impact and the importance of the words themselves to those contemplating the philosophy of government.

Our founders had many things to say that were worth remembering. Some of it was brilliant. They set the stage for our greatness as a nation. Their collective thoughts can help their scions survive the twenty-first century. I am, of course, troubled by the conflicts within their personages. But in one way or another most historical giants are flawed. These flaws, while regrettable, in the majority of cases should not detract from the magnitude of accomplishments. We can respect, study and emulate some of the qualities and achievements of Caesar,

Peter the Great, Confucious, and Voltaire despite elements in their character that we have come to deplore. Similarly, we shouldn't allow the deficiencies of our founders to detract from their wisdom, their eloquence, or their legacy.

In order to balance the scales of our history we should certainly learn more about Crispus Attucks and the many African-American patriots.[5] We should learn about Deborah Sampson and the women who actively supported our Revolution. We should analyze the Iroquois Confederacy, the Cherokee and the Creek Nations as well as the other Native American government systems that offer us so much. The civilizations of Meso-America such as the Maya, the Aztec, and the Olmec influenced the ancestors of our current citizens, and we can learn from them as well. Being inclusive in the study of our origins can only enrich us. But *inclusive* is the operative word. If we exclude, we penalize ourselves and our future.

There are many examples of antifederalists who have been ignored for various reasons. One outstanding antifederalist bears mention even though she has been passed over lightly by most historians. Mercy Otis Warren was born into a prominent Barnstable family in 1728. Her older brother was the brilliant (but unstable) lawyer, James Otis, one of the leaders of the pre-Revolutionary period. Mercy married James Warren who later became speaker of the Massachusetts House of Representatives. She was a friend and correspondent of Thomas Jefferson, Samuel Adams and John Adams as well as other important patriots who respected her mind and sought her advice. She wrote plays that satirized the British colonial government: *The Adulater* (1773); *The Defeat* (1773); *The Group* (1775). She wrote tragedies, poems, and novels. Her masterwork, the widely acclaimed three-volume *History of the Rise, Progress, and Termination of the American Revolution*, was published in 1805. This work describes events, people, and policies known personally to Ms. Warren. A study of her correspondence with political leaders demonstrates the depth of her influence. Some scholars claim that a 19 page pamphlet she wrote outlining individual rights during the ratification battle inspired Madison in his eventual authorship of the Bill of Rights. Mercy Otis Warren didn't have the vote. She lacked many of the rights of her brother and her husband. She has not always been noticed by history. In all these handicaps she was accompanied by millions of our women. It was morally wrong to deny these rights. It has been intellectually wrong to ignore female contributions. The study of Mercy Otis Warren's life and works should be placed on par with the study of those with whom she associated, not only to acknowledge her gender, but also to fully understand the era. That was the conclusion reached by a panel discussion entitled, "The Invisible Founder: Mercy Otis Warren," at the 1988 forum on Women and the Constitution organized by four former first ladies.

There are two concepts involving moral inconsistency that are deeply involved with the development of antifederalism. They are *nullification* and *secession*. Ironically, the first serious brush with secession occurred in the United States when a group of arch-Federalists in New England grew disenchanted with the policies of the Jefferson and Madison administrations which culminated in the War of 1812. These Federalists didn't support the war and they didn't agree with many other aspects of their country's operation. They initiated a move to have New England secede from the union. A convention held in Hartford in the winter of 1814-1815 managed to vote it down. A major part in defeating this secession attempt was played by Harrison Gray Otis, Mercy Otis Warren's nephew.

The main lines of nullification and secession, however, ran through the South. They were, in fact, devices that neatly served the South's way of life, particularly slavery. Under the guise of states' rights, the battle to retain slavery was waged against increasing pressure from the North. Nullification and secession admirably suited the proclivities of a group of states that saw its beliefs increasingly slipping into a minority position. Mainstream antifederalists superseded this moral dilemma by rejecting nullification and secession as part of their doctrine and supporting the integrity of our union. President Andrew Jackson fought a bitter political contest to this end. While he was successful in the nullification crisis of 1832-1833, in the long run antifederalism was unable to survive the states' rights dichotomy. It lost its philosophical cohesion. It slipped into the morass that sought to justify the evil of slavery. Only a war overcame this moral inconsistency, begun perhaps inadvertently by Jefferson in 1798. Even the trauma of the Civil War was insufficient to erase the stigma of prejudice and the quest for state's rights, as the civil rights battles of the 1950s and 1960s illustrated.

A syndicated columnist recently commented upon the difficulty we all have in separating the message from the messenger.[6] He used as an example the Million Man March for African-American males, which was held on October 16, 1995. The march's chief message was that hundreds of largely middle class, family-oriented black men were demonstrating and articulating their values. Among the more poignant expression was a public apology to African-American women for the physical and mental abuse they had long undergone at the hands of their mates. The positive affirmations of this march followed closely on the heels of events with adverse racial implications: the O.J. Simpson trial; the excoriation of welfare as a disease; and the revelation of the statistic that 6.8 percent of all adult black males living in the United States in 1995 were incarcerated. The march's messages of hope and stability were lost in the whirlwind of controversy surrounding the sponsorship of the march by Louis Farrakhan of the Nation of Islam. How people felt about Minister Farrakhan's opinions on various subjects, including his alleged anti-semitism, transcended their appreciation of the march. The message was swallowed by the messenger. Moral inconsistency was allowed to triumph over valid and remarkable expressions. Our history is rife with such examples. It would be a great shame if we allowed their inconsistency to dilute the value of our founders' ideals.

As the columnist noted, I had recently touched on this subject in one of my books.

> A litmus test, in its political context, is a single issue which becomes so important that a candidate's position on it alone determines his or her acceptability to a group of voters...While application of a litmus test may occasionally prove essential, in general it does not produce the free exchange our system requires to remain vital. Discovering common ground, engaging in useful debate, reaching operable compromises all are made more difficult by litmus tests. By galvanizing electorates around strong positions on single issues, litmus tests, more often than not, serve the purpose of extremists rather that leading to a more effective government.[7]

We live in an era where litmus test politics proliferates.

The era of litmus test politics makes accommodating moral inconsistencies more difficult. Either individuals are rejected because of them, or accepted despite them. In neither case is perspective maintained and the message properly evaluated. In neither case is the nation well served.

Hopefully, we can avoid the various psychological traps and accept a selection of principles articulated by our founders for the greatness they represent. As such they can be of immense assistance to us in preparing our society to meet the challenges of the approaching century. Their absence or denigration could do incalculable harm to our prospects for national unity. Moral inconsistency will always be with us. We will have to learn how to better look beyond it so as to discern the value and applicability of philosophical truth.

---

[1] Bernard Bailyn, *Voyagers to the West: A Passage in the Peopling of America on the Eve of the Revolution* (New York: Alfred A. Knopf, 1986), 4.

[2] Connecticut, Delaware, Virginia, Maryland, South Carolina, North Carolina.

[3] Article I, Section 9, Paragraph 1 of the *Constitution of the United States.*

[4] By 1787 in addition to Massachusetts, New Hampshire banned slavery in 1784 and Pennsylvania (1780), Connecticut (1784) and Rhode Island (1784) had voted for gradual emancipation.

[5] Crispus Attucks was a sailor and the first American to be killed by the British in the Boston Massacre of March 5, 1770. There were approximately 5,000 African-American soldiers who fought in the Revolutionary War.

[6] Sean Gonsalves, "Political Acid Test Burns System," *Cape Cod Times,* 19 December 1995.

[7] Charles Stewart Goodwin, *A Resurrection of the Republican Ideal* (Lanham, MD: University Press of America, 1995), 121.

PART II

Antifederalism Now and In the Future

It is always better to form the habit of learning how to see things for yourself, listen to things for yourself, and think for yourself; then you are in a better position to judge for yourself.

Malcolm X

CHAPTER 5

State of the Union — 1990s Version

Everything that grows or changes manufactures a past by realizing a future.

Frederick J. Woodbridge
The Purpose of History, New York 1916

A few brief snapshots of the social, political, and economic climate now prevalent in the United States can bring us from ruminations about the past and plunge us into the cold water of reality. Combining the lessons of our history with the features of our present will lessen the sting of this plunge and help us to determine the texture of the coming century. Author Studs Terkel's interviews in his recent book, *The Great Divide*, declare repeatedly that our young people have no sense of history.[1] It is my intention in this book to bring history to the forefront as a valuable aid in gauging our future merely by the light it can shed upon our challenges.

Identity Crisis

The United States of the 1990s seems to be searching for a national identity. Some of us are looking backwards to a largely Euro-sourced country built upon a Judeo-Christian ethic dominated by white males. Others are looking forward to multi-culturalism with "political correctness" buffering any harshness in the description of past or present events. Understandably, there is a sense of confusion over what is happening and what it means. There is also confusion over how to regard ourselves. It seems as if there is more confusion over these two points than at any time in our history.

Before addressing the subject of government philosophy it will be helpful to get our bearings. What will this country look like in 50 years? What will happen to our economics, our politics, our social structure as well as to our demographics? Many of the conditions that lie ahead of us are pre-ordained. Others depend upon conscious choices. Together they will constitute changes as great as the United States has ever experienced.

In this chapter I will outline some of these changes. They highlight the unfortunate situation that we really don't know who we are. We thought we did as late as World War II. Katherine Newman outlined the most recent transformation of self-awareness precipitated by that crisis in her recent book *Declining Fortunes*. "The war drove home the importance of identifying as Americans, rather than as Italians, Irish, or Jews."[2] Geoffrey Perret described the situation similarly. "It [World War II] was the supreme collective social experience in modern American history. Nothing like it has happened since, for in the unity of wartime a disparate people was fused into a community."[3] Almost as soon as this new sense of national identity and unity began to settle in and become comfortable, events such as the civil rights and women's movements, as well as the Vietnam War, made us realize that we had been enjoying a false sense of security. We began to ask ourselves questions. Should we hyphenate the designation of ourselves, applying some other description first before the term American? Were we really as free and equal as we had assumed? Is our national composition about to take on a radically different structure from that which has existed in our self-images and self-projections? The search for answers and new definitions began in the 1960s. It is continuing.

Demographics

This country is in the midst of several simultaneous demographic alterations. They will govern the way we function. They will determine our national character. They will underlie our social contract.

Fifty years ago the United States was over 80 percent white and composed of people with European ancestry. Fifty years from now the country will be roughly equally balanced between those citizens considered non-Hispanic white and those considered non-white.[4] Fifty years from now less than one-third of our population will have European ancestry.

While I can clearly remember the racial separatism of the *Jim Crow* South in the 1940s and 1950s, my children will experience the mixtures and ramifications of the aforementioned balance as they raise their offspring. *Jim Crow* and other similar evils will be historical remnants to be reviled, even disavowed. In their place could come the unity of the melting pot. Also possible are the sharp divisions of enclavism, elitism, and hatred. If any of these three conditions proliferate, we will be even worse off sociologically than we were 50 years ago. We can see that the path to the future will be cut by many crossroads. The path will also contain many challenges. Our national identity and our sense of optimism may depend upon the directional choices we make during the years remaining in this decade.

Between now and the middle of the next century this country will experience the rapid growth of two demographic groups, the over-65 and the under-18. The elderly will be swelled by the serial maturity of the *baby boomer* generation.[5] The Census bureau projects that over-65-year-old individuals will move from the 11 percent of the voting age population they constituted in 1992 to 13 percent by the year 2000, to 23 percent by 2050. Assuming persistence of current mortality rates the over-85-year-old group will increase even faster, by six times to almost 18 million by 2050.

Fifty percent of all Hispanic Americans and 45 percent of all African-Americans are under 18 today. Both groups have birth rates that are greater than the national average. In fact, since 1989 total new births have amounted to over four million people per year for the first time since the era of the baby boomers. Much of this is due to these two ethnic groups, which together accounted for almost 70 percent of new births in 1994.

The largely white over-65-year-old population will depend greatly for its future support upon young non-white workers. At the same time, there will be a drop in new entrants to the work force due to the shrunken numbers of the *baby buster* generation.[6] By the middle of the next century each worker will have to support about twice as many retirees than a worker does now.

Government figures indicate that the number of workers per retiree will drop from the 3.9 it was in 1994 to 3.3 in 1999 to 2.8 in 2112, to 2.4 in 2030, and to 2.1 in 2050. This will drastically change burdens and attitudes. For example, can we expect poorly educated non-whites to willingly support the benefits of elderly white retirees who may have been instrumental in denying them educational and occupational opportunity? The Concord Coalition estimates that by the first quarter of the new century our workers would have to undergo an 84 percent increase in their taxes to sustain entitlements at current rates of payment for those then retired. They also estimate that by the middle of the next century the costs for Social Security and Medicare (if left unchanged) will consume approximately 50 percent of every worker's paycheck, up from 16.8 percent. Obviously, neither of these developments is financially feasible. These figures indicate the need for a dramatic change in our ideas on benefits, on age, on race, and on education if we are to achieve and to finance anything approaching national unity.

Without unity, meeting the social and economic demands of the new century will be impossible.

Besides the confrontation between age groups, another challenge will arise from the deterioration of and changes in the composition of the traditional family.[7] A divorce rate equal to the marriage rate has weakened the family fabric. We have produced a society in which almost one-third of all babies are born out of wedlock and in which 300,000 children annually reside in foster homes. Part of the problem is embedded poverty. Part of the problem is self-discipline. Our post World War II society has stressed *rights* and *freedoms* at the expense of obligations. We have considered an almost total free range of activities to be our ideal, and have gone a long way towards attaining it. We have largely abandoned faith as outmoded and too restrictive, removing yet another obligation. The family has suffered thereby, as has our responsibility towards it. The result is not only broken homes. It is also the spectre of our elderly residing alone in public and private institutions. It is the trauma of crime and drugs. It is the stress of systemic welfare. It is the social and physical breakdown of our inner cities.

Another challenge is immigration. Few issues have been more integral to the development of the United States. Concomitantly, few issues have proven to be more consistently inflammatory. The May 7, 1964 issue of *The Economist* summarized the problem. "To polarize American opinion, there is nothing quite like the subject of immigration. On the one side are people who think that the current, relatively relaxed policy risks ruining the country. On the other are those who see immigration as the key to America's revitalization."[8] Census figures indicate that while one in 12 Americans was foreign born in 1992, a figure that compares favorably with the one in seven of 1900, a record number of our citizens were born abroad—19.7 million. Immigration in the 1980s (six million legal, two million estimated illegal) approached the previous record decade - the 8.8 million immigrants of 1900-1910. But if current trends continue, ten million immigrants (both legal and illegal) will pour into the United States in the 1990s. Over 90 percent of the new entrants at the turn of the century were from Europe. In the 1980s almost 85 percent were non-European and the figure will approximate 90 percent in the 1990s. This is indeed a new and incendiary situation. The fact that English is now a second language to almost 40 million residents, up from 34 million in 1992 and 23 million in 1980, adds tinder to this pyre. We cannot ignore our new residents. It is unrealistic to think that we can expel them (at least the legal ones). We must seek better methods of accommodation, inclusion and unification, if the United States is to remain healthy and prosperous.

Our final example of the coming century's demographic challenge is urbanization. By Census Bureau estimate 90 percent of the population growth in the 1980s took place in areas classified as metropolitan with over one million residents. By 1990 50.2 percent of this country's people lived in such areas, up from 45.9 percent in 1980. The percentage will grow in the coming century.

However one classifies urban areas it is an enduring failure of our civilization that we have not made them clean, safe, financially rewarding places to live for most of their residents. Conversely, as the post-World War II period has developed, progressively more urban denizens have become exposed to crime, violence, pollution, and economic pressure. In inner cities, disease is burgeoning to Third World levels. Life expectancy is dropping. Education and employment lag far behind the national averages. As a nation we have devoted relatively few resources to these urban problems, thus ensuring their persistence. Urban areas can be cosmopolitan. They can also be de-humanizing and divisive. Crowned by their unreachable suburban diadems they represent both extremes and emphasize our national dichotomy. We can still choose redemptive options, but the one-way route to large scale desperation looms frighteningly close. The resources needed to confront our urban problems are escalating annually.

Economics

We face a series of economic challenges whose outcome will affect the nature of our society in the coming century. The most basic is the challenge to the American Dream at virtually every economic strata.

Embedded poverty is becoming more endemic. Almost 40 million people live under conditions officially described as poverty.[9] Furthermore, a 1994 study showed that 18 percent of all Americans with year-round, full-time jobs had below poverty line earnings. This was an increase from the 12 percent who reported similarly sublinear earnings in 1979.[10] Working poor are growing more common each day. That is an indictment of our system.

However one defines and measures poverty, there is no argument with the fact that a substantial portion of our population lives under distressing conditions and shows little ability to extricate itself. Charles Handy avers that we have made the situation worse through our definition of values. "We made consumption a measure of achievement, unwittingly creating a society of envy, in which to be poor means having less than the average, even if the average is quite high. This is a no-win world, and unintended."[11] We have stigmatized the poor. Michael Katz puts it another way. "In the land of opportunity poverty has seemed not only a misfortune but a moral failure."[12] If Mahatma Ghandi was correct that "poverty is the worst form of violence," a large and growing segment of our population is daily being subjected to a persistent and pernicious physical and psychological battering from their income status alone. Most of these ingrained poor are non-white and 42 percent of them inhabit our inner cities. The appalling conditions under which many of them exist have prompted some harsh observations about our country that we all would prefer not to confront. Andrew Purvis commented that, "a man living in Bangladesh has a better chance of reaching age 65 than a man living in Harlem."[13] *The Economist* reported "in parts of the country a black man between the ages of 15 and 25 is more likely to be killed than was an American soldier in Vietnam."[14] Is this really how we wish to live, and to be remembered? Are we so bereft of imagination that we can find few meaningful ways to express societal compassion?

We also have to ask ourselves as we calibrate our priorities: What are our goals? Are we desirous of improving the standard of living for the majority of our people? Are we interested in the diminution of poverty, or are we merely trying to isolate it? Are we really engaged in insulating our more prosperous segments from the effluvia of the ghettos? The Reverend Martin Luther King, Jr. addressed this question in a sermon delivered at the Washington National Cathedral on March 11, 1968. The title was, "Remaining Awake Through a Great Revolution," and it focused on the ethical choice before us. "There is nothing in that parable that said Dives went to hell because he was rich, Jesus never made a universal indictment against all wealth …Dives went to hell because he passed by Lazarus every day and never really saw him. Indeed, Dives went to hell because he sought to be a conscientious objector in the war against poverty."[15] The current battle over the reform of social services provided to the indigent is only one element of this situation. Ultimately we will have to decide whether or not our nation intends to be a conscientious objector in the war against poverty, and this decision will impact the nature of our social contract.

There is a generational conflict looming. It is the confrontation between the elderly and the young over increasingly scarce national resources. People over 65 currently account for 13 percent of the population. They receive 29 percent of all federal spending, 54 percent of all federal social spending, and account for almost 40 percent of all health care expenditures. People under 18 comprise 26 percent of the population. They receive seven percent of all federal dollars and comparable amounts of other resources.[16] Young families have suffered some relative deprivation as well over the 1973 to 1993 period. "Also over those same 20 years the number of 30-40 year olds who owned homes dropped from 60.1 percent to 50.0 percent."[17] Another measurement is that "since 1973 the real median income of households headed by adults aged sixty-five and over has risen by more than 25 percent, while the real median income of households under thirty-five has fallen by more than 10 percent."[18] The number of young people who have families has declined over that period by 13 percent for heads of households under 30. This is primarily due to the inability to support a family in what is deemed a reasonable manner. All of these figures indicate that as spending on entitlements escalates and available resources tighten, the generational battle will intensify.[19]

Whatever happened economically during the 1980s, and there are widely differing versions, depending on what is evaluated over what period, there are at least four basic and incontrovertible assertions that can be applied to the 1980s and the first half of the 1990s.

First, the gap between the highest earning 20 percent, ten percent or one percent of our population and the corresponding groups at the bottom of the income spectrum widened. One representative statistic was unearthed by Graef Crystal, an expert on executive compensation, who surveyed 424 of our largest companies. In 1974 the typical chief executive officer made about 40 times what his average worker earned. In 1995 he earned 190 times as much.

Second, real disposable after-tax income remained stagnant in the aggregate. Census figures show that the median American worker earned $25,896 per year (in constant inflation-adjusted dollars) in 1979. In 1995 the figure was $24,700, 4.6 percent less.

Third, the share of all taxes paid by the highest earning 20 percent, ten percent and one percent of the population increased while the share of all taxes paid by the comparable groups at the bottom of the income scale fell.

Finally, the level of national debt rose from under $1 trillion in 1979 to $4 trillion in 1990. At the end of 1994 the national debt was $4.7 trillion, or $78,000 for each American family. The annual interest cost on this debt in 1994 was over $200 billion. Interest absorbed over ten percent of national income and over 15 percent of our budget.[20] All those numbers and percentages continue to rise.

These facts provide some clues as to why so-called "economic recoveries" have recently proven unsatisfactory as far as increasing disposable income, reducing core unemployment and lowering debt are concerned, and why the "rich vs. poor" economic situation is proving so difficult to resolve. They also illustrate why the necessary reform of our economic system will have to include substantial spending cuts and comprehensive tax realignment if our country's financial flexibility is to be regained.

The macro economic environment created by these conditions of crushing debt and deficits reduces our ability to respond to changing conditions and needs. The trade and budget deficits each have fluctuated between $100 and $300 billion and in fiscal 1995 the budget deficit alone amounted to 2.4 percent of GDP. The movements have been the result of economic activity, rather than being due to government spending discipline. Consumers are burdened with record levels of debt whose maintenance captures almost 20 percent of their pre-tax income. With so many obligations other than debt built into our spending, such as costs for entitlements and for meeting the requirements of the Americans With Disabilities Act, our deficits cannot show meaningful permanent decline and our budget cannot be balanced without pervasive and fundamental economic reform.

Senator Bob Kerrey, a Democrat from Nebraska, who was co-chairman of the Bi-Partisan Committee on Entitlements and Tax Reform, summarized our financial situation in a recent article.

> Without reforms...the Medicare hospital insurance trust fund will go bankrupt by 2001. In 2013 we will be forced to begin dipping into the surplus in the Social Security trust fund to cover benefit payments an event to be followed by insolvency of the entire fund by 2029...Without reforms, the aging population will catapult spending on retirement benefits skyward so fast that by 2012...every dollar the federal government collects in taxes will go directly to spending on entitlements and interest on the national debt...By 2030 the federal budget will equal nearly 40 percent of our economy, even though discretionary spending will shrink during that period. Today the budget equals less than a quarter of the economy.[21]

It is clear from this summary and the foregoing information that the financial structure of our nation will have to change materially in the coming century. These changes will have to exceed any budget proposals yet seriously considered, and will have to be attuned to a philosophy that can deal with the emerging composition of our country. If the previously quoted figures sound an alarm, they should. No adequate solutions are possible until we are jolted from our suicidal complacency and become committed to an across-the-board reduction in the way our society consumes and despoils its resources—natural, financial, and human.

Politics

It is a fact that people over 65 vote at a 50 percent higher rate than those under 35. There are many obvious reasons for that occurrence. One of them is the free time to organize and to be involved. A result of this phenomenon is that legislation favoring seniors pervades our political system, often at the expense of younger citizens. If the balance is to be redressed and the future of our youth is to be protected, these young citizens will have to organize, to participate, and to vote in far greater numbers than they have to date, and to find ways to impact the system to their advantage.

Another example of effective political organization is the born-again Christian fundamentalists, part of whom are represented by the Christian Coalition. These Born-Again Christians account for 13-14 percent of the total electorate. Approximately 85 percent of them vote. Thus, in the election of 1992 when 55 percent of all registered voters voted, these fundamentalists accounted for almost 22 percent of the total vote. In 1994 when the percentage of voting dropped to 38 percent, their contribution jumped to 37 percent, with a disproportionately high weighting in the South and Southwest. It is no mystery why conservative Republicans from the Sun Belt dominated our House of Representatives. This example illustrates how special interests pay an increasing role in our system. Part of their impact is due to money. More of it is due to persistence, the willingness to pursue issues through endless hearings—and to vote.

Besides the beginnings of generational and religious clashes, with their attendant special interest issues, American politics has recently been characterized by four general traits. First of all, it has endured wide swings of opinion and preference. Whether is was Bill Clinton's 1992 victory over George Bush, who had enjoyed a 90 percent approval rating barely a year earlier, or the 1994 capture of both houses of Congress by the Republicans for the first time since the Eisenhower Administration, our politics have demonstrated that fortunes can change quickly and dramatically.

A second characteristic is a serious flirtation with third parties for the first time since the Henry Wallace and Strom Thurmond ran independently in 1948 and the American Independent Party of George Wallace was placed on the ballot in 1968. The 19 percent of the vote cast for Ross Perot in the presidential election of 1992, and the periodic showing of support for alternatives to the established parties, show the basic dissatisfaction of the electorate. The continued searching for policies and candidates outside the established two-party system demonstrates the public's disillusionment with the politics and politicians of the establishment.

This brings us to a third characteristic. There is widespread disgust with politicians and with "politics as usual." There is no doubt that politicians continue to sink in the esteem of the electorate and that voters are looking for antidotes. Robert J. Samuelson in his recent book, *The Good Life and Its Discontents*, postulates that this disgust is a direct response of the Age of Entitlement. He believes, correctly in my opinion, that politicians have contributed to their own low regard by promising so much that they can only disappoint.[22]

Despite these expressions of frustration, our citizens are not participating either in the process of government or in elections. This constitutes the fourth, the most pervasive and the most disturbing characteristic. In the presidential election of 1992, 55 percent of registered voters voted. Deplorably this was the highest percentage since 1960. In the ensuing elections of 1994 only 38 percent of those registered voted. This contrasts with the nineteenth century when between 1828 and 1900 the number of eligible voters participating in presidential elections never fell below 56 percent. On occasion, such as in 1896, it hit 80 percent. Our democracy is at risk of demise from the disease of apathy. It is that simple. In order to rescue our version of democracy, our citizens may wish to make changes in their political system so that participation in both elections and in government is encouraged. These changes would include a reform of the Electoral

College, campaign finance reform, a change in the duration of most campaigns and, possibly, term limits.

We should recognize, along with writer Michael Barone, that people want more from their government and their elected officials. "The first thing voters seek of government is order—not some arbitrary, authoritarian order, but a rational, predictable order in which ordinary people can raise families, make their livings, participate in their communities and go about their daily lives without fear of physical violence or economic disaster."[23] It sounds like a rudimentary request, but we are a long way from attaining this ambiance of order and security.

There is another element that needs to be restored to our political environment if it is to remain consistent with our democratic, republican foundation. That element is responsible and reasonable debate. This need was eloquently stated by director Mike Nichols (born Michael Igor Peschkowsky in Berlin in 1932) during the course of an Associated Press interview published on March 23, 1996.

> The left and right have to reconcile. The right attacks the left. The left attacks the left...But everybody—parents and children, gays and straights, blacks and whites, and Hispanics should dispense with the attacks. That's the whole idea of this country, Discussion. Dialectic reconciliation. Something very strange has happened to the idea of democracy, which started out with the Greeks, and a reverence for public discussion and questions above answers. Now, all public discourse is nonsense. The only meaningful discourse is in private, mostly secret...there are no questions, only answers. Everybody's beating each other over the head with answers. 'I'm more correct than you.' But that was the idea that you should be able to ask as many questions as possible and discuss them openly. So anything that moves us toward that is a good thing.

Our founders understood dialogue. Their inheritance needs to be redeemed.

Sociology

There are several additional sociological factors that could mold our governing process as we enter the twenty-first century.

The first is the growing tendency toward enclavism spreading throughout our country, particularly along its coasts. People are grouping together economically, ethnically, religiously and generationally. This is not really a new development *per se*. After all, ethnic neighborhoods once formed the backbone of our cities and towns. It is the impetus behind much of this gathering that is unprecedented. In many cases reflex insularity is taking place despite the efforts of government to encourage inclusion, integration, and unity.

It is too often motivated by fear. Its aim is to create the opposite of a melting pot, the safe haven of homogeneity.

Peter Brimelow, writing in *Forbes,* described what is happening.

> The 1990s census shows that international immigration and internal migration are resulting in a spontaneous phenomenon of racial self-sorting in the United States. Only in a few big cities, like New York and Los Angeles, are all racial groups present in force...There are 89 counties that are more than half black...There are 45 counties that are over half Hispanic...There are five counties that are over half Asian...Much of the U.S. interior remains more that 95% white...Of course, immigrants have formed enclaves before. What's new is the scale. The immigrant flow is relatively larger and has lasted longer. What's also new is that with today's easy mobility, it's easier for native-born Americans who don't like living among the newer groups to flee into their own enclaves.[24]

Joel Klotkin, a senior fellow with the Pepperdine Institute for Public Policy and the Pacific Research Institute, has elaborated on this phenomenon.

> Reacting to the cacophony of urban life, millions of Americans seem to be succumbing to what may be called the Valhalla syndrome—a *fin de siecle* yearning for a heavenly retreat, with the promised reward of a simpler, less complex existence. This mass migration could well shape the economic, political, and cultural landscape of the coming decades. As middle-class predominantly white Americans detach themselves from the multi-colored realities of urban metropolitan regions—moving not just to the suburbs but far beyond—the gap between the cities and the world beyond could grow greater.[25]

Ironically, this enclavism is abetted by technology. Sophisticated computer software enables people of like interests to interact without ever leaving their desks. In some ways this is good. But it fosters contact without the development of social skills. People are losing the ability to talk to each other. They are creating cyber-enclaves as well as physical ones.

This trend is not merely exclusionary. It is fostered by a conviction that government has failed. William Eggers, commenting in *Time* magazine about his annual survey on privatization, noted that community associations, ranging from condominiums to towns, have grown from 10,000 in 1970 to 150,000 in 1993, and now contain one in eight Americans. On February 8, 1996 *The Wall Street Journal* estimated that four million people live in gate-guarded, limited-access communities. These communities often provide a wide range of municipal-like services including sanitation and security. "People are saying that if government can't protect them any more or keep their streets clean, then they are going to do it themselves."[26] In one sense this is positive. It is creating government skills and self-sufficiency. But separatism is not positive. Neither is frustration, it induces isolation.

People everywhere are reacting to the perception (or reality) of a deteriorating quality of life, especially in urban areas. They are also reacting to crime which has doubled from 2,180 reported crimes per 100,000 in 1963 to 5,438 per 100,000 in 1993, even though figures for the last couple of years show a slight decline.[27] The young are committing more violent crimes and pseudo-familial youth gangs are spreading across the nation from their headquarters in Los Angeles, New York, or Chicago. In the last five years homicides committed by 14 to 17 year olds have risen 22 percent, while they have declined for other age groups. After years of falling numbers this violent age group is about to explode. There are currently 39 million children under the age of 10 in the United States. This is more that at any time since the *baby boomers* were young in the 1950s. Demographics indicate that the anti-social condition of youth-generated violent crime could be poised for a sharp upturn.

In this country we have over 1 million people incarcerated (including 6.8 percent of all adult black males). This is more absolutely, and relatively, than in any other industrial nation. Yet there is a widespread push for even more prison construction. This paroxysm of fear is often directed specifically against young non-white males who are heavily involved in violence, including the use and distribution of drugs. There is no statistical indication that either the threat or the actuality of incarceration has reduced the violent tendencies of young non-whites, particularly those whose lives seem foreshortened and devoid of opportunity. Fear inhabits all demographic groups, but none more than those who must live side by side with the anti-social miasma of inner city ghettos. It clouds their view of the future. It develops their regard for themselves. It percolates out to surrounding areas. There have to be less costly and more effective answers other than prison. One of these is attitude and its close relative, culture. While the situation is not strictly comparable, it is interesting to note that Arab societies, which have more than their share of urban squalor and poverty, are generally characterized by low crime rates. David Lamb commented on this condition in 1988. "The crime rate is minuscule in every Arab country, even though most use a Western-style legal system. So maybe it is the nature of the Arab culture and the strength of the Arabs' faith, rather than the punishment itself, that account for the absence of crime and violence."[28]

Another sociological factor constitutes an even more ominous threat lurking in our national shadows. It involves the nature of our social contract. The concept of a social contract as a written, oral, or implicit compact among a given group of people defining the rules of their co-existence welled up from the Classical Age. It was filtered through the philosophy of the Enlightenment. It flowed readily to our shores and into our Constitution. Throughout our history the tensile strength of our social contract has been tested many times, but only once, during the Civil War, has it given way and resulted in overt multiplicity. We face such a danger now. We might be nurturing in our midst an alternate social contract.

The embedded poverty that envelops 40 million Americans, particularly the 16 to 17 million that live in our inner cities, has created for them a vastly different perspective on life and the future than that held by most Americans. Violence, crime, and squalor are compounded by inferior education, shortened life expectancy and materially lesser prospects for family and vocation. Poverty-stricken citizens are not new in this country. What is different now from the past is the sheer size of the underclass and its degree of hopelessness. The majority of the core disadvantaged are under-25-year-old African-Americans and Hispanics. Ironically, it is young non-whites who will compose a significant percentage of the reduced number of workers called upon to support each retiree in the next century.

A young African-American or Hispanic-American male who doesn't expect to live to the age of 40 and receives severely restricted opportunities along the tortured path of his brief existence is not likely to have much respect for the life of others. Furthermore, such a person is not likely to be willing to allocate a portion of his or her earnings to fund the retirement of elderly whites. It is alarming to have a large absolute number of our citizens for whom the system of government, the social contract, is just not working. There are millions who will not be educated or employed or housed like the rest of us. For them America is a very different place, as Langston Hughes recognized in the poem that began this volume.

The extent to which this feeling of hopelessness transcends the numbers of abjectly poor and reaches other citizens is the extent to which our present contract is at risk.

If insecure workers or the young who see their future dimming or females who perceive an attenuation of their rights and opportunities join with the underclass, the substance of our contract could alter significantly. Are we capable of creating a spiritual rejuvenation in our underclass, such as the one hoped for by Jacob Riis when he wrote *How the Other Half Lives* in 1890? Our overall lack of financial flexibility; our current lack of political leadership; our apathy towards participation in government; our increasing polarization on issues and our spreading enclavism all mitigate against solutions and escalate the level of risk. It is a very real possibility that this country could enter the twenty-first century with more than one social contract. This would not only be a tragedy, it would be dangerous. However, it is becoming a real possibility. The recent book, *The Winner-Take-All Society*, describes one way the socio-economic center is vanishing.[29] There are a few big winners in most fields and a vast majority experiencing various degrees of not winning. This condition is not a formula for social contract unity. Neither is the growing alienation of corporate America from the national mainstream. They need each other in many ways, and any separation is more than unfortunate. As Robert J. Samuelson has written, "The source of these discontents is simple disappointment."[30] In order to protect our social contract, our national challenge becomes how to transform this disappointment into hopeful anticipation.

A third sociological, as well as demographic, condition is our crisis of gender. Despite the power of the women's movement, despite the very real economic and social advances that have been made in the past 20 years, women remain second-class citizens in almost every respect. They are not currently receiving either the educational or vocational opportunities afforded their male counterparts. In a winner-take-all society, a far lower percentage of women can be deemed winners. This is a potentially malignant condition, especially since our country will desperately need the maximum female contributions—economic, political, and social—if it is to prosper. It is elementary. We just cannot afford the discouragement of our female citizens.

Philosophy

Historian Robert Hughes, writing an essay for *Time* magazine, illuminated the reasons why a coherent, articulated philosophy of government is important for this country.

> America is a construction of mind, not of race of inherited class or ancestral territory. It is a creed born of imagination, of the jostling of scores of tribes that become Americans to the extent to which they can negotiate accommodations with one another. These negotiations succeed unevenly and often fail: you need only to glance at the history of racial relations to know that. The melting pot never melted. But American mutuality lives in recognition of difference. The fact remains that America is a collective act of imagination whose making never ends, and once that sense of collectivity and mutual respect is broken, the possibilities of American-ness begin to unravel.[31]

Our intellectuals and politicians have never hesitated to trumpet the innate superiority of the United States. We have projected our concepts upon the collapsing communist regimes of Eastern Europe and the crumbled dictatorships of Latin America. At the same time our own philosophical thought process is failing us. It appears to be reflecting images seen through a rear view mirror. We are hungry for a coherent, relevant philosophy with which to greet and surmount the next century.

Philosophy, ideals, and concepts do matter. It is the changing nature of America, decried by some, eagerly awaited by others, but inevitable to all, that requires an altered philosophy. We do not have to depart from our history to find one. We do not have to settle for one unsuited to twenty-first century conditions. There is a philosophy of government from our past that may well be more suited to the 1990s than it was to the 1790s. That philosophy is pre-constitutional antifederalism. I believe it can inspire the weaving of a newer, perhaps stronger American social fabric. I have described its origins. I have outlined the environment that awaits its entrance. I have advocated its transposition along the arc created by the pendulum of governmental needs. In the next few chapters of this book I will describe how its tenets can fit the dimensions of the United States as it enters the next century.

---

[1] Studs Terkel, *The Great Divide: Second Thoughts on the American Dream* (New York: Pantheon Books, 1988).

[2] Katherine S. Newman, *Declining Fortunes: The Withering of the American Dream* (New York: Basic Books, 1993).

[3] Geoffrey Perret, *Days of Sadness, Years of Triumph: The American People 1939-1945* (New York: Penguin Books, 1973), 433.

[4] The United States Census Bureau made the following estimates in 1995: The population of the United States will grow from 262 million in 1994 Whites comprised 74% of the people, or 194 million, in 1994. They are projected to be 209 million or 53% in 2050.
African-Americans were 31 million people, or 12% of the population, in 1994. They are estimated to be 54 million, or 13.6%, in 2050.
Hispanic-Americans comprised 27 million people, or 10.2% of the population, in 1994. They are projected to be 96 million, or 25%, by 2050.
Asian-Americans were 8 million, or 3% of the population, in 1994. They are estimated at 32 million, or 8%, by 2050.

[5] Baby boomers are the 76 million people born between 1946 and 1964. Baby busters are the 46 million people born between 1964 and 1974.

[6] Starting at midnight on December 31, 1995 one baby-boomer will turn 50 every 7 seconds.

[7] The Census Bureau estimates that 30% of all families are headed by a single parent. (In African-American families the figure is 58%). That means there are 15.7 million single-parent families. In addition, 9.9 million families are *blended* (including stepparents and stepchildren). Approximately, 4.7 million families are headed by grandparents.

[8] *The Economist*, "American Survey: Return of the Huddled Masses", 7 May 1994, 25.

[9] By Census Bureau estimate the percentage of our population living under the poverty line (earning less than one-half the median income) was 12.8% in 1968; 11.1% in 1973 (the century's low); 13.2% in 1983; 14.1% in 1988; 14.8% in 1992 and 15.17% in 1994.

[10] U.S. Department of Commerce, *The Earnings Ladder,* 30 March 1994.

[11] Charles Handy, *The Age of Paradox* (Boston: Harvard Business School Press, 1994), 10.

[12] Michael B. Katz, *In the Shadow of the Poorhouse: A Social History of Welfare in America* (New York: Basic Books, 1986), xii.

[13] Andrew Purvis, "Why Do Blacks Die Young?" *Time*, 16 September 1991, 52.

[14] *The Economist*, "America's Wasted Blacks," 30 May 1991, 11.

[15] Congressional Budget Office estimates the most controversial element of social services, welfare, was distributed to 14 million persons in 1994. The cost was $12.5 billion to the Federal Government and $10 billion to the states.

[16] Congressional Budget Office figures.

[17] Congressional Budget Office figures.

[18] Peter G. Peterson, "Will America Grow Up Before It Grows Old?" *The Atlantic Monthly*, May 1996, 74.

[19] Entitlements are legal obligations such as Social Security and Medicare to which specific groups believe they are "entitled". In 1994 they accounted for 52% of the federal budget.

[20] Federal Reserve figures.

[21] Bob Kerrey, "Sacred Cow Entitlements," The *Washington Post*, National Weekly Edition, 6-12 February 1995, 29.

[22] Robert J. Samuelson, *The Good Life and Its Discontents: The American Dream in the Age of Entitlement, 1945-1995* (New York: Times Books, 1995)

[23] Michael Barone, "Returning to Toqueville," The *Washington Post* National Weekly Edition, 15-21 January, 1996, 23.

[24] Peter Brimelow, "Al Gore's Lousy Latin," *Forbes*, 15 August 1994, 72-3.

[25] Joel Kotkin, "Beyond White Flight," *Washington Post*, National Weekly Edition, 18-24 March 1996, 26

[26] Jon D. Hall, "The State of the Union," *Time*, 30 January 1995, 57.

[27] The FBI reports juvenile arrests for violent crime went up 68% from 1984 to 1993.

[28] David Lamb, *The Arabs: Journeys Beyond the Mirage* (New York: Vintage Books, 1988), 117.

[29] Robert H. Frank and Philip Cook, *The Winner-Take-All Society* (New York: Free Press, 1995).

[30] Robert J. Samuelson, *The Good Life and Its Discontents: The American Dream in the Age of Entitlement, 1945-1995* (New York: Times Books, 1995), 209.

[31] Robert Hughes, "The Fraying of America," *Time*, 3 February 1992.

CHAPTER 6

A Philosophy for the Knowledge Society

> The old communities—family, village, parish, and so on—have all but disappeared in the knowledge society. Their place has largely been taken by the new unit of social integration, the organization.
>
> Peter Drucker

I first became aware of the term *knowledge society* when reading an article by Peter Drucker.[1] It focused several thoughts that had been floating around in my mind for some time. This article struck me as an accurate description of current and potential developments. In his explanation of this developing society Drucker's analysis has future philosophical implications.

"The shift to knowledge-based work poses enormous social challenges...this is far more than a social change. It is a change in the human condition. What it means—what are the values, the commitments, the problems of the new society—we do not know. But we do know that much will be different."[2]

"A society in which knowledge workers dominate is under threat from a new class conflict: between the large minority of knowledge workers and people who will make their living traditionally, either by manual work, whether skilled or unskilled, or by work in services, whether skilled or unskilled."[3] This is indeed happening. It is already causing divisions and imbalances. We haven't yet figured out how to adjust. We are just beginning to realize what is actually taking place.

Another author that contributed to my philosophical focus was Charles Handy, who described in his book *The Age of Paradox* what new capabilities might be required in a society where "intelligence has replaced land as the source of wealth."[4] Both Drucker and Handy raised a myriad of questions for me. What is intelligence? What is knowledge? What is an organization? What is work? What philosophy can be applicable to the rapidly changing conditions in this country? I will address these questions and some others in this and subsequent chapters.

The standard for philosophical exploration that was set by a social activist, Jim Wallis, is one with which I concur. He summarized the task faced by any governmental philosophy in the coming century. "The success of the American Experiment depends upon us remembering the past, transforming the present, and altering the future. How can we forge a genuinely pluralistic nation where everyone's dignity, contributions and aspirations can be respected and even nurtured?"[5] Indeed. This is what transposed antifederalism can accomplish. Furthermore, it can produce this accomplishment in the knowledge society that is emerging.

My own interpretation of antifederalism may differ from the definitions presented by others. For example, Charles Handy's idea of federalism, which he applied primarily to organizations, comes very close to my definition of antifederalism.[6] Our similar, but diversely named philosophy would build on the principles inherent in Montesquieu's theory of small republics. My concept, as applied to government, would remove power from the center and devolve some of it upon the states, and more importantly upon local entities. While the center would not be disemboweled, it would be bled of some of its functions, personnel, and funding to provide more viable participatory vehicles at the local level.

Local republics, perhaps 2,000 to 3,000 persons in size, would enlist citizen-governors as voluntary, or quasi-voluntary, entrants into the system so that they can operate as many of the factors affecting the local residents' lives as practicable. By this inclusive action as well as by downsizing the relevant entities, representative majorities of relatively homogeneous units could be obtained. These little republics would be bound together in empowered confederations with larger entities such as towns, counties, and states providing essential coordinative functions within the larger republican whole. Thus, would the concepts of Jefferson and Madison be combined in a compound/compact republic. Perhaps more significantly the nature of this structure would encourage, in fact require, participation by our citizens. Increased participation, along with an increased sense of making a difference, would resuscitate our democracy and enable it to flourish with individual citizens once again at the helm.

This small republic system based upon a philosophy of transposed antifederalism fits the structural imbalances we now face, some of which were covered in Chapter 5. Our present society is burdened not only by financial constraints, but also by an anchor of imbedded poverty, which comprises nearly 15 percent of our population. It is constrained by a pattern of rampant consumption through which our six percent of the world's people devour 35 percent of its natural resources. It is polarized by increasingly extreme advocacy, by a disappearance of dialogue and by a scarcity of compromise. Our society is increasingly riven by hatred, envy and fear. Walls are escalating around its enclaves. As these conditions develop, the inevitability of demographic transformation is drawing closer. This society of ours is manifestly philosophically barren while growing increasingly bereft of understanding and compassion. An articulated philosophy may not instantly produce change, but it could produce an attitudinal change.

Technology has exacerbated many of these traits, as noted by William Greider.

> The electronic media—radio and television, and in the emerging future, personal computer networks—produce such contradictions. By their nature, these media empower ordinary citizens—providing access and information that did not previously exist for them, connecting them with distant events and authorities. But it is not clear, as yet, whether new culture created by modern communications will someday lead to a revitalized democracy or simply debase the imperfect politics that already existed.[7]

This is a conundrum of the knowledge society in which our very progress may be leading us in the direction of oligarchy. According to Michael Lind, an overclass, mostly white and male, has brought us to this destination already.[8]

Technology, building upon circumstance, is changing our concept of family, community, organizations and intelligence. It is also, to varying degrees, isolating us. Charles Handy speculates that "loneliness may be the real disease of the next century, as we live alone, work alone, and play alone, insulated by our modem, our walkman, our television...It is no longer clear where we connect and where we belong."[9] Elizabeth Wurtzel, author of *The Prozac Nation*, elaborated on this theme in an interview.[10] "Until I'd traveled a lot, I didn't realize just how lonely this country is. Our national culture is about change, movement, throwing it away and starting over again. It leaves a lot of people feeling isolated and empty."[11] Democracy is a government of rubbing elbows, of heated discussion, of crowded gatherings. Our governmental structure has to fit our philosophy in order to preserve democracy. As we become aware of the knowledge society's outlines, it is increasingly apparent that we have no philosophy to fit this new configuration.

We cannot roll back the impact of technology any more than we can stem the tide of demographics. We can work to adapt. To accomplish that end we have to picture the knowledge elite concentrating on screens, interacting in new combinations—alone but yet electronically connected. Any philosophy for governing in the next century will have to reach them, to move them, and, most importantly, to integrate them. Robert Putnam has remarked that this elite, along with everyone else, has become progressively less involved with their government. "By almost every measure, Americans' direct engagement in politics and government has fallen steadily and sharply over the last generation, despite the fact that average levels of education—the best individual-level predicator of political participation—have risen sharply throughout this period. Every year over the past decade or two, millions more have withdrawn from the affairs of their communities."[12] Is the sense of community, of being in communities, changing into collections of electronic networks? Are these regional, national, and international networks being disconnected from physical communities, thereby increasing the isolation reflected in the glow of a multi-screened America? Are the baby boomers, who have already begun to turn 50 at the rate of seven every second, leading us into a disconnected, egocentric future? Is Christopher Hitchins accurate in his analysis? "In the therapy generation, which scripts even its own lenient satires, you are by all means allowed, if not encouraged to feel guilty. Just as long as you don't feel responsible."[13] Robert J. Samuelson views the situation similarly. "Mass culture is receding before niche culture. Although this is in a many ways healthy, because it offers people more choices, it also fosters social distance."[14] The elites of the knowledge society functioning as the new century's leaders will have to develop a sense of responsibility if this country is to bring its communities back together. The founders as they constructed our governmental foundation presumed the existence of a sense of responsibility, especially among our most advantaged citizens. Perhaps the individualism and the discrete existence that has characterized the boomer generation will help it view others as mere people, not members of groups. This in itself would go a long way towards the reconstitution of communities. However it occurs, communities, associations, and families, by whatever definition, will have to be reconstituted, perhaps in different configurations.

As we try to comprehend the farrago that comprises our socio-economic polity, we can see that our government is becoming increasingly less relevant both to citizens and to issues. Charles Handy perceives the critical problem. "By denying the local smaller loyalty we will kill liberty, incentive, and initiative and rely on the center to be right."[15] Those using the Internet, the fax machine, and talk radio instead of the town meeting or the voting booth are already indicating new proclivities that require philosophical articulation if they are to be effective in healing and unifying. It makes little sense to deny those instincts. We should sculpt government to accommodate and take advantage of them.

If we are actually headed towards the creation of a knowledge elite, we have to search for ways to connect it to the corpus of the people. Emmet C. Murphy and Michael Snell wrote about this latest manifestation of our nation's ongoing elitist-egalitarian power contest. "By too often refusing to live the experience of their people, the 16 million Americans who call themselves professionals threaten to undermine the pluralistic and egalitarian traditions of our country."[16] That is exactly what Peter Drucker is saying. I stumbled across this problem firsthand in my previous professional capacity as an investment analyst. One of my tasks in 1974 was to go to Detroit and learn why, in the throes of an energy crisis, the automobile companies had developed so few models with high gas mileage. In the course of conversations I realized that since all the top executives received the free use of cars plus as much gasoline as they required from corporate pumps, they had no direct idea of what the public had to endure. Unlike the rest of us, they never had to wait in long lines to get their tanks filled and pay exorbitant prices to do so.

I don't believe that we can dissolve this new claimant for the mantle of elitism any more than we could dissipate its many predecessors. It is not really necessary to destroy it. What we can do is construct bridges between this knowledge elite and the rest of America. That way our society can be inclusive and can benefit from arduously acquired expertise without pandering to exclusivity. A likely medium for this process of melding and inclusion to take place is in government. Transposed antifederalism could be the culture in which individuals are brought together to share a common experience. Common experiences are the most effective mortar I know.

At the other end of the socio-economic spectrum from the knowledge elite is the imbedded poor. I have already stated what Ghandi had to say about poverty. Another great thinker, Aristotle, also had some insightful words on the subject. "Poverty is the parent of revolution and crime." We have all witnessed the truth of this statement firsthand as we traverse our urban streets or watch the news on television. Poverty is also fostering the development of an alternate social contract for those who wish to avoid it or escape it but feel rejected or alienated by the current system. This dangerous and divisive prospect is whetted by the tendency of the affluent and educated to ignore and repress, and the disadvantaged to despair. Hannah Arendt believed the disease of poverty to be a cancer slowly destroying our society. "Poverty is more than deprivation, it is a state of constant want and acute misery whose ignominy consists in its dehumanizing force."[17] These dehumanized poor threaten the fabric of our society in a very basic way as recognized by Studs Terkel in one of his interviews for his book *Race*.[18] "It's dangerous to have a bunch of people in a society who've got nothing to lose. I do not think we can afford an underclass."[19] If we can somehow create enough opportunity to penetrate the miasma of poverty, we may be able to bring this perilously disaffected group back under the umbrella of a single social contract. Ensuring a strong unified contract will not require the total elimination of poverty as a condition, but it will require a genuine effort at creation of universal opportunity. To be effective this effort will have to receive a considerably higher national priority than it is currently afforded.

We have other crevasses in our society besides the threats of elitism and poverty. Race and age are two of them. The aftermath of the O.J. Simpson double murder trial and the controversy about the "Million Man March" of African-American men on Washington have highlighted the very different lenses through which the black and white races view their social environment. The tug of war over financial resources between entitlements and education (just to name two contestants) underscores the separate aims of our oldest and youngest age groups. Gender is another source of division. In instance after instance our leaders and our thinkers have failed to emulate Murphy and Snell's "Sitting Bull" and have lost touch with the people. This has deepened existing differences. It has set groups against each other. It has magnified our differences, a task in which a controversy-hungry media has eagerly assisted. A new philosophy of government can reverse this unfortunate trend. It can begin to close the gaps, reforge the unity, and prepare our nation for the demands of the new century.

If the American people are neither perceptive nor motivated enough to bridge the gaps, if these divisions remain, the resulting explosion could be catastrophic. People who have nothing to lose, people who feel abandoned, people who see no hope of improvement, people who are in pain, are more likely to seek the cleansing quality of destruction. Just before his execution for participating in the Haymarket Riot of May 1, 1886, anarchist and editor of *The Alarm*, Albert Parsons, encapsulated the extremism of desperation as he uttered these last words.

> Dynamite is democratic; it makes everybody equal. Dynamite is the equilibrium. It is the annihilator. It is the disseminator of authority; it is the dawn of peace; it is the end of war. It is man's best and last friend; it emancipates the world from the domineering of the few over the many, because all government, in the last resort, is violence; all law in the last resort, is force. Force is the law of nature, and this dynamite—this newly discovered force, makes all men equal and therefore free.

These words would fit the desperate violent mood lurking in the depths of our inner cities. It would fit the mood of terrorists, opposing what they perceive as crushing authority. It would fit in all those places where rays of hope never shine. The words would not seem out of place in right wing militia movements, which seek to exorcise hobgoblins, real and imagined. Unfortunately, they would not be out of place in the expanding pools of frustration seeping into an underclass that perceives few other alternatives. A philosophy of government, widely accepted as sensitive as well as germane, can provide an antidote. It can change attitudes and incorporate realities. It can respond to the many demands for a new society similar to the one presented by feminist Gloria Steinem. "We don't just want to have a piece of the pie. We want to make it a whole new pie."[20] A steadily increasing portion of our citizens wants a new pie. Soon they may constitute a majority. The nation's financial condition and its growing imbalances are signaling that we will have to make a new pie with new priorities and new opportunities but with less abundant resources. I believe transposed antifederalism is up to the task.

Making a whole new pie isn't easy. It has to use many of the materials already on hand. These ingredients can be employed in new and more productive configurations. Youth gangs are an example. They have been a factor in our national life since its beginning. Colonial elders bemoaned the roving groups of rowdy youths. Recently gangs have spread alarmingly throughout the country. *The Economist* pinpointed the socio-economic problem. "The unduckable truth is that the gang crisis is deeply entwined with America's most intractable social failure: the entrenchment of its underclass. Until politicians and the public are ready to attack the problem root-and-branch—until they are ready, in particular, to make a Herculean effort to improve the life prospects of young black men—gangs will grow more powerful and more wicked."[21] That is not the whole story, however. Gangs have provided family and community substitutes. Jim Wallis has related several of the more dramatic occasions when youth gangs have drawn together for positive purposes in his recent book, *The Soul of Politics*.[22] His point, with which I agree, is that many new organisms have evolved to fill the needs and voids of our society. There are new types of families. There are different forms of associations. We are less likely to be able to turn back the clock, to express outrage and disapproval, to stamp these growing organisms out, than we are to help them to adapt. Adaptation for the national benefit can most readily be accomplished under a single, accepted philosophy of government, one that can flow into the many new nooks and crannies of our society.

Self-interest can correct injustice. Compassion can be altruism. A united social contract will benefit us all. Intelligent prioritization can preserve our freedoms. A new philosophy can accomplish these ends but individuals will have to be prepared to persevere in the face of obstacles, while pointing the way to new directions. John William Burgess wrote from the depths of the Great Depression about the contradictions any new direction is likely to face. "The whole idea (of liberty) is that of a domain in which the individual is referred to his own will and upon which government shall neither encroach itself, nor permit encroachments from any other quarter. Let the latter part of the definition be carefully remarked. I said it is a domain into which *government* shall not penetrate. It is not, however, shielded from the power of the *state*. Indeed, the deepest problem of political science has been the reconciliation of government with individual liberty."[23] That is a continuing problem. Extremes are too often being touted by all factions. Our duty as we move into a future underlain with potential turmoil is to promote a relevant reconciliation between individuals and governmental power, which will allow the feeling of making a difference to spread throughout our society. In my view citizen participation is the key to this reconciliation.

I believe that transposed antifederalism with its local bias can most easily reconcile our diverse elements. Charles Handy offers a rationale. "If we want to reconcile our humanity with our economics, we have to find a way to give more influence to what is personal and local, so that we can each feel that we have a chance to make a difference, that we matter."[24] Handy advocates a lessening of power at the center in order to foster what he calls *subsidiarity*. "Subsidiarity means small units, small units with real responsibilities...We need the unit to be big enough to do what it has to do and small enough so that everyone knows everyone else in it."[25] He happened to be writing about corporations, but the comments elegantly fit the situation of local governments and the role of little republics..

In order to foster subsidiary we not only have to devolve power, we must also devolve interest, involvement, and responsibility. Does that mean we should stop thinking about political personalities at the expense of issues? Does it mean that we should lessen our preoccupation with scandal? Does it mean that we should stop talking about what we can *get* and explore what we can *do*? To some degree, all of these are true. In order to make a difference in our own lives, and in our own vicinities, we have to become immersed in their problems. We have to consider issues. We have to focus on remedies. We have to be willing to take responsibility.

Individuals are more likely to participate when they feel significant. They have more of a chance to get this feeling if they know the members of their immediate polity and can meet them regularly. Local government can foster both subsidiarity and involvement. Montesquieu's small republics can be these governments. In most areas they are already in place, if not empowered. The networks of screen watchers, the burgeoning family substitutes, the disaffected and the aspirant elites all can be drawn together in this shared enterprise of local government. They can see the results of their joint activity daily in the multitude of factors that constitute and delineate their lives. Through this process they can create new perspectives from which to view each other.

One new perspective can be obtained by rearranging the way we rate intelligence. Howard Gardner explained his intriguing theory of multiple intelligence in 1985.[26] We will investigate it more thoroughly in the next chapter. However, it does provide a basis for more widespread mutual respect. Robert Ardrey put this perspective another way. "Brain-power represents, in other words, not just the effective organization of your nine billion cells (if you are a human being) but the effective flow of cerebral resource within a community of which you are a part. If that community is divided, heedless of organization, incapable of communication, then the power of the individual brain can no longer be measured in terms of neurological resource."[27] A community is varied; composed of different personalities, requiring different skills. A true community can't all be "just like us." Our standards of achievements and social contract must reflect the need for complementary talents. There can be a multiplicity of measurements, and of successes. In fact, there should be.

We need many types of intelligence communicating and blending with each other. Ardrey perceives another link between the individual brain and its communal government. "The just society, as I see it, is one in which sufficient order protects members whatever their diverse endowments, and sufficient disorder provides every individual with full opportunity to develop his genetic endowment, whatever that may be. It is this balance of order and disorder, varying in rigor according to environmental hazard, that I think of as the social contract."[28] This is the living organism of the small republic – multiple intelligence, mutual respect, balance of order and disorder. These ingredients vary in amount according to the times and with the location. Together they can comprise a philosophy for the conditions that this country will shortly experience.

Power in our nation has never been distributed consistently or evenly. It has moved back and forth along the arc which, as I have noted, is transcribed with centralization at the federal level at one end and local autonomy at the other. I have also noted that when our Constitution was written the founders deemed it necessary to move the power locus from an extreme states' rights position further towards the center. Another instance when the center was strengthened occurred as Franklin Roosevelt assumed the presidency after the election of 1932 gave him a mandate to get the country out of the Great Depression. During the 1930s federal spending grew as a percent of our budget by an order of magnitude.[29] Moves in the opposite direction towards a less powerful center took place, at other times, such as the Populist pressures in the 1890s and the Republican presidencies of the 1920s. The time has come for another journey of significance along the arc. I believe it should be in the direction of more local power. Even President Clinton speaking in the campaign of 1996 has proclaimed that "the era of big government is over." Exactly how it should end and what should replace it are a chief matter for discussion among our citizens today. Hopefully the discussions will continue, and answers will be tested.

It is a contention of this book that at this point in our history more local autonomy is required. It can increase citizen participation in their government. It can take advantage of multiple intelligence. Local governmental organizations can accommodate demographic change and provide an atmosphere of inclusion. This need not imply the end of either representative or federal government but merely advocates their reduction and modification. We would benefit from a regeneration of some of the citizen-governor spirit of our first few decades. Participation could revive our faith in the future and our confidence that we can affect it. The swollen professional bureaucracies and seemingly omnipresent political corruption have caused people to lose their faith in government. The fog of discouragement can be thinned by bringing the process of government closer to home and involving more citizens in it. This action won't eliminate all the bad qualities. People are human after all. But by transporting the power and the responsibility to oversee and correct closer to the individual citizen, we can increase everyone's own sense of relevance and put remedies within their grasp.

A transition of this nature can actually be accomplished more easily than might be imagined. Many small republic-like local government entities already exist in the form of precincts, wards, districts, towns and the like.[30] As the annual (since 1986) Ford Foundation awards for Innovation in American Government have illustrated, many local governments are already setting examples of imagination and sensitivity. Funding streams can be redirected to bolster localities by changing a few fundamental principles, as will be explained in Chapter 8. Citizens are already volunteering in large numbers for governmental, quasi-governmental and *parallel polis* organizations, which Chapter 11 will outline. The situation is far from hopeless but it cannot be attacked under the banner of democracy without individual commitment.

If the small republic units aren't too big but stay in the 2,000 to 3,000 person range, minorities can become majorities. Interaction can replace alienation. Tensions can recede or be tempered. Challenges, even though formidable, can seem surmountable. A difficult transitional task will be that of coordination. Confederations of small republics require sustained dialogue on numerous matters. Larger governmental units such as counties, states, and the federal branches are used to activism, to operation. They will have to develop coordinative skills as their operational roles wane somewhat. In Chapter 12 we will encounter the coordinative skills of the Midwest Community Council, an excellent confederational model. Two aspects of recent devolution are patently unsatisfactory and will themselves have to be transformed. First, the concept of block grants leaves the revenue stream pointing toward the center and the ultimate power in its granting authority. The other is that the basic spirit of devolution has, thus far, been largely exclusionary, reactionary, and resentful. Its basic purpose has been to cut social spending and remove regulation. It has been geared to avoid, not increase, responsibility. When the base of power shifts to the little republics of the grassroots they will have to be inclusive and positive in nature if they are to function effectively. Their small size should facilitate this process if the intention is present.

If we can look forward into the next century with feelings of humanity and optimism, there will be some side benefits. One can be a growing sense of community. This sense was an integral part of the philosophy articulated by all of our founders. Their community existed not only in their backyards but also throughout the nation as a whole. For them community existed not only in the present but also in hopes for the future. Today the feeling of community has telescoped and deteriorated under the onslaught of egocentric individualism. It can be restored in small republics driven by transformed antifederalism lit by the glow of perspective and filled out with the muscle of inclusive participation.

Another ancillary benefit of an optimistic future can be the expression of political conscience.[31] Vacláv Havel articulated it. "A single, seemingly powerless person who dares to cry out the word of truth and then stand behind it with all his person and his life, ready to pay a high price has surprisingly greater power, though formally disenfranchised, than do thousands of anonymous voters."[32] Most of us remember the dramatic picture of the lone Chinese man stopping a line of heavy tanks on a Beijing street during the 1989 protests. This was a living expression of Havel's conscience. "When a person tries to act in accordance with his conscience, when he tries to speak the truth, even in conditions where citizenship is degraded, it won't necessarily lead anywhere, but it might."[33] This is the conscience that has been exhibited by millions of Americans, starting with the patriots of colonial days and continuing through the civil rights advocates of the post-World War II period. Hopefully, we can revive and expand our conscience under a new philosophy. Such growth would provide material assistance in the effort to unify our society.

There are numerous pre-ordained conditions that will persist in the United States as the twenty-first century unfolds. It may be prudent to review some of them as we contemplate the application of transformed antifederalism. This brief review will highlight the atmosphere into which any philosophy, and this one in particular, will have to emerge in the twenty-first century. It will sketch the outline of this philosophy's special applicability.

We covered many of the demographic aspects in the previous chapter. Some of them will apply to religion. As our country is moving towards a rough numerical balance between non-Hispanic whites and everyone else over the next 50 years, some alterations in our religious demographics will result. I will cite several examples. The majority of Catholics are likely to be Hispanic. The majority of Evangelical fundamentalists are likely to be black. There will be more Muslims than Jews. It remains to be seen how severely these religious demographics will affect society. Will they be divisive or unifying? How will they change socio-economic policy? Will they have a political impact?

Financial constraints resulting from the debt and deficit ramifications of our chronic over-spending will restrict our actions and demand strict prioritization. Our entitlement programs, our educational system, our health care, our remaining social spending will all have to be subject to these strictures over the next few decades. Looking at just two figures, relative to our 1995 Gross Domestic Product of roughly $6 trillion gives some idea of how serious the situation is. Our national debt is $5 trillion. Even if the Social Security Trust fund of about $5 trillion is rock solid (a statement open to question due to the fact that it is largely made up of IOUs from the United States Treasury), the system's unfunded liabilities (using the same actuarial techniques applied to corporate pension plans) amount to $12 trillion, an amount over 300 times greater than the combined unfunded liabilities of all private pension funds. Thus, two sets of obligations, the national debt and the unfunded liabilities of the Social Security system, now amount to nearly three times our total domestic revenues. They are both growing, not shrinking. Since the number of workers supporting the youngest and oldest elements of our population will fall dramatically, the pressure on their income streams will be enormous. Properly amortized, the liabilities inherent in our web of entitlements would increase the annual budget deficit by a factor of five.

Urban areas will house 60 percent of our people in the first quarter of the next century, and will be crying out for infrastructure replacement. Our concept of an appropriate lifestyle will be increasingly more difficult to sustain. These are but a few of the characteristics for us to consider. Merely reading them over gives some ideas about how we will have to reorganize our country—physically, intellectually, and emotionally. Cooperation will be vital if any sort of optimism is to be sustained.

We need to ask ourselves some factual questions with philosophical implications. Will we spend the time and money to offer each of our young the opportunity to have an equally first class education? Will we attempt to reduce the percentage of our citizens living below the poverty line? Will we fully fund our entitlement programs and if so, what percentage of the budget should they comprise? How high will our debt grow relative to our Gross Domestic Product, and will interest costs increase as a percentage of our budget? How high will we permit the budget and trade deficits to be, absolutely, and relative to our GDP? Will consumer debt decline from its record high levels relative to disposable personal income, and what will this mean for our obviously low savings rate? What obligations to support retirees will be imposed upon each worker? Will health care spending rise or fall from its present 14 percent of our budget outlays? If it is to fall what implications does it hold for the type and quality of our health care? How high will our tax rates be, and how will they be levied? I think the reader can see that the answers to these and other questions should be formulated by any philosophy purporting to be developed for the next century.

Part of the answer as to why the importance of financial integrity reaches beyond the mere numbers was given by James D. Savage. "A balanced national budget dignified a popular willingness and ability to limit the purpose and size of the federal government, to restrain its influence in the economy, to protect states rights, to maintain the Constitution's balance of powers and to promote Republican virtue."[34] This philosophical answer may be even more important than the monetary one.

Part of that answer can be derived by approaching the questions from the perspective of a totally self-interested, upper middle class white male of my age (57). Even if no sense of community, compassion, or egalitarianism is assumed the answers can be revealing. Health, retirement, and other benefits will not be available as anticipated to such a person unless the workers who have to fund them are well-educated and trained thoroughly enough to contribute to their sustenance. That, of course, presupposes that these workers are so motivated in the first place. Under present financial conditions, a white male of my age has very little hope of collecting entitlements, as offered, for the remainder of his expected life. Without a reduction in debt and deficit levels, without a reversal of the declines in savings rates and productivity, the country will not have the economic flexibility to provide the prosperity and stability that ensures a comfortable existence for those on fixed incomes. If currently disadvantaged groups such as the young, the non-whites, and the female are not made to feel a part of our system and given a future, the socio-economic prospects for those who are now privileged and affluent will surely suffer. A self-interested individual is not likely to be better off if the number of people in our society who feel that they have nothing to lose and nothing to look forward to increases, either absolutely or relatively. A self-interested person is unlikely to preserve anywhere near his present standard of living or quality of life without careful prioritization of scarce national resources and attention to the unity of our social contract. The point is that even for the most insular and self-preservationist among us who are basely expressing their own self-interest, a lack of analysis, compassion and perspective will leave them not only isolated but also bereft of adequate support systems.

We might speculate for a moment about what would happen if nothing changes our current apathy towards government. It's not hard to imagine that continued low participation in elections and operations will hand over increasing control to special interests whether they be corporate, religious, or ideological. It is equally easy to see that the road to oligarchy passes directly through popular alienation from government. It can further be seen that if the semi-volunteer, quasi-governmental organizations that abound everywhere are not included in the process of government in some way, they will gradually form a separate system with their own rules, finances, and objectives. (Italy is an example of a place where this has occurred.) It is reasonable to assume that if this country fragments into more than one social contract, our diversity will turn from an asset into a liability. These are the symptoms and potentialities that any new philosophy must confront.

Conversely, if we are able to assure individuals that they can make a difference, that their input can matter in their communities, we will have a chance to build unity from the bottom up. What might seem disconnected at first actually could become like a pointillist painting— a collection of individual dots, which when viewed from a distance form a beautiful image. Transposed antifederalism's goal would be to strengthen the individual dots and concentrate upon projecting the image. The dots—the local small republics—will strengthen as individuals come forth to become involved. These republics will be as strong as they are broad in participation. Their relevance will come from their physical closeness to the governed. Their strength and relevance can create a beautiful image for the nation as a whole.

Strength and relevance can emerge from a change in attitude. If the individual republic units are small enough and homogeneous enough to permit effective majority rule, they could identify with the thoughts and the writings of that most articulate antifederalist, Thomas Jefferson, and provide a governmental ambiance admirably suited to our current situation. If the republics are small enough, everyone will know one another and be more readily responsive to the needs, opinions, and beliefs of others. If they are both small and adequately funded, they can provide each citizen with the opportunity to positively affect his or her own life. While animosities and tensions will surely exist in small units just as they do in large ones, experience has shown that a recognition of common goals combined with personal interaction can more readily create the tolerance that is required to ensure functionality through compromise. This tolerance is achieved more easily closer to home. In an earlier book I described the mechanics of a little republic system. Essentially, the entities already exist. They are in most cases surrounded and assisted by numerous volunteer and quasi-volunteer organizations. They await adequate empowerment. If this should occur and citizens become accustomed to participation, our democracy can regain its vibrancy.

Transposed antifederalism and its small republics could be considered even more fresh and innovative if they pursue a concept that I call *zero-based thinking*. This concept is derived from the budgeting process where one starts with a clean piece of paper and no preconceived notions, no imbedded costs. Everything has to be justified and built from zero. Zero-based thinking would be used to overcome special interests, prejudice, litmus tests and other impediments that stand in the way of rational, realistic, and compassionate actions. Obviously, like most concepts, it will be difficult to operate perfectly. Even if partially applied, however, it would clear the air of the sentiments that impede solutions and create polarization.

One example of such a thinking process might be that before we conclude that health care is "too expensive," we should build several models from scratch, which would depict how the system would look under different basic assumptions. The goal of each might be to provide exactly the type of care we most desire. Building from the ground up, we might perhaps determine that an assumption to provide ten years from now all modern technology for all procedures to all legal United States residents would cost 20 percent of our budget, up from the current 14. Is this acceptable? What would it mean for other priorities?

If it is not acceptable, what is? Can costs be reduced or will the assumption have to change? Under a different set of assumptions we might develop something similar to the so-called "Oregon Plan." In this system all procedures are ranked according to treatability. Every resident is included in the system but only a certain number of procedures are funded (say 350 out of 500). How will this balance costs and treatment? If economics indicate that we go to an all-capitation system (annual fees per capita as opposed to fees for services), what would this mean for hospital stays, use of specialists and the ability to choose our own doctors? Is this acceptable? Are the savings worth it? New assumptions can be tried but each time the thinking has to return to zero. The concept is not new. It's not complex. But it can work to provide a more comprehensive idea of both economics and social ramifications, and in my view will lead more easily to solutions than merely demanding that costs be reduced.

Education can be another example-area for zero-based thinking. Do we wish to provide each student with a comparable education and similar opportunities in life? If we assume that we need to provide this with no rise in per pupil costs, it could require different curriculums and different financing for districts with different levels of resources. There could also be paths to the objective for districts with varying needs and separate backgrounds. How does this concept sit with us? How would implementation vary? By asking such questions early on, we can avoid complications later. Building toward goals from the ground up should keep us on common ground longer and also produce more responsive results.

A third example for zero-based thinking could be corporate citizenship. We often denounce "corporate welfare" as an unnecessary evil. We often propose sharply raising corporate taxes to reduce "outrageous profitability" or just to produce added revenues. A zero-based thinking approach would be to decide first what we want corporations to do and then determine the most productive methods for achieving these ends. The answers could be to clean up the environment, create jobs, help preserve families as well as to contribute profits and growth. Sweden, for example, has these objectives. It also has some of the world's most successful multinational corporations.[35] Even though Sweden has a high individual tax rate and has had socialist governments for most of the post-World War II period, its companies pay very low tax rates, often well below 20 percent. That is because they get very generous deductions for spending in such areas as pollution control equipment, child care centers, and job sharing by partners with children. Sweden's results demonstrate that it is possible to provide goals for corporations with longer horizons than the next quarter's earnings. As a society we may wish to ask questions such as: "If jobs are a priority and basic research is vital, are companies such as AT&T and IBM really in a better position to serve our national interests than they were before they were downsized?" We don't have to cover all the possibilities here. The point is that we rarely approach challenges in this way. We rarely build thought from the ground up. We are constantly burdened and impeded by the detritus of old concepts (agricultural subsidies or steel import quotas, for example) and short horizons. Hence, we often do disservice to our vital interests in the name of some ephemeral objective. Both our incentives and our rewards tend to confirm these mistakenly narrow and myopic objectives.

Nothing illustrates our national myopia more than our energy policy, or lack thereof. Despite frequent warnings (the 1974 energy crisis and the Gulf War were two examples) we have virtually discontinued development of alternative energy sources. Nuclear power's usage is shrinking due to environmental problems as is coal's. Drilling for difficult, expensive oil and gas reserves has all but ceased due to inadequate returns. Our only policy seems to be keeping prices low (less than half the levels of most industrial nations) and taxes at a minimum, while raising speed limits and curtailing conservation pressures. This has resulted in over 50 percent of our energy needs being met by imports. Economics (such as the spectacular growth of East Asia) guarantee significantly higher prices and possible shortages within a decade. Yet our only political action is for both 1996 presidential candidates to rail against recent gasoline price increases and advocate a removal of the per gallon federal tax. We will richly deserve the economic shock that is shortly to be received.

It is not pre-ordained that our citizens must dissolve into polarized extremes or competing interests before setting objectives. There usually are ways to find and pursue common ground to satisfy most of the requirements of the relevant parties. Often a greater expanse of common ground exists than ends up being a part of the final resolution. The lesson is that if stridency leaps too quickly to the forefront, national goals, even self-interests, can atrophy. Zero-based thinking can provide an antidote.

Our Constitutional Convention of 1787 was an excellent example of this type of thinking. There were a variety of interests present as the convention opened. They were expressed throughout, often forcefully. But the vast majority of participants had the objective of improving the government for the benefit of the nation. They realized that financial stability was vital. They understood that only through restoration of confidence in national government could democracy grow and prosper. They were able to keep these goals in mind as they approached and worked through each issue. They were even prepared to exceed their mandate by scrapping the Articles of Confederation and starting over with a clean slate. The result was a document that fully satisfied no one but contained enough common interest to give it both the strength and the plasticity that allowed it to endure.

I believe that we can apply transposed antifederalism accompanied by an adapted small republic theory, a commitment to politics of conscience, and the judicious employment of zero-based thinking. I believe that by so doing the people of the United States can learn more about matching their desires to their possibilities and can be both united and prosperous the coming century. I believe we can develop policies that preserve families and communities, stimulate our economy and provide security for our citizens. To do that, however, we must regard each other as individual people with thoughts and feelings, not merely members of stereotypical groups. We must regard ourselves as one nation (even if it be a collection of small republics), not as armies of competing interests. I believe we have the innate intelligence and abilities to do all these things. We have the technology. Properly allocated, we have the resources. The question that remains is—do we have the will? Robert Samuelson provides a good place to start to demonstrate such a national will. "Government cannot easily be controlled or command public respect unless there are some limits on its activities that are intuitively grasped and widely supported. These are the limits that have been lost and budget deficits attest to their absence."[36]

---

[1] Peter Drucker, "The Age of Social Transformation," *The Atlantic Monthly*, November 1994, 61.

[2] Ibid., 64.

[3] Ibid., 67.

[4] Charles Handy, *The Age of Paradox* (Boston: Harvard Business School Press, 1994), 199.

[5] Jim Wallis, *The Soul of Politics* (New York: Harcourt, Brace & Company 1994), 112.

[6] Charles Handy, *The Age of Paradox* (Boston: Harvard Business School Press, 1994), 109-148.

[7] William Greider, *Who Will Tell the People: The Betrayal of American Democracy* (New York: Simon & Schuster, 1992).

[8] Michael Lind, *The Next American Nation* (New York: Free Press, 1995).

[9] Charles Handy, *The Age of Paradox* (Boston: Harvard Business School Press, 1994), 259.

[10] Elizabeth Wurtzel, *The Prozac Nation* (Boston: Houghton Mifflin, 1984).

[11] Elizabeth Wurtzel interviewed in *Harvard Magazine*, Nov.-Dec. 1995, 18.

[12] Robert Putnam, "Bowling Alone: America's Declining Social Capital," *Journal of Democracy* 6 (January 1995) no. 1: 68.

[13] Christopher Hitchens, "The Baby-Boomer Wastelands," *Vanity Fair,* January 1996, 35.

[14] Robert J. Samuelson, *The Good Life and Its Discontents: The American Dream in the Age of Entitlement, 1945-1995* (New York: Times Books, 1995), 211.

[15] Charles Handy, *The Age of Paradox* (Boston: Harvard Business School Press, 1994), 130.

[16] Emmet C. Murphy with Michael Snell, *The Genius of Sitting Bull: 13 Heroic Strategies for Business Leadership* (New York: Prentice Hall, 1992), xxxv.

[17] Hannah Arendt, *On Revolution* (New York: Penguin Books, 1963), 60.

[18] Studs Terkel, *Race* (New York: New Press, 1994)

[19] Ibid., 183.

[20] Gloria Steinem as a part of a panel discussion, "Let's Get Real About Feminism: The Backlash, The Myths, The Movement," *Ms. Magazine,* 4 Sept./Oct. 1993, no. 2:43.

[21] *The Economist*, "American Gangs: There Are No Children Here," 17-23 December 1994, 23.

[22] Jim Wallis, *The Soul of Politics* (New York: Harcourt Brace & Company, 1994).

[23] John William Burgess, *The Foundations of American Political Science* (New York: Transaction Publishers 1993), 100.

[24] Charles Handy, *The Age of Paradox,* (Boston: Harvard Business School Press 1994), 109.

[25] Ibid., 141.

[26] Howard Gardner, *Frames of Mind* (New York: Basic Books, 1985).

[27] Robert Ardrey, *The Social Contract* (New York: Atheneum, 1970), 149.

[28] Ibid., 11.

[29] In 1929 federal spending was under 7% of the budget. By 1940 it was over 30%. In 1929 all government spending was 11% of GNP (3% federal, the rest state and local). By 1990 government spending was 38% of GNP (25% was federal).

[30] Charles Stewart Goodwin, *A Resurrection of the Republican Ideal* (Lanham, MD: University Press of America, 1995), 57-68.

[31] Ibid., 39-45.

[32] Václav Havel, "Politics and Conscience", *Open Letters*, selected and edited by Paul Wilson (New York: Vintage Books, 1992).

[33] Václav Havel, *Disturbing the Peace: A Conversation with Karel Hvízdala*, translated by Peter Wilson (New York: Vintage Books, 1991), xvi.

[34] James D. Savage, *Balanced Budgets and American Politics* (Ithaca: Cornell University Press, 1988), 5.

[35] These include Volvo; Astra; ASEA-Brown Boveri; and Ericsson.

[36] Robert J. Samuelson, *The Good Life and Its Discontents: The American Dream in the Age of Entitlement, 1945-1995* (New York: Times Books, 1995), 156.

Part III

Three Antifederalist Examples

The Powers not delegated to the United States by the Constitution, nor prohibited by it to the states, are reserved to the states respectively, *or to the people.*

Tenth Amendment to the Constitution
of the United States (italics mine)

Transposed antifederalism need not be merely an abstract idea. To be worth anything at all it cannot be an academic exercise, but has to be applicable to our daily lives.

As with any philosophy of government, this one will not be imposed in a vacuum. It will have to co-exist with actual socio-economic conditions and improve them for the majority of our citizens.

In this book I present transposed antifederalism as a philosophy that can be operational. This section contains three examples of how it can be utilized in real situations. As a nation we will have to accommodate those demographic and economic developments that are pre-ordained. We cannot just presume that conditions will stay the same or that our wounds will miraculously heal.

These chapters may seem to some readers as if filled with proposals that are too draconian. Others may see the solutions as impossibly impractical, beyond any hope of implementation. There will also be those who consider the suggestions to be moving us in the wrong direction. I see them as absolutely necessary steps if we are to regenerate our democracy with fresh philosophical implants, and restore our socio-economic integrity. It is in this spirit that I cite the following examples.

CHAPTER 7

Education

> Protection of the individual from outward enemies; protection
> through education, of every members right, according to vertebrate
> law, to equal opportunity for developing his potential; and
> protection of members, one from another, as through competition
> they seek psychological satisfaction of their innate needs: these are
> the three functions of order which any society must provide for its
> members if individuals and society are alike to survive...In more
> recent times of technological advance we have recognized or begun
> to recognize the educational imperative, and the inarguable truth
> that the strongest and most durable of societies will be founded on
> the maximum development of its members.
>
> Robert Ardrey
> *The Social Contract*

Generations of Americans, especially those who were recent
immigrants, regarded education with sentiments that approached
veneration. These citizens echoed the sentiments of Palestine refugee
Subhi Lughod, who became a successful television entrepreneur in
Lebanon. "We had a fixation with education because we knew we had
lost everything but our brains."[1] Now it seems that education has
slipped in our list of priorities and is no longer valued as highly. That
is a shame. More than that, it could be a severe handicap if our nation
cannot adequately educate its youth.

Writing in a recent issue of *Time*, Jonathan Kozol accurately
pinpointed the virus invading our educational system and philosophy.
"It has been the axiom of faith in the United States that once a child is

born, all condemnations are to be set aside. If we now have chosen to betray this faith, what consequences will this have for our collective spirit, for our soul as a society?"[2] There will be many consequences, and we will look at some of them.

If we are indeed entering the era of a knowledge society with all of its inherent ramifications, then education will become even more critical to our success or failure than it has been in the past. The soul of our society will be even more dependent upon an adequate educational base. Education, which has always been one of our national cornerstones will play an even larger role in realizing our socio-economic potential.

In this country we have dealt with the twin issues of egalitarianism and elitism since before our founding as a nation. These issues have continually seeped over into the area of education. Many have argued that only the wealthiest, most prominent or seemingly best qualified should receive the full benefits of education. Antifederalist Robert Coram tackled the subject in 1791, favoring equal opportunity all in the areas of education. "But it will perhaps be objected that the minds of some men are capable of greater improvement than others...to which I answer that there is perhaps as great a variety in the texture of the human mind as in the countenances of man."[3] As mentioned in the previous chapter, this theme was recently voiced by academics Charles Handy[4] and Howard Gardner.[5] They both elaborated on the concept of multiple intelligence. In their view individuals possess a number of different skills which are brain-driven, and each type of intelligence can exist separately. None is necessarily connected to or dependent upon any other. These different forms of intelligence include areas such as: facts; languages; analysis; physical or interpersonal skills. The point is that different people may show different attributes at different times without being "abnormal" or "stupid." The necessity for labeling is one of the worst features of our system, as is the failure to recognize different, discrete capabilities and differing paths to "success."

The experience of environmental researchers in Brazil reinforces the contention that there are varied forms of intelligence. "Socono noted that the rubber tappers seemed unusually gifted and grasped concepts quickly, often more rapidly than she could. Her comment isn't rare. Many other students and professors have remarked with surprise on the intelligence of rubber tappers. Sometime during our higher education it seems, we acquire the smug belief that formal education correlates with intelligence. Consequently, we deduce that an illiterate person such as a rubber tapper is dumb and a Ph.D. brilliant. One quick way of dispelling such a mental handicap is to walk with a rubber tapper in his or her forest."[6] There is a plethora of instances where the conventional idea of intelligence wilts in the face of a challenge easily surmounted by a whole different set of skills. Standardized testing, while helpful in some ways, often reinforces labels and devalues alternate capabilities by measuring only one or two methods of achievement.

Handy advocates a related concept—a portfolio of competencies. "Instead of requiring students to reach certain standards before they receive their certificates, we should require *the school* to ensure that the students have reached those standards before they let them go. School should be a place for compiling a portfolio of competencies."[7] This may be getting us closer to the needs of our students in an approaching knowledge society. Maybe we should consider both: evaluating multiple intelligence and requiring a portfolio of competencies; these would provide realistic, flexible alternatives to a standardized core curriculum rigidly administered by grade level.

Christopher Lasch put his finger on the burden of narrowness our educational system now faces. "The whole problem of American education comes to this: In American Society almost everyone identifies intellectual excellence with elitism. This attitude not only guarantees the monopolization of educational advantages by the few; it lowers the quality of elite education itself, and threatens to bring about a reign of universal ignorance."[8] If we enter this new century without recognizing that a multiplicity of measurements for intelligence exists and instead attempt to operate the knowledge society with an elite founded upon a decrepit and an overly narrow education system we are indeed headed for trouble. On the other hand, if an educational philosophy accepts individual responsibility, not social guilt, as the final determinant of conduct, then we shall see some remarkable changes in the curriculum presented to our students.[9] Along with these changes we may also see an improvement in overall performance as well as a greater correlation between education and the needs of our society.

The Provision of Education

Education has been a priority in this country since its inception. As we collectively peer towards the uncertainties of the twenty-first century perhaps no single element is more crucial to our prosperity, or even our survival, than the nature of the education we provide to our young. Our democratic system will not function properly unless our children and grandchildren are educated effectively and equitably.

There is an unfortunate tendency today to overlook the education factor. We too often assume that productivity, that financial benefits, that government or that individual rights can flourish without first ensuring that everyone has the opportunity to attain a quality education. We sometimes forget that our success as a nation to date has largely emanated from the continuous commitment of our leaders and our citizens to the widespread provision of education. The hope and opportunity it offers prompted waves of immigrant families, among others, to insist that their offspring strive to complete their schooling. Our public schools and our higher education system were continual sources of pride for our citizens over the course of many decades. Now these systems are riddled with decay and saddled with inequality. In many areas pride has given way to shame and hope to despair. It is important for us to change this condition and to begin alterations at the local level.

Education retained its position as an example of flourishing localism, even as the country itself was shifting power steadily towards the center. However, lately there has been debate over whether increased federal involvement is required. Proposals such as standardized national testing or a national core curriculum are harbingers. The attempt is to ensure uniform achievement by establishing tools to measure the results of similar content. This is a worthy intent. Possibly some sort of national core curriculum can be constructed to produce the result advocated by Paul Gagnon in a recent *Atlantic Monthly* article. "Something close to national agreement on a vital common core is indispensable to educational equity, to dislodge and replace the empty, undemanding programs that leave so many children untaught and disadvantaged."[10] But, as Gagnon goes on to point out, we have to careful. In an attempt to better our system, we may end up with something like the 314-page standards put out by UCLA's National Center for History in the Schools, which has displeased almost everyone. We also have to be careful that by seeking standards or equitable measurement, we may hinder the recognition of multiple intelligence. As noted above, a "portfolio of competencies" stresses flexibility along with required skills.

We should preserve what has been the uniquely positive aspect of our educational system—its localism, both in orientation and in control. At the same time, we do need to recognize that some problems, such as facility construction, may be beyond the scope of our poorer districts. These problems may call for broader support; from neighboring districts, counties, or even states. They do not necessarily signal that the federal government should become involved or that education should be standardized. In fact, they signal the reverse. Each locality should be equipped for the provision of equal opportunity within a general framework of goals.

I contend that the answers to our educational defects and inequalities lie in reinforcing and replicating this localism, not in diluting it. Anthony Bryk, head of the Center for School Improvement at the University of Chicago, described the unfortunate consequence of not providing this support, using his own city as an example. "We devolved resources and authority down to the schools, but there was no infrastructure in place to support that development. If we're to move beyond where we are now, we're going to need that infrastructure—training for councils, training for principals, looking at issues of incentives and accountability."[11] In the pages that follow we will examine education as a bastion of modern antifederalism, and as a core of the small republic revival of democracy. All the while we should keep in mind Bryk's description of the consequences of inadequate support.

Thomas Jefferson typified the attitude of our founders towards education. He was one of its more forceful proponents as illustrated by a letter to James Madison written from Paris, on December 20, 1787, just as the battle over the ratification of the Constitution was reaching its height. "Above all things I hope the education of the common people will be attended to; convinced that on their good sense we may rely with the most security for the preservation of a due degree of liberty." Nor was this sentiment merely a passing fancy for Jefferson, "As he grew old, he believed more in education as the only hope to teach not only useful skills but to change attitudes, to improve morality and spread civilization."[12]

Jefferson was by no means alone in his sentiments at that time. That leading antifederalist with whom we are already acquainted, Robert Coram, delivered a *Plan for Establishment of Schools* in Wilmington, Delaware in 1791. "Education, then, means the instruction of youth in certain rules of conduct by which they will be enabled to support themselves when they come of age and to know the obligations they are under to that society of which they constitute a part."[13] In other words, we have a duty to inform our youth about the nature of our social contract and prepare them to uphold it.

In our own time a chronicler of social commentary, Studs Terkel, has recorded similar sentiments in his interviews. "Education is the route by which everyone can liberate themselves. When people understand who they are and understand their history, they have more respect for themselves."[14] Few American citizens today would argue with the content of this statement. They might contest its practical implementation, however, as the interpretations of history vary widely. Actually, there is no one interpretation of our history. Differing perspectives produce differing analyses. It is a prime mission of an education system to teach that and explain the nature of and reason for each perspective. That is not "political correctness;" that is common sense.

In fiscal 1994 this country spent $484 billion on public elementary and high school education at all levels. This represents an absolute increase of 444 percent from the $109 billion spent in 1960.[15] Over this same period, spending on public education alone went from $89 billion to just over $400 billion. This amounted to an expenditure of $5,300 for each of the 43.6 million youngsters attending public school. This amount compares favorably with all industrial nations except Switzerland and Sweden.[16] The vaunted Japanese spent less than half of what we did per pupil and the Germans spent about 65 percent as much. Our educational spending in 1994 was almost twice the $250 billion that was spent on defense. In 1994 79 percent of all Americans 25 years old or older were at least high school graduates. Given these facts, why is there such a general perception that our educational system is inadequate? Clearly, the total amount of money is not the whole answer. The answer lies rather in how it is expended. Part comes from the fact that only 50 percent of our funds ever reach the classroom. Part comes from our youngsters spending a smaller portion of their school day on academic matters than virtually any other group of children in the industrial world. Part comes from the large differences in facilities, teachers, and ambiance between districts, often adjacent districts.

We all acknowledge that the solutions to our educational purposes are not simple. Nevertheless, the reality is that for great swathes of our people the methods by which they are educated constitute a woefully inadequate preparation for any sort of life that can be productive to both the national and local communities.

As we pursue this issue of education let us not lose sight of the elements we discussed above — multiple intelligence, a portfolio of competencies, and the creation of personal value through the accumulation of knowledge. These should all be firmly intertwined in the education we provide in the coming century.

Before embarking upon reasons and remedies, let us first amplify the thoughts of Jefferson, Coram, and Terkel by looking at what roles education is being asked to play in our society.

The Role of Education

Emilie Carles, a teacher in the mountains of rural France, movingly described the various roles education might be called upon to play.

> Teaching youngsters to read and write is one thing, it is important but not sufficient. I have always had a loftier notion of school — the role of the school and the teacher. In my view, children take stock of the world and society in the communal school. Later on, whatever their trade, whatever direction their lives take, the mold is already set. If it is good, so much the better, if not, nothing further can be done.
>
> In a backward region like ours, considering the life I had led, what seemed indispensable to me was opening their minds to life, shattering the barriers that shut them in, making them understand that the earth is round, infinite, and varied and that each individual, white, black, or yellow has the right — and the duty — to think and decide for himself. I myself had learned as much through life as through study, that is why I could not judge my pupils solely on the basis of their schoolwork, and why I took into account the way they behaved in their daily lives.[17]

School, then, is one instrument for transmitting behavior, culture and mores, second only to the family (if there is one).

Syndicated columnist William Raspberry has explored a different dimension of education. "So much of the learning that matters takes place outside the school setting...I'm talking about the attitudes and habits that make school learning possible; patience, persistence, self-esteem, reading for fun, the love of learning...they are learned most readily at home...If parents don't value learning and show their children that they do, schools are hard pressed to make up the difference."[18] What do we do if both parents don't exist, or are working, or are indifferent? Do we abandon the opportunities for their children? Or do we rearrange their curriculum to fill in the gaps? Both Carles and Raspberry have highlighted aspects of education which take it beyond mere *ABCs*.

Schools mean different things to different people, and to different areas. They can be havens. They can be families. They can be catalysts. They can be structure. They have to deal with many backgrounds. They have to deal with many concepts of intellect. To do this they must be flexible, responsive, and relevant. In deciding the role of education in our society, and in constructing a curriculum, we must come face to face with these issues. We need to realize that creating equal opportunity from unequal circumstances can require some customization and some imagination.

What happens if there are different moral, ethnic, or religious value systems prevalent within a given district? What happens if there are great disparities among the facilities and resources of various neighboring school districts? How can we blend this kaleidoscope of needs into a coherent educational philosophy for our elementary and high school students who are expected to increase from 44 million in 1994 to 56 million by 2004? When finally formulated, what should we expect from this philosophy and how should we measure the results? All of these questions require thoughtful responses as this nation painstakingly develops a blueprint for its system of education and its educational philosophy.

I have already cited the demographic numbers for the coming century. We know that as the generation of *baby boomers* retires, their sustenance, and that of the country, will increasingly depend upon the efforts and accomplishments of a work force progressively more non-white in composition. Many of those non-whites will be drawn from those groups and areas now considered to be disadvantaged. If they are poorly educated, if they are alienated from the prevailing social contract, how will they support us? How will the United States flourish? How will our democratic experiment continue? Any positive response to these queries will depend upon education; education that is being conducted now. That is why education reform carries such immediacy. In the very near future we must decide what should be taught and how it should be conceived.

We have also to decide how education will be financed. In a report issued in November of 1995 the General Accounting Office estimated that $112 billion needed to be spent, to upgrade the nation's crumbling education facilities. This need has to be evaluated against the fact that Congress in 1995 eliminated $100 million it previously had provided annually for the upgrading of school buildings. Formulating and financing educational policy is perhaps the single most critical issue of our society. It certainly constitutes the foundation upon which all of our other policies will be built. We can begin by constructing some parameters for grappling with this monumental task.

I was recently on a small Bahamian island, off the coast of North Eleuthera, called Harbor Island. The roads were dotted with inspirational signs, mostly supporting faith and knowledge. One sign outside the island's modest primary school blazed: "Don't Lose Sight of Your Dreams." In checking around a bit I found that these dreams were in reality very modest: get off the island; go to high school; get a job; have a family; stay in touch with God. What are the dreams of our students? Are they being fostered in our schools? We have always been a land that encouraged ideals and dreams. Our future depends upon their continuance. Schools should be their primary greenhouses. It is our duty as citizens to create the best possible environment for the nurture of these dreams. It is not merely our duty, it is in our own best interest.

If education is the repository of our dreams, its general availability has been a key to our national excellence and uniqueness since colonial days. I do not pretend to be skilled enough to offer a comprehensive, detailed solution to America's educational challenges. However, I can discuss how education would flourish and function in a governmental system composed of small republics imbued with an antifederalist philosophy. In that context I will offer some ideas mostly originated by others, and apply them to the United States that I envision in the twenty-first century.

The Role of the School

The basic premise that should underlie education in the next century was stated by Charles Handy. "If we don't invest in the intelligence of all our citizens we shall have a divided society."[19] This investment will not necessarily involve more money. It could well require less, as we already spend one of the highest amounts per pupil in the world. This investment does not need to be supported by a larger bureaucracy. In fact, it should need a smaller one, as about half of our combined national school budget now goes to support administrators and other non-classroom service personnel. This education investment will not necessarily demand huge dollops of technology, vast new facilities, or even totally revised curriculums. It will, however, necessitate thought and time and commitment on the part of parents, teachers, administrators, and students, as the needs of each locality are discovered and addressed.

All the research done to date indicates that the single most important ingredient that has to be transferred from our society at large to its 64.5 million elementary and secondary students (43.6 million of them enrolled in public schools) is a sense of caring. This involves caring both for their present and for their future. Principal John Parnell has fostered such an attitude in the Malcolm X Elementary School in Washington, D.C. "Perhaps the centerpiece of his administration is his effort not merely to establish order and civility but also to make the school a place where children feel wanted."[20] Feel wanted—isn't that what we all desire? How many of our young lack the comforting security of being wanted during the school day, not to mention in the home? Making students feel wanted involves little additional expense, but will require major changes in attitude.

It is an undeniable, if often unfortunate, fact that for millions of American youngsters, school, especially the kindergarten and elementary grades, serves as a family substitute. This is true in all demographic strata. It is true for both social and economic reasons. It is also true at different levels in all of the 16,000 independent school districts spread throughout the nation. As we look at education in an antifederalist system this truism will resonate. "The family accounts for educational success and failure far more than the school, let alone the college...the disintegration of the family in much of the West is likely to frustrate government attempts to boost educational results by tinkering with schools."[21] Throughout much of our nation schools will, at least to some extent, have to become surrogate families. This complicates the process of providing education, but it is unavoidable.

We may have to recreate in our school environments many of the lessons formerly imparted within the family structure. It is not sufficient merely to lament the passing of traditional families or their values. We also have to adjust our educational policy to help in their revitalization. How can families and values be recreated by subsequent generations if millions of children never learn what they are? There are a host of children bereft of familial supports who desperately require their replacement. Our entire society will suffer if the most needy districts are not equipped to step up and offer these services. Family enhancement services can be as simple as school lunch or breakfast programs. They can be day care centers provided at the end of the academic session. They can be some sort of a recreation nexus around which young people can gather. This can be as elementary and as economical as the much maligned (by Republicans who opposed President Clinton's law enforcement bill) "midnight basketball." These services can be similar to Project Debut, which provides after school activities for homeless children in Hyannis, Massachusetts. They can be as basic as the provision of a climate for learning to read, learning table manners, or learning to interact. But, in order to bring back families, our schools will have to increase their offerings of family enhancement services, whether financed and staffed by taxpayers or by private volunteers. The dollars expended in this effort will be the most valuable we can spend anywhere, producing the greatest overall socio-economic return.

We also have to recognize, as did the American Association of University Women in its 1992 report, that there is "compelling evidence that girls are not receiving the same quality, or even quantity, of education as their brothers." It is simply common sense that the glass ceiling as well as other gender-based inequalities are best met head-on and conquered in our school system. Equality of opportunity is not just a nice phrase, it is an economic necessity for us in the next century. Women of all races and ethnic groups are key to our national prospects. This policy would also be inexpensive to implement.

An area of opportunity where the economic benefit is less clear and the cost is observably high is special needs education. Special needs education provides an excellent illustration of how a well-meaning, in fact necessary, idea can get out of control when it is inserted into the system in the form of unfunded mandates. This concept was fostered by the Great Society legislation of the mid-1960s to provide educational opportunities, often in the home, for disabled children. It was deepened by the Individuals with Disabilities Act of November, 1976, which required that all disabled students would receive "free and adequate education." Where possible they were to be educated with non-disabled students. The federal government would absorb 20 percent of the additional cost for educating the nation's then 7.9 million disabled students whose total education cost would be $1.1 billion. Under expanded definitions the number of disabled students has more than doubled and the cost of educating them has risen over 100 times in the 20 years since.

When the Americans With Disabilities Act passed in the Bush Administration, it provided greater impetus for special needs education. The January 1996 issue of the *American School Boards Journal* reports that special needs has risen from under four percent of all spending for elementary and high school education in 1966 to 17 percent in 1991. It is close to 20 percent now. This is compared to an increase of just over 396 percent between 1960 and 1993 in all spending for public elementary and high school education. It is evident that a significant portion of the overall increase came from the single category of special needs. The number of public school students enrolled in special education has grown from under two percent in 1966 to seven percent of the total in 1994.

This category of spending has grown geometrically. It has arrived via unfunded mandate. Its costs are inflated by lenient definitions for eligibility and the legal difficulties of challenging program entrants. It is yet another factor pressuring our school systems. We cannot deny our disabled youth their opportunities. At the same time we have to escape financial disaster from programs that are growing much faster than school budgets as a whole. They can produce runaway costs such as those emanating from programs for 1,000 of Boston's disabled students which require funding of over $100,000 per student. We also need to avoid dumping problem students into expensive special needs education programs, something that has earned reprimands from the federal Department of Education for the state of Massachusetts, for example.

There are some things we can do. There will be some requirement for prioritization of special needs as in so many other areas. As with many other conundrums we face, no matter what choices are made there will be some who are offended and unhappy. We have such people now. Above all, we should remember that the problems of special education largely arrive via these programs' status as unfunded mandates. The principle that lies behind them is sound, but open-ended costs have turned them from benefits to detriments.

One difficulty lies in definition. The Americans With Disabilities Act (ADA) states that there are 34 million disabled people in the United States. Yet a close inspection of its criteria yields the conclusion that there are over 90 million Americans who can be classified as disabled. Various mental illnesses, substance abuse, attention deficit disorders, and dyslexia are some of the conditions that legally cause disability. Some impair learning, some do not. Some can be compensated for in the classroom; some cannot. Legally, schools are required to provide education to the disabled, with the states left to decide the exact method to be applied. Overly-broad definition has brought with it crushing financial burdens.

Schools can and should have specialists in learning disabilities on staff for consultation and assistance. Whether there should be as much one-on-one attention to disabled students is another question. In my capacity as docent I have guided many school groups around a museum. In a group of 20 I often have two or even three disabled students, each with his or her own facilitator. They proceed at their own pace, often not that of the rest of the class. They usually require their own explanations, because for one reason or another, they could not understand the one given to the main group. It is difficult enough on a field trip. In a classroom the impediments to general learning and the cost incurred on behalf of disabled students, are immense. Moreover, they fail to prepare these students for the conditions they will face in society.

What staff serving the disabled should be allowed to do, or educational institutions legally required to do, is another area that impacts cost. In her syndicated column of February 2, 1996, Debra Saunders of the *San Francisco Chronicle* tells the story of a suit filed under the Americans With Disabilities Act. A student at a California college has cerebral palsy and is wheelchair-bound due to speech, motor, and visual impairment. She is taking a course in Musical Theater Dance. This student has filed suit because she claims she has not been allowed to dance with other students but only with her Easter Seals aide. The aide is suing as well, claiming having to dance with the student was too "traumatic." Saunders summarizes the issue. "The suit highlights the problem with the ADA. A well-intentioned law, it is so sweeping in its attempt to level all inequities—including those created by nature—that it enables people to sue over slights." The ADA mandates more than equal opportunity. It also encourages lawsuits to define vaguely stated parameters. One of these parameters involves exactly who is entitled to special needs education. In Massachusetts, which has possibly the most liberal policy in the country, a school district challenging the eligibility of a student can spend $35,000 on necessary hearings. Consequently, challenges are rare. Too much of the body of rules applying to disabilities has been determined by the judiciary co-opting the legislative prerogative, and filling the gaps left by loosely-chosen legislation.

This suit noted above, and the costs of similar special education suits, are paid by taxpayers and is a metaphor for special education itself. It is well-intentioned but too sweeping and too expensive. Our special education policy should be significantly redesigned, not only to provide necessary opportunities for those held down by disabilities but also to control costs. Special education is a graphic example, but certainly not the only one, where a well-meaning program catering to a deserving minority threatens to damage the functioning of a system for those in the majority. Localism can be an antidote, but only if it can be accompanied by the courage and the resources to effect prioritization.

Our country has been justly proud that over the centuries it has dealt, generally successfully, with diversity. Today we have more diversity than ever. We have more languages. We have more ethnic groupings. We have the prospect for even a greater number in the future. How will we achieve equity and commonality? In an area that was barely discussed before 1980, controversy now rages over the validity of bilingual teaching versus English as a second language. The deterioration of our verbal Scholastic Aptitude Test (SAT) scores since 1985 is one manifestation of the problem. In 1994 30 percent of all SAT participants were minorities , up from 11 percent in 1973. For ten percent of the test takers, English was not the first language they learned. In eight percent of the cases English and another language were learned at the same time. Roughly 2.6 million of our young students are not English-speaking. In California, where 45 percent of the non-English speakers reside, over one million can't speak English well enough to understand their teachers' lessons. Clearly, we have a multi-faceted challenge. Having English as the national language is only part of the solution. Teaching students in their native languages is, at best, a transitional measure. Bringing the two approaches harmoniously together would be a good place to start. It will require both tact and sensitivity.

Lisa A. Delpit, educator, provides some thoughts on how to make a transition between a native language or dialect to commonly understood English. "To act as if power does not exist is to ensure that the power status quo remains the same. To imply to children or adults...that it doesn't matter how you talk or how you write is to ensure their ultimate failure. I prefer to be honest with my students. Tell them that their language and cultural style is unique and wonderful but that there is a political power game that is also being played, and if they want to be in on that game there are certain games that they must play."[22] English can be unifying. English can be a ticket to political, to professional, or to academic power. It can also be diluting and demeaning. Compromise, sensitivity, and balance are called for in order to preserve our national identity without undue offense. That means instruction in English, accompanied by transitional assistance.

Schools are where this balance can be achieved. Schools are where many of our societal tools are crafted, as well as where the cheapest and easiest adjustments to inequality can be made. Lisa Delpit comments further on this.

> Now you may have inferred that I believe that because there is a culture of power, everyone should learn the codes to participate in it, and that is how the world should be. Actually, nothing could be further from the truth. I believe in diversity of style, and I believe that world will be diminished if cultural diversity is ever obliterated. Further, I believe strongly, as do my liberal colleagues, that each cultural group should have the right to maintain its own language style. When I speak therefore, of the culture of power, I don't speak of how I wish things to be, but of how they are.[23]

The English language has been a major, maybe the major, unifying factor for this nation as it has grown. New immigrants have been integrated by it, and while our culture was being enriched by diversity a common language unified it. That is an inescapable fact and it cannot be disregarded lightly.

As Ms. Delpit has graphically illustrated with language, a characteristic of any educational system is that it will have to prepare its students for life. In September, 1993 the United States Department of Education released a study done for it by the Educational Testing Service entitled *Adult Literacy in America*. It concluded that 90 million of the people in this country over 16, one-half of that total age group, were basically unfit for employment due to their lack of literacy. A Department of Education study in 1992 had previously disclosed that two-thirds of all elementary and high school students were not proficient readers and that only nine percent of all high school seniors can solve math problems that require more than an educated guess. In 1994 only 50 seniors in Boston's public high schools took calculus and almost 40 percent of the city's 15,508 high school students were enrolled in remedial math courses. Distressingly, in many states even math teachers themselves test unacceptably low in their basic skills. Nationwide 25 percent of all students drop out of school before the twelfth grade. The figure is 35 percent for the 6.9 million African-American students in the first twelve grades, and 45 percent among the five million Hispanics attending elementary and secondary institutions. Part of this is due to the conditions of their environment. Part of the high drop out rate is due to the low opinion of education held by these students, their parents, and even their teachers. In a 1995 study, the Public Agenda Foundation learned that only 29 percent of parents and a mere 11 percent of teachers cited education as the key to success. The choices they were given were: education; inner drive; knowing how to deal with people, and, knowing the right people. All were ranked ahead of education by both parents and teachers.

Compounding these deficiencies is another one pointed out by *The Economist.* "The most glaring structural problem with American education is that it does not know what to do with pupils not bound for college."[24] The annual survey of college freshmen conducted by the UCLA Higher Education Research Institute recently found a discouraging trend. In the 30 years this study has been made no year has yielded as high a percentage as 1995 who believe that the individual can't do much to change society. We clearly are not preparing our young for civic life, professional life, or family life. We are allowing the natural optimism of youth to evaporate. In the last chapter we explored the demands of the so-called knowledge society, and how many could be left behind by it, mired into a permanent underclass. Preventing or reducing a permanent underclass through education or in concert with education, can take many forms in many locations. The common thrust would be to prepare as many of our young people for a productive adult life. We don't do a very good job of that today and the onrush of the knowledge society will make the task even more difficult.

How can we provide family extension support and prepare young people for their later lives? A few illustrations will give an idea of what is happening and what can happen. In March of 1991 the Committee for Economic Development published a report called *The Unfinished Agenda—A New Vision for Child Development and Education.* This report, sponsored by 250 leading business executives, called for education to reach out into the community, especially to the poor, and deliver continuing social services in conjunction with school. The York Street Project in Jersey City, New Jersey is one organization doing exactly that. It is privately-funded and provides dwelling space, school, social services, and employment in the same complex for about 20 families. There will have to be many more York Streets if values, education, and parental employment are to be promoted in close proximity, but it is a good start.

A relative of York Street is the Newcomers School proposed for New York City. This high school would serve approximately 1,000 students and their families who are recent immigrants. Parents would be expected to participate in career and family-oriented programs aimed at helping adults assimilate, and preparing youngsters to participate. This type of program can be replicated.

Another program in my home area of Cape Cod would extend help on parenting given to teens and adults. Most of the Cape's 15 towns provide some type of parenting workshop located in the school. One of them, Bourne, is offering workshops held in the homes of selected individuals who are sponsored by the School District and the Department of Social Services. With families more dispersed and with more having two working parents, institutions such as schools are logical locations for bringing families together while imparting services, assistance, and instruction. They are also natural conduits for outreach services.

The traditional role of the school as a place to receive the "three Rs" for a few hours per day has changed. It should be a center of innovation, assimilation, and unification. It may have to replace busy or absent parents, grandparents in retirement homes and cousins scattered across the country. It can be an engine for rescuing our disadvantaged. It can be the vehicle for transmission of our ideals. It can be the barrier at which dissension and division are arrested. With all of these daunting tasks, and more, it is no surprise that major adjustments and fundamental re-orientation are required. Even with all these challenges, schools remain the best single hope for the continuation of our experiment in democracy throughout the next century and the most deserving focus for our collective attention.

Flexibility In Demand

The very nature of our collective backgrounds and educational experiences transmits more than one valuable lesson. Besides illustrating the varied needs of our residents, it highlights the reality that we are facing enormous demographic diversity. This combination would be a challenge even for a nation like the United States which has courted diversity since its inception. Diversity of composition and requirements indicate that our educational system cannot optimally serve its constituency merely by instituting rigid concepts, an inflexible core curriculum or standardized national testing. It should be pliant to accommodate the myriad of demands and proclivities inherent in our society.

This country will attain unity through education not by trying to standardize or attempting to copy the success of other nations, which have their own educational strengths and problems. We will attain unity by laying a foundation of opportunity for each of our groups or segments to find its own path to Americaness. The mere fact that there is a path, based upon education, will permit the process of unification to flourish. Competing against other countries or squabbling over the contents of a required core will not move us forward. Any system that is both inclusive and motivational and which points towards a "portfolio of competencies" will be bound to improve upon the results now generated. A brief look at the possible ingredients of such a system may provide a hint of how improvement could take place.

In 1990 the State of Kentucky passed the Kentucky Education Reform Act. Its intention was to provide more money, a greater equality in the allocation of resources, higher standards, improved curriculums and an acknowledgment of influences from outside of the classroom. Thus far the results are not definitive. But the act was an interesting, positive move that the state seems determined to continue. Its progress is well worth monitoring.

In recent years this nation has been inundated by a variety of concepts and ideas that challenge traditional education. These include multiculturism, political correctness, feminism, and expanded special needs teaching. All have some validity and are accompanied by some complications. It is very difficult to construct a curriculum that simultaneously attempts to right past wrongs, as perceived from a variety of vantage points to address a plethora of new cultural imports, and to provide substitutes for decimated family support. If these tasks are accompanied by the requirement to meet a rigid national standard and do not include a plan for comprehensive district reorganization and refinancing, it may prove virtually impossible to have our educational system adequately serve the majority of our people.

We can change the situation to capitalize on our diversity and our creativity by stressing localism and flexibility. Already there are innovative *Charter* public schools in Massachusetts. There is an extensive voucher system in Milwaukee. Whether vouchers are a viable answer or not remains to be seen but a 1995 Gallop survey shows that 69 percent of the public favors some type of school choice, up from 60 percent in 1989. There are already patterns of intra-system competition. There are 7,291 parochial elementary and 1,296 parochial high schools run by elements of the Catholic Church.[25] These provide popular alternatives in most districts. We have company-owned schools.[26] We have private entities running school systems in cities like Baltimore and Hartford (with, at best, mixed results thus far). We have Fordham Heights Academy in the Bronx, New York, which gives partial credits for non-academic activities completed successfully, and graduates 4,000 yearly. We have interdisciplinary high schools such as the Alan Shawn Feinstein High School for Public Service in Providence, Rhode Island or the California Academy of Mathematics and Science.

There is also Uxbridge, Massachusetts. The school district in that town offers year-round child care. It allows flexible work schedules so that teachers and guidance counselors can meet with working parents. It was the first district in the United States to allow (in 1991) children from outside the district to attend its schools. Its innovative superintendent of schools, Michael S. Roanan, is now proposing measures designed so that his schools will be better able to meet family needs. He is attempting to issue vouchers for books and supplies for at-home tutoring and some at-home classes. Any attempts to bring families and education together are worth watching and dissecting.

There are also various methods for rating both students and teachers. We have tried "race norming," where test scores are compared only within minority groups. We have tried linking the level of teacher pay to accountability and evaluation. The list could go on. Some have been successful, some have not. Flexibility, the willingness to try new approaches, has always been our national strength. There are no easy answers. We should not limit our options in the face of mushrooming diversity, both social and economic. We should not be put off by occasional failure.

As we head into the final half of a decade, which will see 50 million students enter our public schools annually, four million more than had been expected, our resources will be stretched. I will cover finances shortly, but there are some other concerns. First we might consider how we can get more than three million of our six million public school employees into the classroom. This would improve our economics as well as cutting down on red tape. Maybe we could correct the fact unearthed by the National Education Commission on Time and Learning, and released on May 4, 1994, that American high school students spend less time on academics (41% of their day, the rest is extracurricular) than any other major nation in the world. If current extracurricular activities are actually important, and if they facilitate a recognition of multiple intelligence, then maybe more of them should be a part of the regular curriculum. As noted above, we also spend more time and money than most nations on what is called "special education" for physically or mentally challenged students. What are our priorities? How can we initiate rational dialogues to assess them? Where should we place our increasingly scarce resources? What type of flexible education can we best deliver? How can we best employ our people and our facilities? Whatever the particular solutions, or attempts, I believe that they are best tested and accomplished as close to individual localities as possible. I do not believe we can afford to close off any potential avenues. We can't condemn too quickly. New concepts often take time to be proven, and our need for fresh thinking is great. But most of all, the situation cries out for even more community involvement. Both young and old have a vital stake in education. Let us hope that we can all come together to meet its varied and formidable challenges.

Potential Financing Innovations

As stated above, our national resources are scarce, especially our financial resources. If we are to provide adequate educational opportunities for all of our citizens, we will have to make some financial decisions. One of them involves logic. I have argued on previous pages that it is definitely in our best interest to grant our disadvantaged the same opportunities for education available to everyone else. It follows that in some way or some form the wealthier school districts are going to have to provide a portion of the funding to educate members of poorer districts. This is not only logical and equitable but it is also the best investment any of us can make in our collective future. I believe these funding adjustments should occur at the state level or below, preferably below.

The process of revamped financing doesn't have to involve the doling out of subsidies. It can be more innovative. In July of 1993 Michigan abandoned property taxes as the main source of school financing. Property taxes were replaced by raising the sales tax from four percent to six percent, plus raising taxes on cigarettes from $.25 to $.75 per pack. Will this work? The jury is still out. It does bear watching.

In Rochester, New York 33,000 elementary and high school students were placed in a system with school-based management. Most of them were from poor families. One-half came from single-parent households. Teacher pay was linked to performance. There has been friction, naturally, between teachers and the community. The results are still mixed. This experiment, too, should be monitored to see if it improves finances or results.

Texas has instituted a program whereby wealthier districts pay directly for poorer ones. The wrinkles haven't yet been smoothed out, but the State's approach acknowledges the problem. Before too long something similar will have to be employed in many locations, and the Texas results may provide us with guidance.

Lawrence Picus, Assistant Professor for Education at the University of Southern California and Director of the Center for Research on Education Finance, believes states will have to increase their contributions to local budgets. Alan Odden, Director of Finance at the Consortium for Policy Research in Education, a federally-funded organization, conversely sees the need for more central government money (in fiscal 1994 the federal government contributed $20 billion to education, most of it for the disabled and disadvantaged).[27] Picus also emphasizes the need to retain some local financing and decision-making capability. There are many opinions, and, indeed, the emerging solutions will be diverse. While philosophy will determine direction to a certain extent, it can't be so rigid as to truncate promising alternatives.

There are almost as many theories on financing as there are on the proper nature of schools. This is good. There are no magic formulae and money is tight everywhere. Sooner or later the financial debate will come down to four critical points.

1. Should the property tax be used as the basis for public school financing as it has been since 1640? My own feeling is that although this tax will probably have to be supplemented by other financial sources, it constitutes the best source for the large monies required. It is neither totally progressive nor totally equitable, but it is historic and generally relevant. Not all property owners have children. Not all

children are the offspring of property owners. But all members of a given community do, or will, benefit in some way from education. In addition, most school facilities are available for multiple usage in their communities.

Innovations, such as vouchers, are unlikely to provide enough additional monies. Paul Vallas, Chief Executive Officer of the Chicago Public School System, states flatly that "there will never be the money available to make vouchers a substitute for most private sources. They will be supplements or seed money. We are not likely to find an acceptable replacement for the property tax."[28] He is probably correct.

2. Should the bulk of public school monies come from local, state, or federal coffers—or places in-between? My belief is that the financing, and the control should be local, with some guidelines and coordination from central entities. School districts in some states, New York and Oregon among them, set their own tax rates, and have their own tax collectors. This is a structure that could be refined and expanded. Supplementary monies should come from county, regional, or, at most, state sources, if necessary. As was stated, this will be most necessary in the case of the poorer districts. But unfunded mandates, whether they come from Washington or state capitols, are counterproductive, even destructive and in most cases outweigh whatever they are intended to convey.

3. How many activities not in the academic mainstream should a district support? This involves a wide-range of areas, including special education, athletics, shop, art, and drama. Clearly as budgets are tightened the focus of schools will have to be narrowed. But each locality will have to be careful not to preclude the recognition of multiple intelligence and the role it envisages for its particular school system. This will continue the healthy practice of education with a distinctly local flavor. The mix can be different from district to district as each strives to provide the necessary "portfolio of competencies."

4. Coming back to where we started, citizens will have to decide how to increase the capabilities of poorer districts to provide equal educational opportunities. This will require both vision and a broad sense of community. It will also involve hard choices. For instance, we will have to decide whether special needs education can absorb 20 percent of our budgets, and if not what percent and relative growth rate is acceptable. We may also have to choose what publicly-funded extra-curricular activities are necessary, and which ones will have to funded privately. This won't be easy. None of the aspects of the education question is easy.

Thoughts Collected

As the reader can tell, I have raised more questions about our education's future than I have answered. We all will have to keep asking questions, and testing responses, because there is no easy or simple solution. We will have to accept one principle derived directly from our founders. Education is vital to our future. A glance at demographics, one we have already taken, shows why. As the *baby boomer* generation begins to retire on January 1, 1996, around 2010 the number of retirees per worker will begin to accelerate. All of our so-called *entitlements* will become more expensive for each member of the work force, and concomitantly more remote. The link between a satisfactory retirement and a realistic future is education. This dependence upon relevant education is true as the knowledge society expands its influence. Education will be especially critical for those who will make up the majority of our twenty-first century work force: non-whites and women. Equality of educational opportunity can offer our youth a comprehensively more effective preparation for life than it is doing now. In the process all of us will become more secure.

Education has always been a local, antifederalist-type activity. It will have to continue in this form if the system is to be both relevant to and productive for its students. There is no practical alternative to a local-based and financed system of education. Financing may have to employ wider, more broadly cooperative solutions, but the decisions and the responsibilities must remain at the community level if we are to serve an increasingly diverse and disparate student population. It is my belief that by strengthening our local financial and administrative abilities and by opening our minds to a variety of educational possibilities, we can provide better prospects for national optimism and unity in the twenty-first century.

---

[1] David Lamb, *The Arabs: Journeys Beyond the Mirage* (New York: Vintage Books, 1988), 201.

[2] Jonathan Kozol, "Spare Us Cheap Grace," *Time*, 11 December 1995, 96.

[3] Charles S. Hyneman and Donald S. Lutz, *American Political Writing During the Founding Era 1760-1805* (Indianapolis: Liberty Press, 1983), 799.

[4] Charles Handy, *The Age of Paradox* (Boston: Harvard Business School Press, 1994).

[5] Howard Gardner, *Frames of Mind* (New York: Basic Books, 1985).

[6] Foster Brown Ph.D., *Innocence in Brazil,* (Woods Hole Research Center, 1995), 5.

[7] Charles Handy, *The Age of Paradox* (Boston: Harvard Business School Press, 1994.)

[8] Christopher Lasch, *The Culture of Narcissism* (New York,: W. W. Norton & Co., 1979), 145.

[9] Robert Ardrey, *The Social Contract* (New York,: Atheneum, 1970), 379.

[10] Paul Gagnon, "What Should Children Learn?," *Atlantic Monthly*, December 1995, 71.

[11] Anthony Bryk, *New York Times*, 12 November 1995.

[12] Willard Sterne Randall, *Thomas Jefferson—A Life* (New York: Harper & Row, Perennial Editions, 1993), 586.

[13] Robert Coram in Charles S. Hyneman and Donald S. Lutz, *American Political Writing During the Founding Era 1760-1805* (Indianapolis: Liberty Press, 1983), 2:758.

[14] Studs Terkel, interview with William Freeman, *Race* (New York: New Press, 1992), 72.

[15] All figures in constant (1988) dollars

[16] These figures are from the U.S. Department of Education and Labor and are expressed in 1988 dollars. Per pupil spending was $3,500 in 1980. Switzerland spent $5,700 per student. This was a little over 3% of GNP vs. a little over 4% in the U.S. and 4.5% for Sweden (which spent $4,500 per pupil).

[17] Emilie Carles, *A Life of Her Own: A Country Woman in Twentieth Century France* (New Brunswick: Rutgers University Press, 1991), 225-6.

[18] William Raspberry, *Cape Cod Times,* 8 January 1993.

[19] Charles Handy, *The Age of Paradox* (Cambridge: Harvard Business School Press, 1994), 200.

[20] Ted Gup, "What Makes the School Work?," *Time,* 12 December 1992, 64.

[21] *The Economist,* "A Survey of Education: Coming Top," 21 November 1992, 7.

[22] Lisa A. D. Delpit, "The Silenced Dialogue: Power and Pedagogy in Educating Other People's Children," *Harvard Education Review* 58, no. 3, (August 1988): 292.

[23] Ibid., 292.

[24] *The Economist,* "A Survey of Education: Coming Top," 21 November 1992.

[25] Sam Allis, "How Do Catholic Schools Do It? Can Catholic Schools Do It Better?," *Time,* 27 May 1991, 48.

[26] Irene Ricio, "Beyond Day Care: The Company School," *Business Week,* 20 May 1991, 142.

[27] The Department of Education was established in 1980. In that year its budget was $14 billion on 130 programs. In fiscal year 1995 it spent $32 billion on 340 programs. It is hard to measure the impact of the more than $200 billion it spent during those fifteen years when the quality of education in general was plummeting.

[28] Paul Vallas, *New York Times,* 12 November 1995.

CHAPTER 8

Taxation

The message for policy-makers wanting to cut their debt burdens, for whatever reason, is that tight fiscal policies alone are not enough. A little tightening is likely to stunt growth, without any offsetting reward from lower interest rates. And so far, the most successful debt-cutters have been those who are bold enough not to raise taxes, rather, to trim expenditure—and the supposedly sacred areas of spending at that.

The Economist, January 20, 1996

Taxation is a complex and often controversial subject uncomfortably choked with numbers. The natural human inclination is to want less of it for ourselves. Nevertheless, it is, and will continue to be, the main revenue generator for our country. The issue is not whether we should have taxation or even how much it should be (in the aggregate most taxation plans come out to roughly the same overall percentage of GDP) but what form it should take. Taxes can do two things. They can create revenue to support government. They can motivate various groups of people or organizations to operate in a way beneficial to society. They cannot by themselves redistribute income or restructure classes (unless the aim is to force the departure of many wealthy citizens and of corporations due to confiscatory taxes, as has happened at various times in several European countries). Taxes can be an instrument of philosophy, but not its progenitor. Since this book is proposing a philosophy for the twenty-first century, this chapter will approach the subject of taxation with the bias of transposed antifederalism. This bias will lead to the proposal of a national retail sales tax as the core revenue producer for a new system of taxation.

The initial aspect of this discussion is to explore two different concepts of taxation, *progressive* and *regressive*. Contrary to the connotation of their descriptions, neither represents "good" or "bad." Regardless of the type of taxes proposed the aggregate of all state, local, and federal taxes will have to remain in the 20 to 25 percent of Gross Domestic Product (GDP) range unless spending is to be massively reduced. Since 1952 federal taxes have consistently stayed in the 18-19 percent of GDP range, occasionally spiking up to almost 20 percent (1969, 1981) or down to just below 17 percent (1955, 1959). Various state and local taxes add another three to five percentage points to the tax burden's share of GDP. We can rearrange the weighting to change emphasis, or even power. The overall cannot be significantly reduced unless we are willing to accept a radically different budget. Raising total taxes to over 25 percent of GDP would likely bring on unacceptably high levels of protests and avoidance. There are two distinctly different types of taxation reflecting separate philosophies along with enough numbers to provide a factual basis for decision-making.

A *progressive* tax is one in which the rate charge escalates with the amount of the item taxed. Usually it refers to the income tax in which the rate goes up as does the income earned. The current graduated system has five basic rates ranging from 15 to 39 percent. (The top rate was 70 percent as recently as 1980.)[1] The general theory behind this mode of taxation is that as people earn more money they can and should contribute more. In this respect it is somewhat egalitarian and redistributive in nature.

Robert J. Shapiro stated the case for a progressive tax in the Progressive Foundation's report, *Why Fairness Matters: Progressive Versus Flat Taxes.*

> The alternative view of fairness, which supports progressive taxation, stresses people's different circumstances: Taxes are fair when everyone pays according to their ability, and therefore the tax system should exempt the poor and apply to everyone else rates and relative burdens that increase with income...Advocates of progressivity...see progressive taxes as a way to curb concentrations of economic power. In this view, incomes reflect not only people's own efforts but also circumstances beyond their control. Tax progressivity can advance equality of opportunity and real justice by changing the market's distribution of income. The test of a progressive tax is the degree to which, after paying taxes, those at the top are left with a smaller share of all national income than before, and those at the bottom a larger share than before.

A *regressive* tax is one that levies at the same rate no matter what the value of the asset or the level of income. Social Security is our best example of a regressive tax. It taxes everyone at the same rate up to $62,500 of income. Above that there is no tax. Moreover, there is no means test for disbursement. Thus, the upper income groups benefit inordinately. The general theory of regressive taxation is that there should be incentives to earn more money and accumulate assets as this ultimately results in a stronger economy a greater level of investment and higher tax revenues for the government.

Advocates of tax *fairness* generally object to a system that works to the advantage of the more affluent. They tend to advocate measures that are aggressively progressive and designed to redistribute income. Their opponents (epitomized by so-called *supply siders*) point to statistics purporting to show that economic indices rise when taxes are cut.[2] They also note that the higher earners pay a greater share of the overall tax bill when their rates are reduced. These individuals tend to be advocates of regressive taxation. They believe the tax code should encourage free market solutions to most socio-economic challenges. Fairness advocates believe that the more fortunate in our society have a duty to provide for the less fortunate and that the tax code should facilitate this effort.

There are some questions we rarely ask regarding our tax system. Before tinkering with its mechanism, we should give some thought to the fundamental questions of tax philosophy. The most basic is: What do we want it to do? Do we want it primarily to raise revenues? Do we want it to redistribute income? Do we want it to protect the environment, or encourage some other activity we consider worthy? Do we want it to foster savings and investment? These are the questions we need to ask at the outset. We should realize that perfection is not likely. No system of taxation can do everything, but our goals are more easily attained if they are assisted by an accommodative tax structure. Besides the necessity of determining a goal, one other tax characteristic should be recognized. The tax code is more effective if it provides incentives rather than punishment. It is human nature to respond better to encouragement than to punishment. But the incentives have to remain in place long enough to have an impact on attitudes.

If we can apply zero-based thinking to the subject of taxes, it just might be possible to create a system that helps improve our national financial situation. We also could achieve some positive socio-economic results for the future. In the following pages I will discuss some of the options that are available, and then introduce my selection and explain its compatibility with my political vision.

The bulk of tax revenues in this country is generated by income taxes. This tax began in earnest after the Civil War when a federal income tax was levied to help reduce the debt from the conflict. In 1895 the Supreme Court declared a later version of the income tax unconstitutional. In 1913 the Sixteenth Amendment was ratified, instituting the modern federal tax on income. Most of the income tax dollars are collected at the federal level by the Internal Revenue Service. Federal income taxes amount to about nine percent of GDP, slightly higher than the more rapidly growing payroll tax, which now accounts for about seven and one-half percent of GDP.[3] Corporate profits taxes have been steadily shrinking and now account for less than two percent of GDP with other federal taxes adding one percent. The chief reason for the growth of the payroll tax is that it funds Social Security and Medicare. Throughout the post-World War II period various federal taxes have fluctuated between 15 and 20 percent of GDP. Various state and local levies add between two and five percentage points to that figure with total taxation accounting for 20 to 25 percent of GDP. These are the basics of our tax system, which, combined with rising government spending, have produced only one balanced budget in the 35 years since I graduated from college.[4] The next step is to inspect some proposals for changing the system, which, combined with spending cuts, can produce an equitable, financially healthy future for this country.

The introduction of a so-called *flat tax* has received considerable support, especially among Republicans. There are two frequently cited versions of this proposal. One is detailed by United States House of Representatives Majority Leader Dick Armey and United States Senator Richard Shelby. It advocated phasing in over three years a tax rate of 17 percent on all income. A personal exemption of $3,100 would be authorized for a single person, one of $17,200 would be given to a single head of household and one of $26,200 for a married couple. There would be an additional exemption of $5,300 for each dependent. Thus, a married couple with two children would not pay taxes on the first $36,800 of income. No deductions for mortgage interest payments, charitable contributions, state and local tax payments, or anything else would be allowed.

The other major flat tax proposal comes from presidential candidate Malcolm (Steve) Forbes, Jr. who called for the first $13,000 of personal income to be tax-free. There would be a $5,000 exemption for each child. (A married couple with two children would have $36,000 of tax-free income.) After that all earned income would be taxed at 17 percent. There would be no deductions allowed, and no taxes on unearned income. Corporations would pay 17 percent on all profits under both plans.

Obviously, flat tax plans would simplify the process of filing tax returns. However, in 1995 over 70 percent of all taxpayers used the single-page standard deduction form so that, contrary to popular belief, there would be relatively few beneficiaries of simplicity. What would be affected is the approximately $80 billion that individuals pay to accountants and lawyers for tax advice, compliance and avoidance. Flat tax proposals have been criticized for being regressive and for hitting the middle class particularly hard.

A look at some facts can determine where the real flat tax problems lie. Studies show that 60 percent of all income is earned by people making between $20,000 and $100,000 annually. Approximately 18 percent of all income is earned by people in the $40,000 to $75,000 range. This latter group pays 30 percent of all income taxes. Those in the top one percent of all earners—over $200,000 per year in income—paid 27 percent of all income taxes in 1995. It is evident that individuals earning over $40,000 per year pay 57 percent of the tax bill. If their taxes are reduced dramatically, there will be severe pressure on the government's revenue stream.

Let's take a look at deductions and how they are employed. Most of the interest deductions, about 55 percent, are taken by people in the $50,000-$100,000 earning range. The same is basically true for those deducting property taxes from federal returns. Conversely, the higher earners accumulate the most deduction for charitable contributions and state income taxes. Items such as oil well drilling allowances and depreciation on forests, real estate, or capital equipment are also mainly used by the wealthy.[5]

Thus, before we get to mortgage deductions, we can see that the middle class is vulnerable to elimination of deductions, for taxes and interest deductions that directly impact their daily life style, while the higher earners would lose those deductions used to motivate particular programs or activities. If corporations lose deductions for interest and fringe benefits and have to pass the costs on to employees and consumers, the lower and lower-middle earning groups would suffer proportionally greater penalties. The wealthy would suffer some loss of deductions (and their basic income taxes would decline) but the programs that are supported by these deductions would be hit even harder. This look at deductions illustrates that there will be winners and losers with every proposal. Furthermore, it will be virtually impossible not to adversely affect the middle class in some way, despite what our politicians would have us believe. The other element we have seen thus far is that any reduction in taxes for upper-middle and high earners will have to stimulate economic growth (as proponents suggest) for there not to be a revenue shortfall.

The most controversial element of the flat tax proposals, beside the allegation that it benefits the wealthy, is the proposed loss of the mortgage deduction. Our national housing market is valued at about $8 trillion. About 64 percent of all Americans live in owner-occupied homes. Around 60 percent of all homes carry a mortgage. About half of all homes were bought with less than the usual 20 percent down, so that their base of equity is thin enough to be at risk from price declines. There would likely be at least a temporary decline in most housing markets as the mortgage deduction was reduced or eliminated.

Most of the United States' 27 million homeowners who take a mortgage deduction earn between $40,000 and $100,000 per year. These middle class people typically have half their net worth tied up in their homes. As noted many of them have thin equity cushions. However, the amount of the deductions they take is relatively small. The top five percent of taxpayers take 44 percent of the tax benefits from mortgage deductions, about $2.2 billion per year. These people are most likely to own high-priced homes which are the ones estimated to be hit the hardest by price declines resulting from elimination of deductions. Approximately 75 percent of all homes valued at over $250,000 are in seven states: California; New York; New Jersey; Connecticut; Maryland; Virginia; and Florida. If the mortgage deduction is eliminated, the high wage earners in those seven states will suffer the most absolutely from housing price drops. The middle class will be hit the hardest relatively if the experts are wrong and prices for median-cost housing drops and doesn't recover quickly enough to restore the home equity which constitutes most of their net worth.

Another criticism is that a flat tax would result in a loss of tax revenues to the government. Forbes himself admits his proposal would produce $40 billion less in revenue than the current income tax system. Citizens for Tax Justice claims the shortfall would be $200 billion. In 1995 the federal personal income tax will yield about $600 billion, 11 percent of total household income. The investment firm of Goldman Sachs estimates that the rate necessary for a revenue neutral flat tax would be 23 percent. Some others say a 25 percent rate would be needed. The assumed growth rate for the economy as a whole is key. The accounting firm of Coopers & Lybrand estimated that the economy would have to grow for a decade at five percent annually (twice its current rate) to keep the flat tax rate under 20 percent without widening the deficit. Most estimates indicate that elimination of the mortgage deduction would require three to four additional percentage points to be layered onto the flat tax rate to keep the revenue to the government from falling. A flat tax rate of 20 percent would be consistent with tax history but might not be enough to ensure revenue neutrality, unless economic growth accelerates sharply.

The benefits claimed, in addition to simplicity, are that savings and investment would be encouraged for both business and individuals. This might be offset by at least temporary changes in the pricing of assets such as residences and municipal bonds. Therefore, if the aim were to make a flat tax more equitable and progressive, some exemption or package of exemptions might have to be granted for the lower and middle income groups. Some of the homeowning groups would need to be able to deduct a few mortgage payments for at least a short period of time. The basic flat rate would definitely have to be higher than 17 percent to offset revenue loss from the deduction. In summary, 17 percent is probably an unrealistically low rate to have any chance at revenue neutrality without massive spending reductions. Changes in many asset values, a tough transition period for charities, and disproportionate penalties for the middle class would be hard to avoid. So would a sharp increase in the deficit if the rate were under 20 percent. If this were accompanied by a windfall to the wealthy, the nation could be polarized even more than it is currently.

Three other income-oriented proposals, again mainly by Republicans, have been made to effect partial reforms and to induce greater levels of saving and investment. The first is elimination of double taxation on dividends. Dividends are taxed now when earned by the corporation and again when received by the holder of securities. The proposal would eliminate the tax to security owners. The majority of security dividend income is received by high earning individuals. The second proposal involves reviving the investment tax credit on machinery and equipment when they are purchased by corporations. In the past these incentives have only worked when kept in place long enough to facilitate planning. Too often they have been rescinded before this period has been reached. The third proposal would reduce or eliminate the capital gains tax from its current level of 28 percent. A related proposal would index the cost of assets to inflation so that the owner would only be taxed on real appreciation. These three proposals all have some merit in the narrow areas where they are focused. It is hard to avoid the contention that they inordinately benefit the wealthy and large corporations. Indexing the value of assets seems to make the most economic sense if proposals are introduced discretely and not as a part of a system. Not undertaking a comprehensive tax review and only inserting narrow changes would, I believe, be a mistake at this stage of our economic development.

While there is much impassioned rhetoric on the issue of taxes, the facts are often twisted to bolster a particular theory. There are some things we can identify as closely approximating fact. The one percent of people earning over $200,000 per year on an average pay about 60 percent of all capital gains taxes. Despite all the statistics about the absolute number of people owning homes or shares, the indisputable fact is that the affluent would benefit most from a reduction in capital gains taxes. It is also indisputable that when tax rates have been cut for those in the higher income brackets, as they were in the 1980s, these groups' relative share of total tax payments has risen. On the other end of the equation, there is no credible evidence to support the claim that reducing income taxes increases savings or investment. From the end of the 1970s to the middle of the 1990s both savings and investment as a percentage of Gross Domestic Product dropped precipitously.[6] Savings as a percentage of disposable personal income dropped at an even greater rate. Without getting too complicated, there is no conclusive data to indicate that fluctuating tax rates impacted anything more than the short-term timing of transactions during this period. On the other hand, researchers such as Ethan S. Harris and M. A. Akhtan of the New York Federal Reserve Bank find a relatively high long-term correlation between the size of budget deficits and the rate of savings, which is critical for investment.[7] A high statistical correlation over a long period of time has been found between the establishment and increase of entitlement benefits and a decrease in the propensity for individuals to save. Focusing on deficit reduction, accompanied by the necessary adjustments in entitlement programs, outlined in the next chapter, will go a long way towards reversing the decline in the savings rate. It would be indeed a shame to make significant changes in taxation only to find that the desired ends would not be achieved. Worse than a shame, it would promote national unrest if proposals enacted were perceived by many to merely be giveaways to the already wealthy and powerful, and would put the middle and lower earnings groups even further behind.

Out of this often daunting array of figures we have learned a few things thus far that may assist in the formulation of any tax policy. Out of the cascade of data two conclusions in particular jump out. One is that the wealthier, higher income segment as a whole pays taxes that are a significantly higher percentage of the total than the percentage of the population they comprise. These individuals in general have greater flexibility to move their income streams around. Thus, measures designed to exact high taxes from them generally prove counterproductive, merely depriving the nation of valuable income. As has been proven in this nation and others, placing punitively high rates on the rich, for whatever reason, is less economically sound for the people as a whole than providing encouragement for the affluent to increase earnings, spending and concomitantly, tax payments. Conversely, any gamble that lowering taxes for this group will spark an economic surge is socially and politically risky.

A second conclusion is that no tax system can avoid hitting the middle class. This is due to the very definition of the economic group, its size and its share of the national income. The object of any system then has to be equity along with revenue maximization. Another objective can also be the facilitation of a particular structure of government. What taxes should not be asked to do is "soak the rich" or give undue and uneconomic advantage any particular group for political purposes. Now let us move on together to consider an entirely different philosophy of taxation, which may be more appropriate in the coming century.

Another classification of taxation is levies on the *consumption* of goods and services. This type of tax is particularly suited to the philosophy of antifederalism since it can more easily be collected at the state and local level, thus keeping the monies needed by these authorities from being funneled through the center. In pursuit of this concept we will investigate user fees, a national retail sales tax, a value added tax (VAT) and other means by which taxes on consumption could be implemented. We will also probe the relative progressivity or regressivity of the several consumption tax proposals. Finally, we will dip gingerly into the unknown waters of the potential financial impact on individuals, on localities, and on the country as a whole.

The basic theory is simple enough. The most desirable conditions to add incentive are: earning, saving, and investing. These should carry little or no tax burden. Spending, especially on luxury items, is less desirable, proponents say. Of course, our economic system is currently geared to encourage spending, especially on luxury items. As long as some provision is made to isolate lower income earners from taxes on necessity items, it makes very little difference to this theory what a person earns. It is what that person spends that regulates taxation.

User fees are straightforward in design—you use something, you pay for it. They can be as local as the cost for a permit to moor my boat or use the nearby landfill. They can be as widespread as taxes on gasoline, which go into a Highway Trust Fund. If the fees go directly to pay for a related service—my mooring fees being used to pay the Harbormaster, for example—they meet the criteria of tax "fairness." If they go into some type of general revenue fund, not only do they not meet that test but they can become regressive. Governor Weld of Massachusetts proposed such a diversion. He recently sent to the Legislature a proposal to take as much as 85 percent of the state's cigarette tax revenues away from anti-smoking programs and use them to finance a state income tax cut. There are some in Congress now advocating using the revenues in the Highway Trust Fund (generated by interstate tolls) to offset the budget deficit. User fees at all government levels have been invaded and diverted, negating their original purpose and turning progressivity into regressivity.

Ideally, user fees can be adjusted to fit local needs. In an optimal situation they would be paid into a fully-funded account. This account would keep the principal intact to meet future requirements and pay for current costs out of interest-earned and appreciation. Social Security and Medicare Part A are examples of funds that are supposed to operate this way—but do not. Both of them have allowed funding to fall so that expenses have at least partially been met out of current revenues. If user fees are diverted, or have other monies utilized to supplement them in supporting a relevant service, they forfeit some of their claim to fairness. I believe that channeled into properly-funded accounts and supporting related services, user fees can be a valuable and equitable revenue source. Due to their ability to focus and be collected locally they can be important financial foundations for transposed antifederalism.

The Value Added Tax (VAT) is used throughout the European Community (in conjunction with income taxes). It involves charging a fee at every stage of production and distribution for the amount of value added (approximately sales minus non-wage costs) to all goods and services. This feature renders the tax virtually self-policing since every transaction is reported twice, by two different parties (each wholesaler's revenues are a retailer's costs). The consumer pays on goods and services, like a sales tax. There are four main objections, however. One is that the administration of its multi-layered system is costly and complex. Another is that VAT is regressive, unless exemptions are made for necessity items that can provide relief for lower income groups. These exemptions might drive the required rate prohibitively high. A third objection is that this type of levy will often compete and conflict with state and local sales taxes. The fourth is that there is no statistical evidence that this type of taxation encourages savings.

Senator and presidential hopeful, Richard Lugar of Indiana, proposed early in 1995 that this country replace the federal income tax, the capital gains tax, gift taxes, and inheritance taxes with a national retail sales tax. He proposed a rate of 17 percent on retail sales, excluding food and medicine. The taxes would be collected by the states, 45 of which already have sales taxes. For example, consumers in Atlanta, Georgia, with a six percent sales tax, would pay a total tax of 23 percent at the same time and to the same local cash register, when they purchase a product or service. The only federal tax left to pay under Lugar's system would be the Social Security payroll tax. This would make the 110,000 employees and $7 billion budget of the Internal Revenue Service (in 1995) largely redundant. It would also, theoretically, boost savings substantially.

Another version of the national retail sales tax was introduced early in 1996 by a bipartisan group of United States Congressmen. They would institute a 15 percent tax on goods and services sold at retail, with a rebate provided for those whose earnings are under the poverty line. They advocate repeal of the Sixteenth Amendment (establishing the federal progressive income tax) first and then passing a national retail sales tax bill. Economist Lawrence Kothikoff of Boston University conducted a study showing how this tax would not only be revenue-neutral but would substantially raise living standards. One way this could be accomplished was stated by one of the bill's co-sponsors, W. J. "Billy" Tauzin. He calculated that American manufacturing firms would rid themselves of the "hidden taxes" they are now paying (presumably for the provision of benefits and for some regulatory items) and foreign imports (with no hidden costs built into their price) would be charged the same retail sales tax, thus leveling the playing field. This would negate the need for most protective tariffs, and increase jobs in the United States.

Many of these assertions have yet to be proven. What is important is the philosophical change, from income to consumption, and the different emphasis it would produce. Of course, it would have to be shown that the new system would be revenue-neutral with the old. We will address that further on.

There is yet another proposal in this general category of consumption taxes. In fact, it is a bridge between income and consumption taxes. It is called the national consumption tax (called by some the consumed income tax, or the savings deduction). It was originally sponsored in 1994 by Senator Sam Nunn of Georgia and Senator Pete Domenici of New Mexico, who entitled their bill the Unlimited Savings Allowance (USA) tax. It would operate in the following manner. For both corporations and individuals all purchases of goods and services would be subtracted from gross income. A tax, employing a progressively graduated rate scale, starting at eight percent and escalating to 40 percent, would be paid on the difference.[8] For individuals, all savings and investment would be tax free (i.e., not included in goods and services). There might also be some exemptions made for necessity food, housing, and medical items. Deductions for some educational expenses have also been proposed. For companies, all capital equipment and inventories would be expensed in the year acquired. Labor and financing costs would not be deductible. The tax on the difference between gross revenues and costs would be 11 percent. The corporate version of this tax makes considerable sense; the individual less so from the standpoint of antifederalism since the central collection function would be retained.

This bill could simplify the tax process, depending upon how deductions were enumerated. It would be collectable at the point of payroll dispersal, which might make it easier to collect than a sales tax. It would provide the option of introducing progressivity into the rate scale. Since they would not be taxed, it might promote new savings and investment although the income therefrom would be taxable.

There are some basic questions that have been asked about consumption taxes. One is whether they could generate enough money to replace present income tax and payroll tax revenue and not increase the budget deficit. In other words, what rate would it take to make them revenue-neutral? Bruce Bartlett of the National Center for Policy Analysis estimates that the national sales tax or the consumed income tax would require rates of about 20 percent to accomplish this task. There is general agreement among economists with this contention, although legislative proposals run three to five percentage points lower.

Another question is whether poorer or younger families, which tend to spend the largest percentage of their incomes on necessity items, would be disproportionately penalized, as would the elderly who live on fixed incomes. The answer is that they would, and that some adjustment to alleviate this situation would have to be made. The adjustment would either be in the form of exemptions or rebates. Younger families also save less than the higher earning middle-aged groups. They would thus benefit less from provisions made to encourage savings. That is a fact and if savings are to be fostered, they are most likely to come from other demographic groups, as they traditionally have.

The Economist recently made some insightful comments about our present tax system.

> One compelling objective of tax policy is to make taxes as neutral as possible: rather than punish some productive activities a lot, punish them a little. America's system (and that of most other countries) violates this principle in three ways. It applies different tax rates to different activities. It favors consumption over savings, discounting investment in productive capital. And it applies high marginal rates to people with high incomes, discouraging effort. A system free of these distortions would also be much cheaper to

administer. (Most experts reckon that the cost of complying with the present system is well over $100 billion a year.[9]

I agree with these criticisms and objectives.

No tax is perfect. There will always be defects and biases. The total cost to the public will be roughly similar. In the end the selection of tax format is likely to be based more upon philosophy than any other single factor. That is why I generally favor taxes on consumption rather than those on income. In particular, I lean towards a national retail sales tax. This tax would be collectable at retail sites and thus would enable funds to more easily remain in localities. It would fit the philosophy of transposed antifederalism by allowing monies to remain local without being collected by a federal agency and funneled through Washington, D.C. If this tax is supplemented by a network of dedicated, fully-funded user fees (which could include an energy tax with money flowing into alternate fuel development and conservation, and an inheritance tax with its monies going to supplement Social Security) and have its impact on lower wage earners alleviated by some rebates, it could meet the first test of "fairness." It would also possibly promote savings and be reasonably progressive. A rate of 15 to 17 percent at the federal level, supplemented by user fees and other state or local levies of approximately another five percentage points, would be sufficient to be revenue-neutral with the old system but still remain within the historical band.

Those high wage earners who wished to live at a much lower standard that their incomes might justify in order to build savings would be free to do so. It would benefit the country. The power of the Internal Revenue Service, if it were retained at all, would be diffused. Local governments would absorb more of the collection responsibility and the financial muscle. Accountability would move closer to citizens' homes. They, in turn, would have to step forward and become involved to make the system work.

A technique has been advocated to project what the effects of particular economic policies, especially tax cuts, will have on future growth rates. It is called dynamic budgeting. These growth rates can then be factored into the budgeting process. It can give rise to some distortions, as one might expect. Actually, it is not new. Alexander Hamilton used much the same process in compiling our nations' first budget under the Constitution. Dynamic budgets for integrating a national retail sales tax or any consumption tax into the revenue process should allow for a transition period until people get comfortable with the new system. A five-year hiatus in economic growth would be a reasonably conservative projection.

A national retail sales tax would be a new concept. It would thus be hard to figure out in advance what the impact upon various economic sectors might be. The rates set would probably require adjustment. This should be anticipated, as should reams of alarmist rhetoric. We also have to realize that no significant long-term change in the savings rate is likely to occur without a reduction in the budget deficit and a revamping of the entitlement policies. All we can do is make our best judgments of desired outcomes, effect the tax policies most likely to produce them and be prepared for alterations. That is how we have operated our country since its beginning.

Corporate taxes should also be of the consumption form. They would fit better into the national consumption tax, the consumed income format outlined above, promoting those activities which are considered to be in the national interest. Deductions could be allowed for investment in plant and equipment, for protecting the environment, even for increasing jobs and providing day care centers. This would give companies an incentive to invest in those areas which we badly need and conduct themselves in ways deemed beneficial to society. It would also remove deductions for interest costs and thereby encourage financing from internal cash flow rather than through adding the leverage of debt. This restructuring of the tax system can eliminate those forms of "corporate welfare" that complicate and antagonize without meeting national objectives. Corporations are vital to our economic health but they should also be responsible, and zero-based tax thinking can nudge them in that direction.

The chief aims of a tax code oriented towards consumption would be to facilitate localism, simplify the overall structure, generate a revenue stream large enough to operate a fiscally-conservative government and produce fairness from top to bottom. This is, of course, a tall order. It has to begin with our willingness to prioritize so that we can operate within the scope of our financial resources. It will require citizens to step forward and participate so that our democracy, and its expression through local government, can work effectively. Rearranging an out-of-date and badly skewed tax system will not be easy. Our citizens will require large doses of perspective and persistence in order to make a new system work. If this country can generate the type of debate where various interest groups delay their advocacy or protests until an overall philosophy has been agreed upon, our decision process will be greatly improved. A national retail sales tax for individuals, coupled with a national consumed income tax for corporations, could assist this nation with its objectives in the twenty-first century. It could gradually re-energize and motivate our people and our economy.

---

[1] In 1980 the top rate was 70 percent. It was reduced in the 1980s to 28 percent by 1988; raised to 31 percent in 1990 and raised again to 39.6 percent in 1993.

[2] "Supply side economics is little more than a new label for standard neoclassical economics," said Art Laffer in Victor A. Canto, Douglas B. Jones, and Arthur Laffer's, *Foundations of Supply Side Economics: Theory and Evidence,* Academic Press NY, 1983, p. xv. Robert Bartley in *The Seven Fat Years and How We Can Do It Again,* The Free Press, NY 1992, p. 55-6, elaborated further. "What counts is government control

over real economic resources whether it commandeers the resources by taxing or buys them with bonds. Or it's not government borrowing that crowds out the private sector, but government spending." Bartley continues, explaining that "the essential point is that the supply of credit is not fixed. The savings pool available for borrowing expands and contracts with the fortunes of the economy." Supply siders argue that cutting income taxes is the best way to create economic growth.

[3] United States Internal Revenue Service estimates. In 1960 the payroll tax was about 2 1/2 percent of GDP, the federal income tax was about 9 percent, the corporate profits tax about 5 percent and other federal taxes about 2 percent of GDP.

[4] The only year the budget was balanced was 1969.

[5] Sources for figures are the Joint Committee on Taxation and the Internal Revenue Service.

[6] The savings rate for the country as a whole averaged 8.1 percent of GDP in the 1960s. In the 1970s it dropped to an average of 7.2 percent. In the 1980s the decline was sharper, to an average of 3.9 percent of GDP. Net domestic investment averaged 7.3 percent of GDP in the 1960s. In the first half of the 1990s it averaged 3.5 percent of GDP.

[7] Joel Slemrod, editor, *Do Taxes Matter* (Boston: MIT Press, 1991).

[8] Taxable gross income would include wages, salaries, and other forms of compensation. It would include interest, dividends, and receipts on the sale of securities.

[9] *The Economist*, "America's Tax Reform: A Better Way to Pay," 13 January 1996, 32.

CHAPTER 9

Entitlements

> Increasingly freedom is defined as the accumulation of rights and entitlements as well as license for any form of self-expression and gratification. The notion of self-imposed or socially expected service to society has become unfashionable.
>
> Zbignieiew Brzezinski
> *Out of Control*[1]

Entitlements Defined

Over the last few years federal programs providing certain specific services have been much in the news. They have been the cause of battles over funding and battles over whether or not these programs are inherent citizen's rights. Collectively they have been called *entitlements*, implying a legal or moral contract between the recipients and society. They have become focal points for passionate debate among proponents and opponents of their sustenance, even their continuation. What are they?

The initial tranche of entitlements came out of the Great Depression and Franklin Roosevelt's New Deal. They were contained in the Social Security Act of August 14, 1935; which was composed of a collection of programs including Old Age Survivors Insurance, Disability Insurance and something called Aid to Families With Dependent Children, which we refer to as Welfare.

The Food Stamp Act was added just prior to World War II—on May 16, 1939, two weeks after I was born.

Lyndon Johnson's Great Society brought forth Medicare, basic hospital insurance for those over 65, and Medicaid, medical insurance for the needy and disabled not covered by Social Security. Both were signed into law on July 30, 1965.

These programs were initially conceived as a safety net for the indigent. They were designed to keep people afloat if their economic condition temporarily precluded obtaining those basic essentials necessary to keep them alive and functional. The programs were designed to sustain people in their old age if their families couldn't take care of them. Nobody predicted how long the average life span would become. Nobody envisioned that the American family would disintegrate. At their creation nobody foresaw that gradually most of the entitlements would come to be co-opted by the middle class, who would grow to envision them as rights. This evolution has produced a definitional dichotomy. Democratic Senator Daniel Patrick Moynihan says of Social Security, "It was envisioned from the beginning as a social insurance program." At the same time Republican Congressman Bill Archer calls it an "earned right program."

Whether they are considered social insurance or middle class perks influences the cost of entitlements. It also influences their political malleability. Refining these definitions will play a critical role in the determination of our political health in the twenty-first century. In this chapter these programs will be described. Some solutions will be suggested. The complete picture is so complex and the programs so entwined throughout our socio-economic structure that an extensive volume would only begin the unraveling process. This chapter's intent is to bring us face-to-face with some truisms and start us thinking about remedies. During this discussion it will become evident that I lean towards Senator Moynihan's definition and that my solutions would require extensive revisions.

Entitlements and the Economy

In fiscal 1995 the United States federal budget amounted to just over $1.6 trillion and our Gross Domestic Product approximated $6 trillion. The four key entitlement programs were funded as follows: Social security—$357 billion; Medicare—$178 billion; Medicaid—$176 billion and Welfare—$26 billion.

Interest on the national debt of $4.9 trillion amounted to $235 billion. Thus, these four entitlements plus interest on our debt made up 60 percent of the budget, up from 29 percent in 1963. The budget, or all federal spending, amounted to 21.3 percent of GDP, which includes all domestic revenues. All government spending (federal, state, and local) amounts to 34 percent of GDP. The budget deficit was $163.5 billion in fiscal 1995. As mentioned in an earlier chapter, the level of national indebtedness has arisen from our inability to balance more than one budget since 1961. If no adjustments are made and even if economic conditions are stable, the deficit, due to the evolution of programs, will trend up over $200 billion by the end of the decade.[2] It will increase annually, after a likely decline in fiscal 1996 and possibly fiscal 1997, due to the nature of in-place programs and demographics. These estimates assume annual real economic growth stays at the 2.5 percent average registered since 1973. In fact, my own belief is that real growth will prove to average a considerably lower rate between 1996 and 2000. Both the Democratic and Republican plans for balancing the budget assume economic growth rates higher than the average of the last 20 years in their estimates. Their projections are thus likely to fall short for that reason and the fact that most of the individual budget categories contain estimates that are on the optimistic side. Spending will most likely have to be more vigorously attacked than any current plans suggest if the budget deficit is to be eliminated approximately at the century's turn.

It can be readily seen that no credible deficit reduction program can take place without addressing Social Security, the two medical programs and the national debt. By way of comparison, defense spending was $260 billion in fiscal 1995. All spending for education, both private and public, was about $300 billion. Spending on all forms of health care (including Medicare, Medicaid, and about half of the Social Security funds) was just over $1 trillion. Federal spending on health care comprised just under half of the $1 trillion and that was the amount included in the budget. Virtually all of it was in the form of entitlements. Thus, entitlements and debt are clearly the runaway areas to control if we are to once again enjoy financial security as a nation. As will be shown during the unfolding of this chapter, the situation is serious enough to require significant changes, not merely a tinkering with growth rates.

Senator Robert Kerrey of Nebraska, Co-Chairman of the Bi-Partisan Committee on Entitlements and Tax Reform, speaking in 1995 characterized the nation's situation in the following manner. "Our fiscal problems do not exist because wealthy Americans are not paying enough taxes. Our fiscal problems exist because of the rapid, uncontrolled growth in programs that primarily benefit the middle class." The middle class has been a enormous beneficiary of this country's creation and dispersal of entitlements. Despite the popular conception, the middle class today versus 50 years ago is better off financially, lives longer, has better education and health care, and has a more assured retirement. Much of this is due to entitlements.

Entitlements in Outline

In order to understand what might be done to revise them, we first should take a brief look at each of the major entitlement programs. With this perusal we may better comprehend how entitlements work and where they are headed.

Social Security is the biggest, and most emotionally charged, of the entitlements. It is viewed by seniors as the fulfillment of a long-standing contract. Young people regard it as one of the principal instruments for eviscerating their American dream. In a way, both are correct.

Over 44 million individuals receive Social Security payments starting at 65 (62 for early benefits), an age that will rise very gradually to 67 by 2027. These benefits are indexed to inflation (specifically, to the Consumer Price Index). Monies for these payments are collected through a 12.4 percent tax (half from employers, half from employees) on income up to $62,500. Over 139 million workers and their employers paid $345 billion to Social Security in 1995. In fact, most workers in this country pay more in Social Security taxes than they do in income taxes. Costs and unfunded liabilities for Social Security have been increasing at about a 12 percent average annual rate over the past two decades.

Medicare covers 33 million elderly and four million disabled persons. Its income is generated by a combination of taxes and premiums. Its disbursements are supervised by the Health Care Financing Administration. Medicare funding and disbursements are divided into two parts.

Part A covers hospital bills. These costs are covered by payroll taxes of 1.45 percent each to employers and employees (for a total tax rate of 2.50 percent). Part A accounts for about 60 percent of all Medicare expenses.

Part B covers doctor bills. One-quarter of its revenues is generated by a premium of $46.10 per month paid by employees. The other three-quarters come from general tax revenues.

Costs for Medicare have been growing at ten percent per year.

Medicaid is a joint federal-state program designed to provide care for 36 million indigent persons who have to meet a test of limited earnings and assets. About 40 percent of its payments go to nursing homes and about 25 percent to hospitals. The largest group of recipients is single mothers with children. Medicare, too, has been growing at approximately ten percent annually. Thus, the total of Social Security, Medicare, and Medicaid programs has been growing at a rate four times greater than that of the economy as a whole over the past 20 years.

Welfare is a relatively small program. It covers 15 million people, mostly single mothers with children (almost ten million of those covered are children) and costs a total of $26 billion. Those who advocate its reduction contend that the aggregate of programs based upon the recipient's limited means (e.g., school lunches, homeless shelters, foster care, the earned income tax credit) totals over $300 billion. Due to its nature—paying people who don't work, prohibiting a recipient to cohabit with a spouse or a mate—it has been a lightning rod for criticism and target for reform. Most people who oppose welfare are upset by those who remain on it for extended periods. The most controversial cases are those where generations of women remain welfare recipients. Teen mothers are a prime candidate for this permanent or semi-permanent status. The Population Reference Bureau's report, *The United States at Mid-Decade*, states that there are over one million teens who get pregnant every year, and teen-aged mothers bear a third of all the children born out of wedlock. About one-half of all teen mothers go on welfare within four years. At any given time over one-half the women making up the total welfare caseload gave birth as teens.[3] However worthy or successful any re-engineering of this program might be sociologically, it is unlikely to make much financial difference to the budget, although at some stage improved productivity from those now receiving welfare payments could make an economic impact.[4] In fact, the various state programs proposing major changes—Wisconsin, Michigan, Massachusetts, for example—are not expecting significant financial savings. In the initial stages at least, their proposals would actually cost more money. These states are targeting a change in the attitudes about and the ability to perform work. One of their biggest challenges, if their programs are successful, may be to find jobs for those coming off welfare.

The Pulse of Entitlements

Entitlements are in financial trouble. In 1995 the Office of Management and Budget (OMB) estimated that the growth and the magnitude of our entitlements threatened national economic stability. According to its figures, if the entitlement programs remain unchanged and Gross Domestic Product averages about three percent real growth annually (half a percentage point above the average of the last ten years), all federal revenues will be consumed by entitlements by the year 2012. Furthermore, OMB estimated that by the year 2000 three program—Social Security; Medicare; and Medicaid, plus interest on the national debt—will preempt 80 percent of all federal spending. These are frightening numbers. *Washington Post* columnist Robert J. Samuelson described the situation neatly. "The real question is not whether the welfare state survives. It will. Hardly anyone wants to revert to unfettered capitalism. The real question is whether it can gradually rein in its over commitments—or whether it will do so convulsively as the result of crisis."[5] Our recent history indicates that crisis convulsions are more likely than steady application of discipline.

I have already cited the ongoing decline in workers per retiree. That will be dramatic. In 1950 there were 16 workers for every person over 65. Now (1996) there are four. This will fall to 3.1 by 2015, to 2.5 by 2025 and to two by 2050. This decline has resulted from the fact that the post-war baby boomers have been the first generation in our history not to replace itself in the population pool. The fertility rates dropped starting in 1971 when they fell below replacement levels and have essentially stayed there with only a slight upturn showing in the 1990s.

Additionally, lives of seniors have been prolonged far beyond what was expected when the entitlement programs were established. Finally, due to lavish ladling our of benefits, indexing of these benefits to inflation and poor financial management, costs have run amok. Costs and obligations have grown to the point where if the combined committed Social Security, Medicare, and Medicaid benefits are paid to all people now in the work force without alterations, the total payroll tax taken out of salaries will have to jump from its current 14.9 percent (12.4 percent for Social Security, 2.5 percent for Medicare) to 40 percent within 50 years. By the end of this decade these three programs alone, if left unaltered, will add a minimum of $200 billion a year to the budget deficit. By the year 2030 OMB estimates that the combined annual cash deficit of Social Security and Medicare will be $1.7 trillion. A glimpse of the instabilities within each program may lead us towards some remedial alternatives.

Social Security is the largest network of programs. Economist Herbert Stein has amplified upon the above analysis.

> Another way to look at the finances of the system is to ask what would happen if no new workers entered it but all present retirees continue to draw their benefits and all workers now covered continue to pay their payroll taxes and later draw their benefits. Calculations have been made on that basis. They show that the future liabilities of such a system exceeded present and future assets by $7,119 billion at the end of 1990 and that this excess had increased by over $1 trillion in 1990. This means that a very large fraction of all the benefits to be paid in the next seventy-five years will be paid by the contributions of workers not yet in the system.[6]

It is mind boggling to contemplate the increase in unfunded Social Security liabilities at the rate of at least $1 trillion per year. The unfunded (above the Social Security Trust Fund) liabilities are currently at a level of $12 trillion, twice the GDP. The prospective workers that will be called upon to shoulder the burden of retiring, mostly white baby boomers will be largely non-white. Even in the event that it will be financially possible for them to pay, will they be willing to do so?

In addition, it is becoming increasingly evident that the combination of pensions, savings, and social security that workers are counting on to finance their retirement will not be adequate to maintain their current standard of living. Kenneth E. Feltman of the Employer's Council on Flexible Compensation put it this way in a recent survey. "For many people, that means the standard of living that we are used to is going to have to decline in our remaining working years in order for us to have a decent standard of living in retirement." This standard will not be helped by the fact that the number of Social Security beneficiaries is expected to double by the year 2040.

The trustees of the Social Security trust funds estimated in their 1994 Annual Report that income would drop below payments in 2013. They further estimated that their reserves would be depleted by 2029 when the demands of payments will bankrupt the system. The year 2029 is when, if current trends continue, federal spending will comprise 40 percent of the budget, up from 29 percent in 1995.

The current "surplus" in the Social Security trust funds of around $5 trillion is merely an accounting gimmick. The funds are not really on a financially sound self-sustaining footing. To begin with revenues are transferred directly to the Treasury's general pool with an IOU placed in the trust funds. When the day comes that the IOUs have to be redeemed, the government may or may not have the financial revenues to honor them. In the budget crisis of 1995-1996 Secretary of the Treasury Rubin was dipping into various pension and trust funds to provide the funds (unconstitutionally many said) to stave off a default of the national debt. Whether this trust fund surplus is illusory or not is almost academic. Let's assume for a moment that the $5 trillion trust is rock solid. If the same accounting rules that are required of corporations were applied to the Social Security trust funds, unfunded pension liability would have to be shown (and amortized). This unfunded liability is enormous. As mentioned above, most actuarial estimates indicate that by the end of 1995 it was at least $12 trillion, more than twice the stated surplus, more than twice the national debt, and twice the Gross Domestic Product. This is the figure if no more workers enter the system, and it is staggering. A company with an unfunded pension liability of twice its revenues would be teetering on the brink of insolvency. Social Security is only one of many financially-troubled government programs. It is not the only program in the entitlement network.

The issue of a contract is at the heart of the concept of entitlements. Seniors (supported by their lobbying group, the American Association of Retired Persons) often contend that they were given an implied promise by their government to supply them with Social Security payments throughout their lives, regardless of what they paid into the system. An average earner who retired in 1994 will get back all contributions plus interest in eight years. For workers who always earned the maximum, the payback time is about 11 years. The average couple with one wage earner who retires in 1996 will receive about $125,000 more in Social Security benefits over the remainder of their lives than they paid into the system. The average man who is 65 today is expected to live to age 80. The average 65-year-old woman is expected to live past 85. These numbers were not anticipated when the program was established. Even if a contract is assumed, it wasn't this lavish.

Even more important, is making such a promise to all workers, regardless of income, financially sound and equitable? Economist Thomas Sowell compares this to a savings account. "I have been faithfully putting money into a local bank for more than a decade, but if I present the teller with a withdrawal slip for a million dollars, the bank is not about to honor it."[7] If all its customers presented such withdrawal slips, it wouldn't be long before the bank was out of money. What an unfunded pension liability represents is the sum of all the likely withdrawal slips. We have been allowing retirees, regardless of need, to withdraw far in excess of their deposits. This is a practice that will most certainly break the bank.

Three other issues impact Social Security costs, and to some extent those of other programs as well. One is a liberalization, by legislative and legal action, in the definition of disability. Between 1984 and 1994 the population of the United States rose 11 percent. In that same decade the number of individuals legally considered to be on disability rose 40 percent. Disabled persons are entitled by law to a wide range of payments—for education, for health care, for retirement.

Another issue is the fact that 28 percent of the over-65-year-olds receiving Supplemental Security Income assistance were legal aliens. In 1995 that amounted to 700,000 legal aliens collecting this money. Payments to legal aliens from a variety of programs are estimated to total $30 billion over the balance of the decade. (e.g., Pell grants for low-income college students were paid to 390,000 legal aliens in 1995 and cost $662 million.) Illegal aliens are a bigger burden on the health care system than on Social Security, but both categories of aliens regularly drain our coffers. No other nation is this generous to non-citizens.

A third issue is that Social Security payments are 100 percent indexed to inflation, as represented by the Consumer Price Index. Research from the Federal Reserve indicates that this index has overstated inflation over the past decade by between .2 and 1.5 percentage points annually. If all the federal benefits programs that are indexed are taken together (Social Security is the largest), each one percentage point change in the Consumer Price Index impacts the budget by about $6.5 billion annually. All three of these cost factors should be addressed, and controlled.

How about Medicare? The Congressional Budget Office estimates that by 2030 the 33 million workers that are over 65 and are now receiving Medicare will have grown to 70 million Medicare recipients. It further estimates that 1995 outlays of $178 billion, which accounted for 11.7 percent of the budget, will have grown to $458 billion, or 18.6 percent of the budget, by 2005. The Bi-Partisan Committee on Entitlements and Tax Reform estimated that the Hospital Trust Fund would be in deficit by 1996 and exhausted by 2002. In fact, the fund went into deficit in 1995. This deficit will not only be the result of expenditure growth, but also is another example of excess withdrawals.

For example, the average recipient retiring in 1995 will take $100,000 more out of the Hospital Trust Fund over his or her remaining life than was paid in through his or her Medicare taxes. Another factor impacting Medicare is the enormous expenditure made for terminal patients. In 1996, 30 percent of Medicare's budget was for goods and services used in the last year of a patient's life.

Medicaid is growing just as fast as Medicare. It is supposed to be the health insurance system for the nation's poor. The largest chunk of its money goes to maintain 1.6 million elderly people in nursing homes. The occupants of nursing homes are usually old and sick. Over the coming several decades we know that the population is going to grow older, and probably sicker. This doesn't bode well for the economics of Medicaid. One of its most controversial features is that it requires people to meet its asset tests in order to qualify. So individuals often have to "spend down" to reach the $5,000 per person asset limit. This seems to many to be an unwarranted waste of financial resources. Either they are poor and have to be helped, or they are not. The program shouldn't have artificialities built into it. If some other type of program needs to be fashioned to meet long-term care needs, it should be discussed.

Welfare, and the related means-dependent programs for the disadvantaged, are also growing faster than the economy. The strategy so far employed by Congress has been to drastically cut them at the federal level. The responsibility, sometimes accompanied by block grants, has been devolved to the states. The result is that in this program especially, but also in others, the original inspiration for entitlements, the indigent, have fared particularly poorly. That is not surprising since they have relatively little political clout. Medicaid in particular is crowded with artificial poor, a middle class elderly attempting to meet minimum asset tests. The ironic consolation is that even those who have had clout will shortly be joining the poor in bemoaning discontinued or reduced benefits as available resources dwindle and Social Security and Medicare benefits will become curtailed.

Economically, the message is clear. Entitlements are in serious trouble and have to be drastically altered to survive. Philosophically, the prevalent message has been similar to that sent by President Lyndon Johnson when signing Medicare and Medicaid into existence on July 30, 1965. "No longer will older Americans be denied the healing miracle of modern medicine." In other words we are entitled to all that technology offers, regardless of what we contributed, regardless of what it means to the financial health of the nation. The transition to a more fiscally and socially responsible philosophical attitude is what will come next. Hopefully, that transition will be smooth. Most likely it will not. Many who have been counting on these programs are likely to be disappointed.

Entitlement Solutions

It would be presumptuous of me to pretend that I have perfect, balanced solutions to the economic, social, and philosophical questions surrounding entitlements. It would be equally foolhardy to contend that nothing needs to be done. A number of corrective suggestions have been published recently. We will peruse a few of them in this section, highlighting the areas that seem to make the most sense.

There have been several mechanical adjustments proposed for Social Security. All of them, in some form or other, will probably have to be adopted before the end of this century. Raising the eligible age is one of them. As noted, a very gradual rise to 67 will take place by 2027. A sharper and more rapid rise will likely be needed. The fact was mentioned above that benefits are linked to the Consumer Price Index. It has been proposed that the CPI itself be reduced. This will not be enough. Over the next ten years benefits, even a reduced level of benefits, will need to be de-indexed. It has been proposed that a means test be administered prior to disbursement. It has also been proposed that benefits be taxed for those with higher incomes. Currently, each individual can receive up to $11,280 per year in outside income (income from investments is not counted in this amount) before having Social Security benefits reduced at a rate of $1 taken away for every $3 earned. On March 30, 1996 President Clinton signed a bill raising this outside earning limit to $12,500 in 1996, and increasing it to $30,000 by 2002. This bill will increase effective government payments on over 70 percent of the proposed income to one million recipients between ages 65 and 69 who receive Social Security. It will cost this country about $7 billion per year. Currently, only half of all Social Security recipients have less than $11,280 per year of income. Allowing people to collect Social Security no matter what their income level defies logic, and sound financial practice.

Refusing to tax incomes over $62,500, not means testing disbursements, not counting investment income when compiling benefit limitations, increasing the allowable amount of outside income, smacks of the most irresponsible type of special interest pandering. The principle of means testing has been called wrong by some. David R. Henderson, a research fellow at the Hoover Institution and associate professor of economics at the Naval Postgraduate School, cites two ways in which it manifests its errors. One, he says, is that it is inherently unfair, penalizing the person who might save and invest versus someone with the same lifetime income who spent it all. The second problem in his mind is that means testing "reduces the incentive to work and encourages people to hide income." These comments show worthy sentiment but are economically naive. His suggested remedies are to increase the eligibility age, from 62 to 65 for early retirement and from 65 to 70 for standard. He would also lower the marginal tax rates on older people by eliminating the earnings test while making all benefits taxable.[8] Unfortunately, the arithmetic of these adjustments doesn't even begin to attack the mountain of costs created by rising benefits and unfunded liabilities.

There have been several different plans for privatization or semi-privatization. Some degree of privatization seems inevitable. One plan was put forth by Professor Karl Borden of the University of Nebraska. He would offer a deal to all individuals under the age of 47. If they agree to give up their rights to Social Security, they wouldn't have to pay the Social Security tax and could put an amount equal to 12.4 percent of their pre-tax income (a combination of the employer and employee tax rate) into an Individual Retirement Account type instrument free of any taxes. This would reduce the future strain on Social Security, increase savings, and improve returns (as the trust funds have underperformed even the Treasury Bill yield compounded over the last 20 years). Other countries, notably Chile, Australia, and Sweden have instituted some privatization of their Social Security equivalents with enough success that serious study is called for. Anytime taxes show promise of being turned into private investments, while improving the health of the overall system, a close inspection of possible implementation strategies is warranted.

The 13-member Advisory Council on Social Security, which was appointed in 1994 to make recommendations to the Social Security Administration, advocated in its report of February, 1996 three separate plans for partial privatization. Six members of the panel proposed that the government invest up to 40 percent of the Social Security Trust Fund (assuming, of course, that there is something besides IOUs in the fund) in equities to obtain a better long-term return. Five panelists sponsored a Chile-like system. Under this proposal workers would create personal savings accounts funded by five percentage points of the 6.2 percent of payrolls that employees pay in Social Security tax. Employers' five percentage points would pay for a flat $400 per month (in current dollars) benefit. The remaining 1.2 percentage points from each contributor would go into the traditional system. The final two panelists would gradually reduce benefits and create mandatory retirement accounts by adding another 1.6 percentage points (.8 each from employer and employee) to the current tax. These accounts would be invested in equities. All three plans are similar in pointing out the necessity for privatization.

I believe that privatization is inevitable but there are transitional questions that have to be addressed. The current system has one redistributive aspect to it. Workers who have earned the minimum wage get a higher ratio of pension income to lifetime wages than a higher wage earner. Would this be continued? The redistributive aspect is more than counterbalanced by not taxing salaries over $62,500 and not means testing disbursements. Would these contradictions be ironed out? Any plan involving equities contains capital risk. Who would bear that risk? Would it be the government or the potential beneficiary?

The result could be some sort of multi-tiered system. United States Representative Mark Sanford of South Carolina outlined a hypothetical transition. Let's assume the old system ends at midnight 1999. Those receiving benefits would continue to do so. People 50-years-old or older who are not receiving benefits could either stay in the system and continue to pay Social Security taxes or choose to opt out and take the present value of their contributions as a zero-coupon Treasury Bond and deposit it in an individual retirement account. Those in the 30-to-50 age group could make a choice: stay in the system or take half the present value of their contributions to date. There will be hiccups in the transition. That is unavoidable. A transition will be necessary, however. The sooner it is effected, the less dramatic it will have to be.

Once a private, or partially-private system is in place there will be one more hurdle, besides the one of the risk of the equity investment. The pension consulting firm of Rogers Casey did an in-depth survey (released in March 1996) of company executives in charge of administering 401 (k) and other retirement plans. This survey revealed that employees are not adequately funding their retirements. According to the respondents: employees aren't signing up for the plans in sufficient numbers; employees aren't contributing enough; and employees aren't allocating their money appropriately. While a transfer to the private sector will ease the Social Security budget crisis, it will create new challenges and new requirements. People will have to contribute, and they will have to pay some attention to investing, at least enough to pick a responsible advisor.

Privatization might conceivably provide surprising benefits. Economist Martin Feldstein argues that changing Social Security from a pay-as-you-go system whose assets are invested in United States Treasury obligations to a funded system whose assets are invested in wealth-producing private sector assets would materially aid overall economic growth. In fact, Feldstein calculates that GDP could be increased by three percent per year ($220 billion based upon 1995 figures) by such a metamorphosis.[9] This assertion, if proven true, would make a major difference in our economic outlook.

In the previous chapter we advocated applying the proceeds of all inheritance taxes to the Social Security Trust Fund. Philosophically it would make sense. One of the reasons we have a Social Security crisis is the break up of the family and the concomitant lapsing of elderly care within the family. Funneling inheritance taxes into the fund would somewhat correct the generational imbalance. Financially, it would not be particularly significant but every little bit helps, and change could prove to be important.

Medicare, which is health care for the elderly and disabled, is the subject of an emotional political debate at the moment. Most of the alternatives offered either attempt to reduce Medicare's rate of growth or to fold the program into a larger health care provision system. It seems likely that whatever the ultimate form of health care in this country,

Medicare will require serious restructuring if it is to survive what Martin Corry, director of federal affairs for the American Association of Retired Persons, describes as "the baby boom generation hitting Medicare like a tsunami." There have been a number of suggestions made which purport to cut Medicare costs. When analyzing any proposal the distinction needs to be made between those that would only slow its runaway growth and those that would actually reduce costs. Most proposals being considered today would only accomplish the former, and that won't be enough.

Part A provides coverage for hospital costs. It is a huge factor for the industry as the average hospital receives one-third of its revenues from Medicare. You will remember that it is funded by a payroll tax. Most Medicare recipients believe that their taxes (both payroll for Part A and general for Part B) plus accumulated interest over their working lives have paid for the benefits that they eventually collect. In fact, on average these payments only cover 26 percent of the benefits. In order for Medicare to pay for hospital costs by the time all baby boomers have retired in 2030, payroll taxes would have to almost triple from their current levels. These necessary cost increases are so large that Part A Medicare really can't survive on its own. Realistically, becoming a portion of an overall solution is the only logical outcome. This solution will almost surely involve capitation, prioritization, more home care, less visits to specialists, and more preventative medicine. The recent announcement that Medicare will no longer pay for lung reduction surgery (at $18,000 to $25,000 per operation) to alleviate emphysema is only the opening salvo in the barrage of prioritization and re-organization that will engulf, and probably dismember Medicare over the balance of this decade.

Part B provides coverage for doctors' bills through a monthly fee, plus use of general tax revenues. The proposed Republican Medicare plan calls for the monthly fee to rise from 1995's $46.19 to $53.70 in 1996 and $88.90 by 2002. This would save an estimated $49 billion cumulatively over the seven years from 1996–2002. If Medicare remains in place, a fee increase for Part B is a virtual certainty. In all likelihood the Republican increase would be an absolute minimum. Fees would likely be scaled so that higher income earners pay significantly more than those in lower brackets. It will also be necessary to make recipients of funds pay more than the 20 percent of most doctor's bills that they pay now. The eligibility age will probably be raised as well so that recipients will be over 70 before getting any payments. All of these measures for both parts A and B are necessitated by imminent insolvency, which the surprise announcement of an operating loss for fiscal 1996 only brings closer.

Another avenue of Medicare cost reduction is the area of compensation to doctors and hospitals. If the fee-for-service system stays in effect (which is unlikely), both doctors and hospitals will find their margins squeezed even further. Those patients receiving home health care will likely have to pay more for it than they do now. The provision that allows state Medicaid programs to pay premiums, co-payments and deductibles for four million low income elderly receiving Medicare may well be rescinded by financial difficulties at the state level, forcing these costs to be borne by the Medicare system. States are running out of money for health care even faster than the federal government.

That brings us to the most probable outcome. Our entire fee-for-service health care system is evolving toward some form of capitation plan. (National health care, managed care, or health maintenance organizations are all capitation based). These plans all involve the principle of capitation, which is payment of a fixed fee (one proposal is for $5,200 per year per individual) for a service that would stress prevention, short hospital stays and less visits to specialists. Only ten percent of Medicare recipients use such an option today because they vastly prefer using their own doctors. If costs are to be controlled, this will have to change. We are one of the last nations in the world where individuals can choose their own doctors, unless they elect to pay for that privilege themselves. Capitation, in any form, will be unpopular at first, but eventually it will be seen as the best way to provide economic care in the face of daunting demographics, and the United States will follow most of the world away from fee-for-service. Medicare will be a part of this capitation system, its fee-for-service days are likely to end before the new century begins.

Medicaid is the joint federal-state program created to provide care for the indigent through state organizations. The largest chunk of its payments go to nursing homes for the care of the elderly and the disabled. This program, more than any of the three considered here, provides the clearest contrast between original intent and recent development.

Medicaid was created to care for the indigent. That is why it contains some of its present controversial provisions, such as "spending down" assets against costs-for-care until a minimum level has been reached. These provisions are obviously offensive for those expecting to receive a middle class entitlement. They make a lot more sense as a part of a safety net for the poor. Looking out over the next 25 to 50 years it seems clear that if we wish to rescue our entitlement programs financially, they will either have to take on more private aspects (e.g., IRA clones replacing Social Security, capitation replacing fee-for-service health care) or return to their original purpose of sustaining our disadvantaged rather than serving our middle class. A truncated Medicaid may survive with specific focus on our poorest citizens.

Of the households headed by individuals 65 or older, 42 percent have incomes of $15,000 per year or less. These are the people Medicaid, Social Security and even Medicare were designed to assist. Most Medicaid patients can be helped through state programs setting their own criteria for eligibility, level of service and matching of federal funds. Currently, the states match from 50 to 80 percent of federal Medicaid funds. It this is to continue, virtually all states will be forced to drastically tighten their Medicaid eligibility criteria.

All of the programs outlined above, plus Welfare, will have to be immediately revamped. The Medicaid and Medicare programs will most likely be a part of an overall healthcare redesign. Social Security will probably be at least partially-privatized. States will assume control of Welfare. In this manner it will be possible to retain at least a portion of the implied contract with our middle class, while providing a safety net for the indigent. But the situation is very serious. If financial collapse under a demographic attack is to be averted, reform must come swiftly and comprehensively. Hopelessness is not foreordained. If we are prepared to be innovative in rethinking our objectives, we must move rapidly to implement the reforms.

Entitlements and Antifederalism

Budget deficits are now $165 billion and seem headed over $200 billion before the decade is over. The federal debt ceiling has just been raised to allow the amount to exceed $5 trillion with annual interest costs expected to top $250 billion. Consumer installment loans (other than mortgages) are devouring 11 percent of the average worker's pre-tax income, before interest and principal payments. The average American household has an outstanding balance of credit card debt alone of $3,900, and the nation's total load of credit card debt is $400 billion, with rising delinquency rates. In this economic climate of progressively reduced financial flexibility, median real personal income has dropped 15 percent since 1973. With the number of workers per retiree falling, unfunded liabilities for Social Security growing, and insolvency looming for Medicare, the scope to increase taxes in order to pay for entitlements is small. If this vast realm of middle class entitlements is to be maintained, even in a severely reduced form, without entirely gobbling up the budget, new thinking involving comprehensive restructuring is called for.

Transposed antifederalism would philosophically support both privatization and localization. Given the necessity for entitlement cost cutting, privatization and localization may be our best chances to accomplish that mission with preservation of service somewhat approximating current levels. That means Social Security would largely be converted to a tax-free individual savings plan, which would be administered locally. The bulk of Medicare, and some portions of Medicaid, would be transferred to capitation plans (some of which would be private and local) as part of an overall health care restructuring. The state organizations in place to operate Medicaid would be in position to administer the remainder of Medicare and Medicaid under the guidance of a reduced Health Care Financing

Administration. Federally-funded entitlements would cover those aspects of Medicare, Medicaid, and Social Security applicable to the older, less flexible beneficiaries or the truly indigent. These attenuated federal programs could be financed by reduced taxes and premiums paid directly into fully-funded trusts to ensure their financial integrity.

Welfare is already in the process of being localized. Largely volunteer *parallel polis* organizations are providing increasing segments of the spectrum of social services. As charities adjust to the realities of a new tax code they will retain their role as important supporters of social services. This country does not have the financial wherewithal to continue those social services without their support. We can provide fully funded health and social services to the indigent (with the interest earned from established funds). Middle class entitlements, if still desired, will have to be coordinated with the private sector. There simply is no realistic alternative.

For those education and social service programs that remain in the public sector, some sort of realignment to improve efficiency is badly needed. There are 240 different federal programs for education and job training alone, a ridiculous defiance of common sense management. United States Representative John Porter and Senator John Coats suggested a Project For American Renewal. This multi-bill program would fall into three general areas. 1) Fathering, Mentoring, and Family: The Mentor Schools Act; The Role Model's Academy Act; The Family Reconciliation Act; The Family Housing Act and The Family Fairness Act. 2) Community Empowerment: The Maternity Shelter Act and The Family For Independence Act. 3) Effective Compassion: The Medical Volunteer Act; The Community Partnership Act; The Compassion Credit Act and The Comprehensive Charity Reform Act. This structure may or may not be specifically what is called for but the overall thinking is. We can continue to be a compassionate nation, but government remains the last over-staffed and poorly organized element of our society. We can no longer afford it.

Our system of entitlements could be redirected to meet the twin principles of efficacy and fiscal conservatism. They could provide the disadvantaged with a full range of services. They could move the more affluent towards privately-supported retirement and health benefits. They could make the tax revenues underlying middle class entitlements more equitable in nature. This would begin to lessen the pressure on a system grossly overburdened with future obligation. It would also move administration, and in some cases control, closer to the individuals affected. A financial crisis could thus be transformed into a more manageable situation utilizing the basics of antifederalist philosophy, coupled with elementary managerial common sense.

There is no painless solution. We have dug a deep hole for ourselves with no easy exit. I believe the methods suggested above would offer an opportunity to provide needed services while improving our finances. I believe they would remain consistent with our ideals. Fifty years from now our descendants will be receiving entitlements under a materially different system. We can only hope that it rests upon a sounder, more realistic social and economic foundation.

---

[1] Zbigniew Brezezinski, *Out of Control: Global Turmoil on the Eve of the Twenty-First Century* (New York: Charles Scribner's Sons, 1993).

[2] Estimates are just that. The development of demographics and entitlement programs indicate the upturn in fiscal 1997. Economic growth rates play a large part in deficit estimates. For example, over the weekend of December 9-10, 1995 the Republicans, using Congressional Budget Office estimates, raised their growth estimates and trimmed $100 billion from the projected cumulative seven-year deficit and thus eliminated at one stroke that much necessary spending cuts. The Republican estimates for the GDP went from 2.4 percent annually to 2.6 percent. The Democratic Clinton Administration and Budget estimates projected growth of 2.8 percent as a real annual average. The reverse side of this is that if economic growth turns out to be disappointing over the balance of the decade (an occurrence I deem to contain at least a 50 percent probability), then the deficit estimates and spending cuts proposals will turn out to be too optimistic. Then, aside from a savings on cost-of-living adjustments, the entitlement funding crisis will turn out to be more pressing than is indicated in this chapter. Between 1947 and 1972 our economy grew at an average annual real rate of 3.6 percent. From 1973 to 1995 the rate was 2.5 percent on average per year.

[3] The numbers are provided by the Department of Health, Education and Welfare.

[4] Even when food stamps at $37 billion; the food program for women, infants, and children, which is just over $3 billion; and school lunches, which cost $4.5 billion are included, Welfare-related programs are well under $100 billion.

[5] Robert J. Samuelson, "Perceiving Our Future," *Washington Post National Weekly Edition,* 25-31 December 1995, 5.

[6] Herbert Stein, *An Illustrated Guide to the American Economy* (Washington, DC: The AEI Press, 1992), 224.

[7] Thomas Sowell, "A Legal Con Game," *Forbes,* 27 March 1995, 60.

[8] Martin Feldstein, *The Missing Piece in Policy Analysis: Social Security Reform,* National Bureau of Economic Research working paper no. 5413.

[9] David R. Henderson, "The Sneak Attack on Seniors," *Fortune,* 4 March 1996, 60.

PART IV

New Century Idealism

What is a civil society? I think it is a society with a large measure of self-government, where citizens assume their role in public affairs. Citizens must shoulder their share of responsibility for social development. Civil society is a social space that fosters the feeling of solidarity between people and love for one's community. There are various minority needs that representative democracy cannot, in its present form, safeguard. Civil society encourages ordinary people to participate in government, thereby strengthening relations between citizens and their state.

Václav Havel
May 25, 1994

CHAPTER 10

In Praise of Ideals

Ideals are like stars; you will not succeed in touching them with your hands. But like the seafaring man on the desert of waters, you choose them as your guides, and following them you will reach your destiny.

Carl Schurtz
Address
Fanueil Hall, Boston
April 18, 1859

Throughout its history the United States has been the heartland of idealism. This idealism has been expressed in word, in deed and in thought. It has rippled out from our shores like stone-fed waves on the surface of a pond. Idealism has been considered one of our most endearing and admirable traits. However, its application in our nation has become ever more selective. We invoke its name when justifying military incursions into places like Vietnam, Somalia, and Bosnia. We trumpet our attachment to "family values." Yet the numbers of our disadvantaged continue to multiply, along with divorces, babies born out of wedlock, and abuse rained by family members on each other. Our commitment to involvement with democracy is disintegrating in a paroxysm of egocentricity and neglect, as are our founding ideals.

In this era of pragmatism and *real politik,* idealism has almost become a nasty word, a quality to be derided and reviled. How did this happen? What does it mean? Can Americans and their ideals ever regain their once comfortable relationship?

We are caught up in a maelstrom of profit in the name of progress and in the determination of winners. To be recognized as number one is more important than to determine right or truth. This message blares forth from our media, resonating over shattered families, crumbling ethics, and miasmic cities. We are becoming a nation of enclaves; protecting what is left of past achievements, clinging to the remainders of tattered expectations. We are constantly seeking to stretch above the rubble of shattered lives, to be recognized for finishing first in some measurable way. This is a far cry from idealism.

We trumpet rights in flashing neon while obligations rusticate in dust filled corners. Self has overawed community in many thousands of incarnations. Faith is regarded with technological skepticism as an impediment rather than a conduit. In the moments of our greatest success we simultaneously find ourselves bereft of ideals and despairing of the future. We are shamed by the dissenters from communism in Czechoslovakia or the Tiananmen students in China who clung to ideals at the risk of their lives.

All this has come over the land that has boasted the Declaration of Independence and the Bill of Rights. It has descended over the champion of the downtrodden and the absorber of massive migrations. The storm clouds of unrest almost obscure the beacon of liberty that has guided millions in far flung lands, warming both poets and economists with its rays. As citizens of the United States of America we cannot afford to let this happen. We cannot stand idly by as our bulwark of ideals vaporizes and drifts away into the mists of philosophical mediocrity. We cannot allow class conflict to ripen while the standards that have led this nation are employed for individual convenience rather than community service. We cannot permit the myopia of greed to obliterate the perspective of justice, eclipsing our national interest in the process.

It is not too late. Remedial action is possible. In an earlier book I argued that the four pillars of family, community, tradition, and faith were the necessary foundation for a vibrant civilization.[1] While they have become badly eroded in our society, they are not irreparably damaged. Ideals can shore them up for the twenty-first century if we begin today.

As we seek to rediscover our ideals we should perhaps remember some of Montesquieu's principles, which infused the thoughts of our founders. "Montesquieu identified liberty with a life lived under the rule of law. A man is free only when he limits his doing as he wishes to activities not forbidden by law...Doing as one wishes in a society is self-destructive or self-contradictory: men in a position to do as they wish in a society are not free because they are threatened with force, violence, and death."[2] This was the sense of community that persisted in Philadelphia in that magic year of 1787.

In addition to *liberty* we have always stressed *happiness* as an ideal. Our founders, all of whom were familiar with the works of

Montesquieu, meant something far different by *pursuit of happiness* than do the self-indulgent, sybaritic individualists of today. "For Montesquieu...civil society exists not for the sake of creating happiness but for the sake of protecting the means to happiness, or the means to each individual's avoidance of unhappiness."[3] Avoiding misery is quite different from the self-gratifying materialism that currently pervades many strata of our society. The scramble for material gains has left large swaths of our people to endure the tribulations of poverty. In addition, many of those who have attained those coveted material rewards have been unable to avoid the stresses of unrequited personal lives. Clearly, something is missing.

One missing element underlines Montesquieu's view of what constituted liberty, and reinforced his respect for laws and community. "What is liberty? According to Montesquieu it is not independence, which is just doing what one pleases, but rather the condition that causes people to feel that their person and their property are secure...Montesquieu never mentioned rights, natural or artificial, but only a deep assurance of personal security."[4] Very few of us have that assurance. Although we presume to tell the world about the virtues of our democratic vision and our capitalism, we radiate insecurity in a myriad of ways in our daily lives. Few of us feel physically secure. We build prisons, carry guns, and employ private guard services. Financially, we worry about the security of our pensions and benefits, of our institutions, and of our jobs. Progressively less of us respect the law as we watch it flaunted by our leaders and by our corporations. We feel individually exposed as our families and our communities disintegrate around us. We retreat behind walls of isolation and protection fearing the importation of drugs, products, and people. We are wary of being drawn into foreign entanglements with murky parameters. This is a far cry from the confidence of our past. I believe the weakening of our idealism constitutes a significant portion of the different ambiance we are experiencing.

Obviously, recapturing ideals is far easier said than done. Nevertheless, it can be done, and it has been done. Perspective is a key ingredient. We can't make good decisions for the benefit of our nation and our communities if we persist in only looking as far as the next election, or the boundaries of our immediate circle. A longer view and wider scope are called for. While self-interest isn't inherently a bad thing, it can lead to unfortunate developments if too narrowly, or too short-sightedly, defined. I have already used the example of senior citizens not always grasping the fact that their future benefits depend upon the ability, as well as the willingness, of young workers to provide them. If these young workers lack education and access to jobs how will they bear an increasingly large burden of retiree benefits? This attitude on the part of some seniors reflects a lack of perspective. It demonstrates lack of perspective not to seek a balance between development and the environment, not to pursue an inclusive society, or not to eradicate gender bias. Exercising the muscles of perspective can lead us a long way towards the re-establishment of our ideals.

We can benefit further by looking beyond our immediate environs to some sort of larger community—be it a neighborhood, a village, or a nation. Over the course of our history hundreds of thousands of Americans have given their lives for the sake of broader communities and the ideals that supported them. Failure to acknowledge this sacrifice by refusing to practice inclusion and acceptance amounts to a betrayal. Our social contract has been successfully built around the central core of community, liberally laced with tolerance. Our founders and the philosophers they revered envisioned it thus. A sense of community and the unity it provides are a part of our superstructure of ideals and are vital to our existence as a nation. There are many avenues we can follow to relocate it. These paths should be taken without delay.

Another of our founding ideals is equality of opportunity. Right from the beginning this was a keystone of our national credo. Associate Supreme Court Justice John Marshal Harlan eloquently stated the principle of equality of opportunity in his dissent from the verdict in *Plessy versus Ferguson* in 1896. "The white race deems itself to be the dominant race in this country. And so it is, in prestige, in achievements, in education, in wealth and in power...But in view of the Constitution, in the eye of the law, there is in this country no superior, dominant ruling class of citizens. In respect of civil rights, all citizens are equal before the law, the humblest is the peer of the most powerful." We have always felt that opportunity bred optimism, just as inclusion reinforced strength. No matter what deplorable conditions our citizens had to endure they were confident that their children or their grandchildren would have better lives. That led to the enthusiasm and the positive energy that settled frontiers, developed industry, and spread education. It is tragically destructive when people feel that there is little reason to hope and that their heirs will be worse off than they. That is the unfortunate situation for much of our citizenry at the moment. It promotes the antithesis of idealism, cynicism and despair.

Our collective quality of life is bound up with the ideals of liberty and happiness, in their original connotations. If we assume liberty to mean the operation of a social contract under rule of law, it provides a framework for each individual to relate harmoniously with others. If we understand happiness to mean freedom from misery, this harmony can extend to cover most of society. If individual license extends only so far as it doesn't infringe upon the general quality of life, problems of the environment, of poverty, and of crime can be looked upon in this context. So can areas such as violence in the media. Values and ideals are not put in place to restrict, or even to exalt, as much as they are to ensure that the gears of social interaction mesh smoothly. We should remember this philosophical fact before dismissing idealism as impractical and morality as binding.

I am deeply convinced that ideals are neither corny nor inhibiting, but absolutely necessary to a truly free society. I further believe that by removing the film that now partially obscures many of our original ideals we can strengthen our national fabric and improve our outlook on the future.

Transposed antifederalism has its ideals taken from the legacy of its philosophy. Foremost is the ideal of citizen-governors, inherited directly from the Roman republic. As our nation was being founded it was assumed by most parties, but antifederalists in particular, that each individual voting citizen (defined by the standards of voting at the time) would periodically and temporarily participate in the process of government. There are many ways to accomplish this. Most of them exist at the local level. People can run for public office. They can serve on boards or committees. They can go to meetings and discussion groups. They can help campaign actively for issues and candidates. They can be included on juries. They can vote. The bottom line is that either our citizens can feel involved and that their involvement can make a difference in the way their lives are governed, or democracy as we have known it is in danger. With only 38 percent of registered voters participating in the last major election, and special interests running rampant over our legislation, it would appear that this danger is upon us.

Whether expressed through family, extended family, or community, the antifederalist ideal has been self-sufficiency. That doesn't necessarily mean raising vegetables in the back yard. It does mean not automatically turning to central government for everything. Many aspects of the issues that are at the heart of today's controversies, such as the environment, health care, and crime, can be handled without first putting out a call for federal assistance. We have abdicated too much to our representatives while we spend our time on more pleasant, or more profitable pursuits than monitoring government. We should be ready to try some local remedies before crying out for federal aid, and we should start by holding our local officials directly and daily accountable for their actions. We have gotten out of the habit of doing this. We have permitted too many of our decisions to be rendered beyond our personal attention at great distance. We have become too accustomed to griping after the fact. The machinery of self-sufficiency has been allowed to rust. It can be unlimbered by acknowledging responsibility.

There are many positions in government, or quasi-government, that can be filled by antifederalist type citizen-governors. A slew of boards exist to assist various government functions. There are also many offices, both elected and appointed, which do not have to be filled by career politicians and bureaucrats. Our private institutions and corporations can make it easier for people to move back and forth between them and government without damaging their job prospects. We no longer have the military draft. President Clinton's Americorps has remained small and experimental. Programs like the Peace Corps and Vista are not what they were. Service to the nation or to the community, which used to be widespread, is now minimal. Most citizens spend entire lives in which their only brush with service to their nation, state, or locality is an occasional stint of jury duty. That is not the way this country was constructed, not what our founders envisioned. The ideal of service needs to be restored for democracy to flourish.

If ideals can be refurbished, attitudes can change. Optimism, enthusiasm, energy, and positivity are all attitudinal. All of them, as well as many more qualities, can change with mental states. Anyone who observed South Africa before and after the election of Nelson Mandela has witnessed the miracle of attitude change. Problems may not vanish in the face of such change, but considerable progress can be made. We have experienced this phenomenon often throughout our history. Two examples are the initial administrations of Andrew Jackson and Franklin Roosevelt.

We can change our national attitude in the coming century as well. This new century will contain many formidable challenges. An optimistic attitude would be a powerful asset in meeting them. Idealism can foster this attitude, as its key ingredient, especially if it includes a growing conviction that individuals can make a difference. Antifederalist ideals can be instrumental in pursuit of this ideal of individual significance.

I sincerely hope that by showing a willingness to participate, and to accept obligation, we can make our democracy flourish. In so doing maybe we can live up to the words of perhaps the greatest speech ever given, Abraham Lincoln's Gettysburg Address. "That this nation, under God, shall have a new birth of freedom, and that the government of the people, by the people, and for the people shall not perish from the earth." I firmly believe that with the re-establishment of its ideals the United States can once more become what our Pledge of Allegiance promises: "One nation indivisible, with liberty and justice for all."[5] If this chapter sounds like an impassioned plea; that is exactly what it is.

---

[1] Charles Stewart Goodwin, *The Third World Century* (Lanham, MD: University Press of America, 1994)

[2] Thomas L. Pangle, *Montesquieu's Philosophy of Liberalism* (Chicago: University of Chicago Press, 1973), 109-110.

[3] Ibid., 189.

[4] Judith Shklar, *Montesquieu* (Oxford: Oxford University Press, 1987), 86.

[5] The Gettysburg Address was delivered on November 19, 1863. The Pledge of Allegiance was created by Francis J. Bellamy, editor of *Youth's Companion* magazine, to be first given at the dedication of Chicago's Columbia Exposition on October 12, 1892.

CHAPTER 11

Volunteers on Tap

Shore found out great truths, which are lamentably not yet in general circulation. One is that government programs, no matter how lavishly funded, are not enough. The other is that private charity cannot take up the slack. The missing ingredient? Citizen involvement. Only volunteers willing to feed, tutor, visit, encourage, and instruct can pull the country out of the mire, he thinks...

Volunteerism as an indisputable element in putting the country back together is not yet chic.

> Mary McGrory, writing about author and
> social activist, Bill Shore, in her syndicated
> column of 22 November 1995.

We have long been known as a nation that understands the virtues of mutual assistance. Alexis de Toqueville reporting on his journey of 1832 noted this fact. "When an American asks for the cooperation of his fellow citizens, it is seldom refused; and I have often seen it afforded spontaneously, and with great goodwill. If an accident happens on the highway, everybody hastens to help the sufferer; if some freak and sudden calamity befalls a family, the purses of a thousand strangers are at once willingly opened and small but numerous donations pour in to relieve their distress."[1] From the nation's beginning cooperative efforts requiring donations of time, ranging from barn raisings to volunteer fire departments, have been frequently recorded in the annals of our history.

A coalition of philanthropic organizations called the Independent Sector estimated that in the mid-1990s approximately 95 million

Americans, 48 percent of all adults over 18, volunteer for something during the course of a year. The largest group of volunteers comes from the 35 to 45-year-old age sector, 55 percent of whom donate their time. However, they do advise that the number of volunteers peaked in 1991 and has declined five to seven percent since then. The Independent Sector further estimates that there are approximately 100,000 associations of various types to which Americans belong. Peter Drucker estimated that one out of two adults works at least three hours per week as a volunteer in some social activity.[2] Karen Paget has made the assumption that the various extra-governmental organizations contain 15 million active members. The Salvation Army estimated that during the Christmas season of 1995 over six million Americans would rely on it for help in their celebrations. It further estimated that at least one million volunteers would assist the Army in its efforts. Whatever the precise number of volunteers actually is, and however many organizations these individuals actually belong to, we can see that the amount is substantial. The United States is a country where volunteerism is almost endemic. This can provide a solid base for future efforts to assist and supplement formal government.

One other truism is becoming painfully evident. Government can neither provide all of our social services nor ensure maintenance of an adequate quality of life. The financial resources are not available. The inclination is receding. This could turn out to be considerably short of the disaster some suppose if volunteers are available to fill a portion of the gaps. Robert L. Woodson, president of the National Center for Neighborhood Enterprise, has observed this in action. "If devolution is to make government more cost-effective and efficient, authority, resources and trust must be vested, ultimately in individual taxpayers and community organizations...Merely reducing or eliminating federal programs won't do the trick. Another essential component of a new populist strategy must be to create politics that support and promote grass-roots programs of mutual support."[3] Citizens, private organizations, the *parallel polis* if you will, can grow to operate in the areas left untended by federal and state pullbacks. One such program was developed on Cape Cod and encouraged by Barnstable County. The Cape Cod Cooperative Extension, supervised by local businesses, organized to collect antifreeze and keep it from poisoning the environment. In 1995, its first year of operation, the program collected and recycled 1,400 gallons. The same spirit pervades many of our social and environmental organizations but it will have to extend even further. The arithmetic informs us that in some form or combination the private sector will have to step up and assume a large share of the burden if our social and environmental services are to be maintained. If the private, or semi-private, sector responds this development could trigger a chain of positive responses. Such a development would be very consistent with democracy and republicanism.

Before methods for encouraging volunteer organizations can be determined, the role of charity needs to be studied. It is a powerful force in our economy. The *Chronicle of Philanthropy* estimates that in 1995 some $108 billion will be doled out through charitable contributions. That will amount to an average of about $265 per person residing in this country, and equal to about 1.3 percent of the nation's pre-tax personal income. That number is not as solid as it appears. According to the Independent Sector, slightly more than 30 percent of the combined income of charities comes from various government sources. Government funds are being cut. Furthermore, some tax proposals, specifically called flat tax and taxes on consumption, would eliminate deductions for charitable gifts. Lester M. Salamon, director of the Institute for Policy Studies at Johns Hopkins University, and Alan J. Abramson of the Aspen Institute, studied both the Congressional and White House proposals for balancing the budget in seven years. They concluded that charity groups would lose between $140 and $150 billion cumulatively from these proposals over the 1996-2002 period. Charitable giving is at risk. At the very least it will undergo a possible painful transition.

In addition, most private charities are not tightly managed with salaries and other administrative costs often eating up over 50 percent of the revenues. Too large an amount of charitable monies is spent on areas such as basic research, where an immediate impact can't be obtained. This is particularly true in the area of health care, which accounts for slightly over ten percent of all charitable funds collected from the public. Professor and author James T. Bennett has researched the situation.[4] He realizes that health charities, and indeed all charities, will have to concentrate on filling the role most suited to them. "Health charities must return to their charitable roots and do what no other group in society can do: organize volunteers to help needy disease victims."[5] Ultimately this shift can be very beneficial, but first adjustments will have to be made. Nonprofit hospitals, which depend upon government payment for 48 percent of their revenue from patient care, according to the American Hospital Association, would be among the hardest hit. Their need for volunteers to augment their services is already acute.

Assuming the army of volunteers can be energized, expanded and funded, partially by charity, in a way to support environmental and social services, there could be a positive chain reaction that would contain at least five basic elements. A look at these elements in turn will give us some clues as to the nature of potential remedies.

The first and most obvious beneficial reaction can be a broadening of those people involved in assisting their fellow citizens. With participation will naturally come greater interaction, understanding, and unity as people learn that they can rely upon each other.

A second link in the chain can be that individuals will develop more confidence in their ability to affect their own lives. They will be dealing directly with some of society's most intractable problems. While there will undoubtedly be frustration attached to this effort, there will also be a sense of doing something of satisfaction from progress achieved. Consequently, community spirit should be reinforced.

A third element can be the development of local leadership skills. Volunteer efforts will entice leadership from individuals and in locations where it had not previously existed. This will add credence and confidence to any attempts at self-government.

A fourth positive development can be the prioritization that should emerge. Our nation has been characterized over the post-World War II period by a tendency to expect everything. Resources have been so abundant that little prioritization has been necessary. Now that is no longer the case. Broad involvement of the public in environmental and social services will make them aware that priorities have to be set, and hone the skills of sifting and deciding.

The fifth chain link can be the gradual blending of *parallel polis* type volunteer organizations with the institutions of local government.[6] It can be in this manner that the republican ideal of antifederalist localism will become a reality as government learns how to nurture and tap this powerful source of energy.

The next step is for us to explore methods by which this antifederalist local ideal, manned largely by volunteers, could come about. There are already thousands of organizations largely composed of volunteers, dealing with our main social and environmental challenges. For example, in New York City alone the number of neighborhood civic associations has grown from 3,500 in 1977 to 8,000 in 1995, according to the Citizens Committee for New York City. They and other similar groups throughout the nation perform many functions. They supplement education. They combat drug use and crime. They alleviate the strictures of poverty. In dozens of ways they seek to preserve and improve the environment that surrounds us. Many of them have been successful in a variety of milieus, and can be emulated or duplicated.

Increased pressure on the time of many professional citizens, coupled with increased individual egocentrism, has caused a drop-off of willing volunteers in many traditional organizations, such as Parent-Teacher Associations. This drop-off was dramatically characterized in the ABC Evening News American Agenda segment of February 13, 1996, which focused on a PTA in Colorado. Potential volunteers seemed to be discouraged by the regularity of evening meetings and the inflexibility of scheduled activities. The news program also showed which volunteer networks are flourishing. It featured Hands On Atlanta, which was started in 1989 by 12 friends to provide social services. Now there are Hands On organizations in many cities. The Atlanta chapter has a $1 million budget, 17 paid staff members and a mailing list of 11,000 volunteers. These volunteers can call up at the last minute and find out which of the 187 projects, such as soup kitchens, park cleanups, and tutoring programs are going on that day so they can help.

This flexibility and convenience also characterizes New York CARES, which is a clearinghouse designed to connect volunteers with projects around the city. It started in 1986 with six people and now has a mailing list of 13,000 names. Its format has been replicated in 26 cities with a total membership of almost 100,000. Most of these volunteers are professionals between 25 and 45 in age. Michael Krasner, an associate professor of political science at Queens College in New Yo k, has studied why young people are volunteering for such organizations. "The decline of other institutions, the decline of political parties, the decline of Democrats in New York City, and the disinclination of people, particularly young people, to join political parties, are helped by the perception that civic associations are clean. They are not seen as dirty dealing or political."[7] This is the wave of the future for environmental and for social services—flexibility and adaptability, and attracting younger enthusiasts.

Grammercy Place Shelter in Los Angeles is another example of an innovative volunteer-supported organization. It provides a full range of counseling, job training, day care, room and board for homeless parents. The residents can learn, can work to earn "shelter money," and can have the majority of their welfare checks put into a savings account to provide a cushion for when they re-enter the work force. This type of effort becomes even more necessary when one realizes that throughout our nation women with children make up 62 percent of the homeless family units and children under the age of 18 comprise 11 percent of all homeless persons.

James C. Crimmins recently produced a miniseries for public television entitled "The American Promise," which depicted a variety of results that can be attained by citizen organizations working through volunteers in local settings. Each of Crimmins' examples portrayed an organization that was close to Robert Woodson's description of grass-roots virtues.

> Their power lies in several characteristics that these grass-roots organizations have in common: They are created by individuals who live in the same neighborhoods as, and have a heartfelt concern for, the people they serve. These leaders have a personal stake in the success of their programs and are available to their constituents long after the 9 to 5 workday comes to a close. Many have conquered the same problems that they are helping others to overcome. And nearly all of their programs incorporate elements of spiritual renewal and the re-establishment of values.[8]

Such organizations are flourishing all over the country in places where each of us can witness and participate in their activities.

Further evidence of this grassroots support is the International Union of Gospel Missions, which operates 250 missions that provide 27 million meals, nine million beds and 13 million pieces of clothing annually to homeless persons in the United States and Canada. The

Salvation Army operates 6,000 different types of shelters for over nine million people each year. There is no reason why these models can't be extended even further than they already are. They can be based on the examples like the ones cited above, which are volunteer driven.

The really difficult part is to figure out how to make the transition from a federal government, which is of necessity cutting back and a network of private charities, which is feeling financially pressured, to an adequate system of local assistance based upon volunteerism. No one would pretend that this will be easy. It seems reasonable to assume that by the time we enter the new century charitable funds can be sustained at a level above $100 billion after an initial adjustment in giving patterns is made (after all, tax-deductibility is only one of the many incentives for charitable giving) and that their impact can be improved through increased and judicious utilization of volunteers. Demonstration of results will help sustain contributions from those whose time or money is being sought.

An excerpt from the *Solutions Local* newsletter published in Mashpee, Massachusetts in December, 1995 gives a hint of how the process can begin. "Solutions Local forms a network of caring people who help each other whenever possible and it produces a spirit of cooperation and volunteerism in the communities it is part of." These caring people can create some combination of private efforts (both work and money), corporate contributions, charitable funding, and assistance from governments—either directly or indirectly via tax incentives. The key to success will be the ability to create effective prioritization of targets to be served, plus efficient mobilization of available personnel and financial resources with which to attack them. Mobilization will definitely include skill in fundraising and the operation of an organization flexible enough to encourage volunteers.

What can 95 million people accomplish if properly directed? What can $100 billion-plus of charitable funds purchase in terms of environmental and social services if the spending is focused? What impact could this $100 billion make if the percentage devoted to salaries, benefits, and administration could be reduced by ten, 25, or even 50 percent? What revenues could the taxation system produce if it were rearranged to empower localities? What number of jobs could be created for those people not fully employed such as our growing number of elderly citizens? Maybe the answers to these questions will be negative and the organizational results will be disappointing. We'll never know unless we try. Our current programs aren't working too well. Our societal problems are not vanishing, they are growing. Our people have demonstrated their willingness, even eagerness, to volunteer. Let's see what happens if we expand the use of this resource.

There are two distinct pools of people that are dramatically underutilized. One is the unemployed, largely contained among the ranks of the poor (especially the young urban poor). The other is the elderly, often left with little to do after a productive life. Localism could deploy both in the campaign to supply social services.

Retired people make excellent volunteers. They have accumulated skills over a lifetime of service. But often they need extra income, especially if their expected benefits are at risk. Two Massachusetts towns—Chelmsford and Provincetown—have developed programs to provide tax abatements to senior citizens in exchange for community service. Under these programs senior citizens can work up to 100 hours per year in their communities for wages equal to $5.00 per hour. The $500 earned would then be applied against their property taxes. Seniors can perform numerous tasks consistent with their experience and physical condition. Obviously, these programs can be adjusted, or expanded, it they show promise.

Most of the proposals designed to get people off welfare are not designed to save the government money, but to get people working. Most welfare recipients live in neighborhoods that are run down, prone to crime, laced with drugs, and desperately needing social services. If those now on welfare or suffering unemployment can be redirected towards the rehabilitation of their communities, everyone will win.

There are approximately 33,000 case workers employed in the United States, largely in child protection matters. They are dramatically overworked. This situation highlights only one area where volunteers could supplement government services. Los Angeles County employs about 2,000 case workers, the largest single concentration in the country. Over the past decade over 40,000 children of the county have been removed from abusive families. The cost of this activity reached $7,672 million in 1995 (37 percent of which was provided by federal funds).

In the process of combating the tragedy of child abuse, Los Angeles County has developed a landmark family preservation program that started in 1993. By 1995 it served 10,000 children, utilizing 23 separate "networks," each providing up to 22 services. These networks are community-based and are extremely labor intensive. Obviously, most neighborhood residents who are potential volunteers (or hirees) are not qualified to stand in for social workers. But they can help deal with the massive administrative burden (logging files onto computers, updating, filling out forms). Similar networks, bolstered by volunteers, can be utilized throughout the United States. The same principle can be applied to other services.

Most inner cities have vast areas that appear as if a war just ended. The need for rehabilitation of physical facilities is extensive. Thousands could be employed in relatively low-skilled tasks if the rigidities of governments and unions can be overcome. Corporations and governments will eventually receive a beneficial impact if formerly unproductive individuals begin to acquire some skills as well as the ability to operate in a regular and organized fashion in job-related settings. This eventual impact will justify some investment, as the biggest problem in getting people off welfare seems to be training them in proper work habits. The required investment is not likely to be major. Corporate America can provide valuable moral and financial assistance in this training process. Corporations can also be a source of committed, skillful volunteers for a range of activities that will be beneficial to the community. This can bring communities and corporations closer together. As was noted in a previous paragraph, corporations will be more able to support their professional employees' volunteer activities if the organizations they serve are flexible enough to accommodate busy schedules.

Volunteers can contribute to the betterment of their immediate neighborhoods, and of their own quality of life. This will serve to bring them more into the mainstream of the governing process. As citizens start to feel that they can make some headway against their most pressing problems and be productive to society, their attitudes will change. They will grow more optimistic. The power of a changed national attitude, especially among the disadvantaged, should not be underestimated. As it percolates upward from the grassroots, the momentum from a growing number of positive individuals can build both esprit and unity. Cohesion and cooperation can replace division and advocacy. If 100 million Americans can see themselves really making a difference through volunteering, the United States can be revitalized. Moreover, people can feel good about their own contributions.

As people cooperate, work together, and learn to prioritize, they will be acting in the national interest. If we all begin to think of what we can do rather than what we can get, positivity and cynicism can be transformed into energy. At first glance it may seem naive to suppose that platoons of citizens, many acting on a part-time basis, can replace or supplement professional bureaucrats in the provision of services. It may even seem merely another way of cutting government. It is in fact the opposite—the preservation of democracy through popular involvement. In this way government can actually be made more relevant and more immediate. The delivery of services that might otherwise be curtailed by attempts at economy might restore that sense of republican virtue so prized by our founders. Civilizations can be revived from the torpor of diffusion with focus like this. Both the disadvantaged and the sybaritic can develop pride, and with it create hope in areas where it couldn't flourish before.

It's not as if this electric revival wasn't happening anywhere. It is, in many places, some unlikely. It is not as if we are bereft of resources. We are just employing them inefficiently. It is not as if we don't have citizens who serve at the local level. We have millions of them. They are in a position to blend the *parallel polis* and local government to produce a more energized and optimistic future in the coming century. Volunteers can be a catalyst for the resurrection of our historical governmental values. I have seen it happen.

1 Alexis de Toqueville, *Democracy in America* 2 (New York: Vintage Books, 1958), 185.

2 Peter Drucker, "The Age of Social Transformation," *Atlantic Monthly*, November 1994, 75.

3 Karen Paget, "Citizens Organizing: Many Movements, No Majority," *The American Prospect,* Summer 1990, 47.

4 James T. Bennett, "Unhealthy Charities: and Hazardous to Your Health and Wealth," *Insight*, 24 June 1993.

5 James T. Bennett, "Charities Ignore the Needy in Reversal of Robin Hood," *Insight*, 16 October 1995, 26.

6 *Parallel polis* is a term first used by Czech philosopher and mathematician, Vacláv Benda, in his essay "The Parallel Polis" which Vacláv Havel credits when he included this term in *The Power of the Powerless: Citizens Against the States in Eastern Europe*, edited by John Keane, London, Hutchinson 1985, p. 20. It refers to those organizations essentially performing the functions of government but operating outside it.

7 Pam Belleck, "In Era of Shrinking Budgets, Community Groups Blossom," *New York Times*, 25 February 1996, 34.

8 Produced by KQED, San Francisco and initially aired on public television on the 1st, 2nd and 3rd of October, 1995.

CHAPTER 12

Positive Policies

The right motive for toleration is the recognition that all religions are quests in search of a common spiritual goal and that, even though some of these quests may be more advanced and more on the right lines than others, the persecution of the 'wrong' religion by a *soi-disant* 'right' religion is of its very nature a contradiction in terms, since by indulging in persecution the 'right' religion puts itself in the wrong and denies its own credentials.

Arnold Toynbee
A Study of History

The key to the American Progressive tradition, where it works best, has been the view that government's highest purpose is to strengthen the capacities of individuals to achieve self-reliance and to nurture the country's rich network of civic institutions that are independent of both the state and the marketplace. Some of the greatest achievements of the Progressive tradition—the GI Bill, civil rights laws, student loans, minimum wage laws—were aimed not at making government powerful, but at making it easier for individuals to seize opportunities and to strengthen their own community.

E. J. Dionne, Jr.
*They Only Look Dead: Why Progressives
Will Dominate the Next Political Era*

The Nature of Positive Policies

It is legitimate for the reader to ask: "What are positive policies in the context of our daily government?" The answer is that they are the opposite of polarization, extremism, and individualism; which are all expressed at the expense of the community. An example of positive policies was demonstrated by Harvard Law School professor Mary Ann Glendon in her capacity as Chief Vatican Delegate to the Fourth United Nations World Conference on Women. Her public comment on the conference's position paper was a positive policy incarnate, as one excerpt illustrates. "We found many things to affirm in the document. The Holy See is proud to associate itself with these parts of the document."[1] There was no dwelling on differences, no underlining of antagonism. Positive policies are about finding common ground. They are about expressing opinions, but seeking broad areas of agreement. They are about respect and understanding overcoming opposition.

I first heard the term used by a friend, Todd Souza, who is from a nearby town. He runs an organization called *Solutions Local* and publishes a newsletter of the same name. Several quotations from this newsletter indicate his views. "There is so much negativism in the media, especially on TV and the larger newspapers, so I thought people might like to hear more about positive things...We will share information and highlight the positive events and contributions made in local communities...When we have a positive attitude we open a door to unlimited possibilities. Our everyday actions seem to have a purpose." Statements about positive attitudes can sound simple, but they are fundamental to achievement and to the realization of potentials. All of us function better when buttressed or encouraged by positive words.

The Need for Positive Policies

Think for a moment how each of us reacts to positive reinforcement as opposed to negative criticism. Think what it does to our outlook to see a constant stream of crime, violence, and corruption in our news media. Think of our initial response when someone attacks a position we believe in and feel strongly about. A significant part of our suggested philosophy for the coming century is the achievement of a national attitude change. This can be facilitated by accentuating the positive, by seeking agreement, by building unity.

Too often in our country today we tend to follow litmus-test politics. We hold up a single issue, such as abortion or entitlements, and base our support, our interaction, our representation on this one issue. No matter how individually valid or worthy any person's position on a particular issue might be, litmus-test politics breeds confrontation, separation and antagonism, as well as intellectual attenuation. We ought to be able to get beyond that. We should be able to develop a talent for inclusion and for compromise to help our country to flourish.

The present national mood is summed up in the November 29, 1995 version of the popular comic strip *Calvin and Hobbes* by Bill Watterson. Both Calvin and his stuffed tiger/friend Hobbes are reading the newspaper. Calvin says: "These are interesting times. We don't trust the government, we don't trust the legal system, we don't trust the media, and we don't trust the each other! We've undermined all authority, and with it, the basis for replacing it! It's like a six-year old's dream come true!" Hobbes dejectedly replies: "Interesting is a mild way of putting it." That is the situation in a nutshell. If we as a nation are to rise above the level of six-year-old's fantasy, we will have to learn about the practice of positive policies.

Starting on January 1, 1996 one baby-boomer (someone born between 1946 and 1964) turned 50 every seven seconds. Christopher Hitchens, writing in *Vanity Fair*, chronicles this generation's need for positive policies as he quotes Ralph Whitehead, a demographer from the University of Massachusetts. "If there's one thing that has come through in all the interviews and focus groups I've done with boomers, it's that these people have big egos but weak identities...the typical baby-boomer is like a balloon stretched very tight. The air is the big ego and the thin, tightly stretched rubber is the identity. One pinprick and you're gone."[2] This generation, which will be increasingly responsible for our society needs a positive climate to be effective, even more than the generations preceding and following it. It also needs something else, mentioned as well by Hitchins. "In the therapy generation, which scripts even its own lenient satires, you are by all means allowed, if not encouraged, to feel guilty. Just as long as you don't feel *responsible*."[3] Taking responsibility is a positive policy that has eroded in our current society of blame.

Opportunities for positive policies arise daily in meetings, hearings, conversations, and a plethora of other interactions. Whether it be commenting on the news, participating in a PTA meeting or operating on the Internet, all of us can and should practice finding positive ways of getting along with each other. The alternative, a deepening of divisions and antagonisms, is too horrible to contemplate. The institution of positivity requires only an attitudinal change; no legislation, no court cases, nor complex financing are necessary. While altering the national mind set is by no means a simple matter, it is something that is within the reach and capabilities of us all.

Characteristics of Positive Policies

The characteristics of positive policies are relatively straightforward and they dovetail neatly with transposed antifederalism. Perhaps the foremost characteristic involves a willingness to engage in dialogue with the object of discovering common ground. That means interacting in a search for things that bind, rather than divide. One of the thorniest issues in my home region of Cape Cod is the struggle between protection of the environment and its use for commerce or recreation. In November of 1995 a landmark conference was held. The National Park Service, custodians of the Cape Cod National Seashore, invited two-dozen individuals, with often competing ideas about off-road vehicle usage, to have a dialogue with the intention of arriving at a consensus on regulation. Over the past few years the National Park Service's enforcement of the Endangered Species Act to protect the nesting areas of the piping plover was one of the issues that aroused the ire of many campers and sport fisherman in particular. This conference managed to attain unanimous consensus on a new set of regulations by means of a new process called "negotiated rule-making." The negotiations took almost three months and began with all parties being pessimistic. Gradually, a settlement was reached by seeking a solution that could provide some benefit to all parties. This initial demonstration of negotiated rule-making captured common ground by always keeping the need for solution in view. It demonstrates how positive policies can impact our policy making.

Another example of people with diametrically opposed beliefs coming together occurred in the Bettendorf-Davenport, Iowa area. A group called Common Ground was formed to discuss the various aspects of the abortion issue. It is still very much a work in progress. Solutions have not yet been formed. What has been found, though, is mutual respect and the ability to engage in rational dialogue.

Nobody can expect perfection or total altruism in our society. However, we can expect a social conscience, in the Havelian sense, or the republican virtue advocated by our founders. In fact, if we don't develop these qualities our nation could disintegrate under the pressures of inevitable change. Unity and optimism may be recaptured through belief in something greater than self, our community and our national collection of communities. The onrush of demographics is assured. Our finances may take decades to restructure. Our attitude towards fellow citizens and about our prospects can be changed in a heartbeat. Sometimes it takes a cataclysmic event such as a war or disaster to unite a nation. It would be a shame to await something of such terrible magnitude if the same ends can be accomplished through adopting positive policies. In every political campaign, and every opinion-sampling poll, our citizens are signaling their disgust with the polarization of negativity and their longing for increasing doses of positivism. The time has arrived to put those expressed desires into practice. We have many complex tasks before us that could take years to accomplish creating and spreading positivity is easy by comparison, cerebral rather than material.

Implementation of Positive Policies

Negative and egocentric attitudes have wrought one particular condition that urgently needs to change. This condition was discussed in Chapter 5. It is the very real possibility that we could develop more than one social contract. Our national polarization on key socio-economic issues, our practice of exclusion, and our inability to conduct meaningful dialogue, have conspired to place our carefully crafted social contract at risk. We are constructing two very different systems of values and opportunities, a situation of danger for any nation. It is especially dangerous in a country that has prided itself on, has boasted in fact, of its egalitarian qualities. It is particularly dangerous with a leadership cadre, even if it were trusted and respected, that speaks to and for a relatively narrow band of the population. It is dangerous for a nation whose existence has teetered on the brink of disaster whenever significant holes have appeared in the fabric of its unity, exposing the inherent flimsiness. I believe that these dangers can be ameliorated, and possibly avoided, by immediately implemented policies of positivity.

Positive policies operate best at the local level. There they fall directly within the purview and spirit of antifederalist philosophy. There they can operate among people who know each other. There they can function smoothly with those organizations that Vacláv Havel termed the *parallel polis*, and that are critical to the operation of any democracy. One such organization is a San Francisco homeless shelter called Raphael House. It was described by syndicated columnist Debra J. Saunders on November 24, 1995. She noted that Raphael House was started by the Rev. David Lowell in 1977 to help those who satisfy two criteria: immediate need and the desire to work within a highly structured environment. Those families that wish to heal "find an important opportunity to rebuild their lives in the midst of a support network that they previously may have lacked." They receive education, regular meals and job training, all amidst togetherness. This is one manifestation of a positive approach to family values. It provides an ambiance for reclamation not condemnation.

Another positive member of the *parallel polis* is the Adult Re-Entry Program at Cape Cod Community College, especially its Women in Transition Program. This program is run by single mother Dorothy Burrill, and approximately 40 percent of its clients are single mothers on welfare. Its program provides counseling, extensive personal support (especially in the first semester) and post-graduation advice. It creates a sense of community that encourages those who are often destitute and desperate. The positive reinforcement moves women off the welfare rolls, but more importantly gives them hope for the future. This is the type of attitude that is replicated numerous times by numerous organizations throughout our country and should be expanded geometrically.

Yet another example from close to home is the New Hope Parent Aide Program in Sandwich, Massachusetts. It strives to help some of the 97,000 children reported to the state as being abused last year (versus 84,000 births). The organization is mostly staffed by volunteers who donate four to six hours per week. Its motto is: Helping Parents Helps Children. The task required is intensive interaction with families, especially single-parent families. Children, parents, volunteers, and the community all benefit from the organization's positive efforts.

In 1990 volunteers from seven churches in Harwich, Massachusetts got together to form the Harwich Ecumenical Council. Its aim was to reduce the problem of homelessness by raising private funds to provide transitional housing rather than motels and shelters. The group has developed a network of houses to rent, established an affordable child care center, and set up a mortgage foreclosure program to help families in danger of losing their homes. Over the years the council has prevented 500 families from becoming homeless and hopes to purchase ten duplex houses. The Harwich Ecumenical Council is implementing positive policies every day.

The Midwest Community Council coordinates 500 block associations of Chicago's West Side. As such it functions as a confederation of little republics and as an excellent example of local government structure. Each of these associations is part of a larger grouping containing ten entities. There are 50 of these in the entire council. Studs Terkel interviewed the then council president, Nancy Jefferson, about the workings of the grouping of ten. "We take in ten blocks. We visualize that as a little town. Each has a president. We have somebody who is over all. He is sort of the Mayor of those ten blocks. Everybody begins to get involved in everything: garbage disposal; traffic lights."[4] This is positive policies in action. This is individuals making a difference.

Former Secretary of Health, Education and Welfare, founder of Common Cause, and director of the Urban Institute, John W. Gardner, has consistently been working to create positive policies. His latest effort began in 1992 with the founding of the Alliance for National Renewal. This alliance brings together 60 community building organizations. Through the power of combination the alliance is building on the efforts already made by many community based social programs. In March of 1995 *The Dallas Morning News* characterized its work in a series of articles on local self-help. "Across the country a growing number of Americans have stopped complaining about government. Together they are working to find new solutions to some of the country's most pressing problems. They are beginning a national movement—about community, about citizenship, and about the role we all have in shaping our national destiny."

This is what we can hope for from positive policies. They can give people a sense of making a difference in their own lives. They can feel more in control and consequently more optimistic. Such feelings are in all of our interest. They can thus help preserve our environment, help ensure our financial benefits and generally improve the quality of our lives. If they achieve those ends they can be important ingredients for a national attitude change. I believe that all we require for such a change to take place is a feeling that we all are in the same boat and that we can so something about it. In fact, all we need is to expand upon the efforts of those who are already doing something.

The Dialogue of Positive Policies

There are no precise records of the Constitutional Convention of 1787. The best legacy is the notes taken by James Madison during the proceedings, which were for the most part secret.[5] Although there were several distinct political and philosophical factions represented among the 55 delegates, their dialogue radiates a remarkable perspective, a sense of community, and a willingness to compromise.[6] In the privacy of the convention floor they frequently adopted or accepted positions contrary to those they had advocated publicly. Virtually all the time they respected the society as a whole (as they understood it) and considered the future in every decision. The 71 percent consensus among all appointed delegates which was achieved was an outstanding monument to the positive dialogue. It is one to be emulated. John Adams wrote Hezikiah Niles on February 12, 1818 stating his opinion about our coming together as a nation at the Convention, and in the 12 months thereafter. "To unite them [the 13 states] in the same principles in theory and the same system of action was certainly a very difficult enterprise. The complete accomplishment of it, in so short a time and by such simple means, was perhaps a singular example in the history of Mankind. Thirteen clocks were made to strike together. A perfection of mechanism which no artist had ever before affected."[7] This mechanism was the result of a dedication to positive politics.

I have found in my own political or civic discussions that the common ground, if discovered, usually exceeds the space occupied by extremist rhetoric. It is the task of our leaders to discover and promote it. Unfortunately, leadership is heading the other way. Moderates are withdrawing almost daily, leaving the field to polarized factions that represent vocal, albeit committed, minorities. The broad swath of moderation is not only shrinking it is all too seldom heard from. If we can tap it, consult it, draw it out, compromise may yet overcome rigor. If we can develop ways of talking positively with each other, instead of ranting at each other, we will have a better chance of dealing with our problems and creating unity in a functional society.

Other countries have the same difficulty. A tragic manifestation of this was the assassination of Israel's Prime Minister Yitzak Rabin. Rav Marjav Yubuda Amital addressed some Yeshiva students just prior to boarding a bus where they would all attend Rabin's funeral on

November 6, 1995. "We can continue, even while disagreeing, to find the will and the strength to build the State of Israel. Despite our differences of opinion, we still have much to unite us...If someone does not share our religious commitment, it does not mean he has no values, and it does not mean that he has no just claim to our love." That is a plea for positive dialogue emerging from a situation, momentarily at least, even more explosive than our own.

There is a small groundswell in the direction of positive politics. It is beginning to build in this country and in some of those organizations I have collectively called the *parallel polis*. People are tiring of uncompromising advocacy, especially when it gets in the way of implementing remedies. They are frustrated by the venality and unresponsiveness of many elected officials. They deplore the huge interstices in government social programs where compassion is absent. Citizens are slowly beginning to take civic action back into their own hands, where they perceive a void of caring.

When contemplating a future for positive policies I have two avid hopes. The first is that the positive process spreads, overcoming divisions, disagreement, and inhumanity. The second hope is that a positive feeling begins to seep into the structure of government. Perhaps some *parallel polis* organizations will themselves become a greater part of government bringing with them attitudes of positivism. What can happen and can spread is an initiation of dialogue, with consensus, and not advocacy, as its end.

Small republics, small enough to possess an homogeneity of interest, can assume responsibility if they are empowered. Their deliberations can look to enable, not prevent. They can foster idealism not ideology. This is what happened in the Midwest Community Council. My hope is that these kernels of positivism can sprout from the nurturing soil of localism and flourish in the salubrious climate of republican participatory democracy.

These are my hopes. I am convinced that they aren't completely unrealistic because some encouraging development is taking place. It will be our collective challenge to support those organizations moving in a positive direction, to set an agenda leading to consensus, and to seek unity through inclusion, not by proscription. We have done all of these things as a nation in the past. It is not beyond our capabilities to produce a positive environment for the future. Indeed, our very existence may depend upon it.

Positive Policies in Operation

Assuming that we have empowered small republics, how can we instill positive policies within them? There is no easy or pat answer. The first step is to find or create an organization that can be ecumenical enough to cover the entire community over a broad range of issues. In

Sandwich, Massachusetts, for example, there is the Sandwich Youth Task Force. In other areas it can be a civic association. It might also be an organ of government. It is important for this organization, which can be called a citizens' council or something similar, to convey its purpose, to adopt a positive, inclusive format right from the start. It should agree to eliminate negatives and conflict from discussions and seek consensus whenever possible. In its formation it can set the proper tone by including all segments of the community regardless of positions previously taken. The intent of this council in all of its functions is to bring people together, to have them relate as human beings, to put aside divisiveness and to search for common ground.

To that end a variety of activities can be sponsored, just to bring people together where they can interact. Regular coffeehouse meetings can be one. Another could be a talent or drama show. A third could be a neighborhood block party. Still another could be some sort of benefit. Support of an athletic team or event could be a fifth. The intent is merely to involve people of various factions, opinions, or economic status in a joint effort through which they can relate. After interaction and shared experience can come productive change built upon commonality.

When discussions do occur great care should be taken to make certain that they remain positive, that divisive issues aren't allowed to intrude. What can then happen is that people learn to view others merely as people, not as representatives of some interest. Problems that once seemed mountainous can start to shrink. When individuals or groups don't feel that are going to have something imposed upon them or decided without them, they start to relax and can consider joint solutions. It often turns out that the perceived common ground is wider than was initially supposed, that the divisions are less severe and that the problems are less intractable. The whole technique, from inclusive council to shared activities to joint decisions, is designed to create an atmosphere where teamwork can flourish and people can regard others as individuals with fears or uncertainties similar to their own. In such an atmosphere meaningful action can occur, reason can prevail. It does work. I have witnessed it.

Ironically, the fact that our technological society has abetted individuality can prove to be a benefit if it doesn't lead to isolation and exclusion. People accustomed to looking at computer screens or catering to their own needs may be more inclined to view others as individual entities, not as part of a group. Obviously, individuality can be carried to an extreme but it also can be useful. Blending individualistic and interactive talents can further group dynamics. Communities can grow again, and they can be based upon principles of equality. To the extent that this condition spreads, we can escape the possibility of rule by an oligarchic overclass.

A final and key element of the positive political process is communication. It can and should assume many forms including the media and the Internet. One very successful organ of communication is a newsletter, like the one published by Todd Souza's Solutions Local. This newsletter, like his discussions, will only carry positive articles. They can be written by a variety of people representing all facets of the community. At first it may be regarded with some skepticism. People may not know what to make of it. Gradually they will be drawn in by the positive tone, by the ability to exercise their own talents, by the revelation of the many things that are going on, and by their desire to interact. Businesses will sponsor columns. Organizations will look to it as a way to outline their activities. Individuals will have a way of monitoring the community pulse without having to engage in or be subjected to rampant advocacy. Loneliness will be overcome as will ideological isolation.

This in a nutshell is the practice of positive policies. It can demonstrate that deep down citizens don't want to bitterly oppose each other. It can show they don't want the stress of uncertainty and mistrust. It can create an ambiance for citizens to come together in the pursuit of common goals. The fans at a high school football game show that. So does the audience at a play. People enjoy being together and being positive if they are given the chance. It is our challenge to create a structure of government, and of society, which is designed to give our people that opportunity.

Antifederalism: A Reprise

I have suggested that antifederalism of the pre-constitutional, pre-Jeffersonian variety be transposed along the arc of the pendulum to the twenty-first century. This version of antifederalism contains no support for the principles of nullification and secession. It would involve citizens in government. It would seek to generate positive approaches to the issues affecting our daily lives. It would thrust upward from the grassroots, and multiply.

The philosophical basis for this brand of antifederalism primarily emanates from Montesquieu, especially from his theory of small republics. These small republics would be of a size to create a homogeneity of interests so that when empowered they would be able to exercise influence upon the factors affecting their existence. They would do this by the implementation of majority rule, which would also ensure accountability. By providing a sense that people mattered they would also encourage citizen participation. In fact, without extensive participation in both elections and the mechanism of governing these republics wouldn't function properly. Through this participation citizen-governors will become used to looking at issues in terms of functional solutions, not as ideological positions. It is amazing how practical people can get when they have to deal with a budget and that budget directly affects their taxes. This practicality is reinforced by inclusion and by positivity.

Standing firmly behind the principle of citizen participation is the idea that rights come with obligations. This key tenet of democracy has been too often overlooked by our current society. Combining obligations with participation would be designed to strengthen and to preserve our great experiment in democracy through the socio-economic turbulence that may lie ahead.

Three critical concepts would bolster the practice of transposed antifederalism. The first is *positive politics* which would create a new national ambiance. The second is *zero-based thinking,* which would enable us to view issues with fresh perspectives and with absence of preconceived conclusions. The third is the acceptance of *multiple intelligence.* This acceptance would enable us to perceive our citizenry in a new light that would seek to discern areas of excellence, not to classify for relegation. If these concepts are employed within our small republics and then throughout our nation, it is likely that a widespread change of attitude can take place that would prove beneficial to the United States in the twenty-first century. It could rival the major emotional turning points that have pulled our people back from the depths of despair and spurred them on to greater levels of unity and achievement.

Corporations and the Wealthy

It is very tempting to view corporations, particularly large corporations, and the affluent as our society's villains. They commandeer resources and benefits. They exert undue influence. They transfer burdens to others. Many of these assertions are correct. But they aren't the whole story. What is more, they leave unanswered critical economic questions.

How can an important source of our nation's discretionary cash flow, corporations and the wealthy, be included in the positive process without succumbing to the condescension of paternalism? How can these two elements of our society be transformed into catalysts for growth and unity? How can they find themselves in the socio-economic mainstream?

It is a shame that these two significant elements of our society can be regarded by many as counterproductive. It is an even greater shame that in so many instances they act as if their interests and those of the nation were separate. The plain truth is that if this country is to support the type of lifestyle that it seems to demand, contributions from corporations and the affluent will be vital. Nothing good will be achieved by penalizing them or driving them away. We need to find ways to encourage and include them.

Just prior to Christmas of 1995 a fire devastated the Methuen, Massachusetts-based mill of Malden Mills Industries Inc., which is the country's largest producer of Polartec and Polarfleece fabrics. The damaged mill employed 1,800 of the company's 3,200-person work force. About 1,000 employees were put out of work by the fire. At this point the tragedy begins to turn positive.

The owner of the 130-year-old company, which was founded by his grandfather, is Aaron Feuerstein. He regarded his company's $400 million in annual sales as directly attributable to the dedication of his workers. "I don't consider them like some companies do, as an expense that can be cut. I know in the long run that what I am doing today will come back tenfold and make Malden Mills Inc. the best company in the industry." What Feuerstein was "doing today" was promising to continue his displaced workers salaries for at least two months and their health insurance for another three months even though he had no legal or contractual obligation to do so. "Why am I doing it? I consider the employees standing in front of me here the most valuable asset the Malden Mills has."

Aaron Feuerstein was not making a philanthropic gesture. He considered himself to be acting in his own best interests. The response of his workers indicated that he might be correct. They applauded the pledge to reopen the mill. Furthermore, they believed the company would be repaid many fold—in the long run. Perspective is the quality that can separate sound business decisions from paternalism. It can connect self-interest and community interest.

Obviously, companies should not deliberately engage in or continue policies that are uneconomic. What they should do, though, is employ enough perspective to determine what actually is economic. Most companies are motivated by short-term outlooks to which their bonuses are tied. They are responsive to the quarter-by-quarter reporting requirements of the stock market. I was a part of that culture in my 26 years in the investment business and saw many a corporation subjugate its long-term interests to the immediate blandishments of professional investors. How necessary was it for AT&T or IBM to cut jobs and research? Was it just to please investors? Will these companies or our country be better or worse off for those actions ten years hence? The answer is, as usual, somewhere in between. Some jobs should have been retained. Some research should have been continued.

As was noted in Chapter 8, corporations don't have to be eleemosynary to consider the environment, the workers, or the community. They can be given incentives. The incentives can be financial. They can be psychological. They can be patriotic. The moral is that corporations do not have to be bad citizens. They can take positive measures, which will ultimately be in their own best interests. As this country's most responsive generator of discretionary cash flow it would be a very good idea for all citizens to have corporations acting for the benefit of the nation at large. Forcing or regulating them to do what is "right" is not the optimum method. It may be necessary in some instances, but an eager accession to the general will with joint objectives would be much more preferable.

As with corporations, the wealthy are often depicted as greedy, selfish, and evil. Sometimes they are. Along with their reception of many financial and non-financial benefits, they also provide the backbone for charitable giving and non-profit institutions. They, along with corporations, are much more able than ordinary citizens to move their cash flows around (even out of the country) to avoid requirements and situations that they deem hostile. As was previously noted, attempts to raise tax revenues by "soaking the rich" are rarely successful. The wealthy have too much financial flexibility to be caught in that net. All those policies accomplish is to drive away the support that many areas of our economy require.

What we need is to encourage wealthy citizens and corporations to do those things society deems to be beneficial. Those might include saving, investing, donating, and hiring, as well as other things. Incentives can come through the tax code. They can come via social conscience. They can develop out of shared experiences and goals. They can arise from national pride. For them to arise from somewhere is essential.

History, in this country, and around the world, has shown that government regulation or financial compulsion does not work well with the wealthy or with corporations. These entities respond to such pressures either by vegetating or by leaving. Positive encouragement works better. Our financial situation is such that we will need all the cooperation we can get from our financially solid elements if we are to withstand the stresses of the next century. It would behoove us all to develop creative methods for bringing both wealthy citizens and corporations together with other elements of our population to positively achieve common ends.

Participation and Positivity Can Make a Difference

Many of us who are citizens of this country feel removed and powerless when regarding our government. We are acutely aware that the United States of the 1990s is being consumed by negativity. We are continually inundated by divisiveness. We polarize instantly around significant issues. We blame. We accuse. We sue. Our dialogue has dissolved into advocacy. We construct litmus tests as conditions of support. Even worse, we have watched idly as the ingredients of power — funding, influence, decision-making — have slipped from our grasp to reside far from the average citizen in the hands of bureaucrats, special interests, and entrenched politicians. We have developed a multitude of questions with virtually no ready answers. We have growing doubts about whether our nation can prosper through the coming century. We are concerned for those who follow.

Before the twenty-first century is half over the majority of our population will be non-white. Almost half of our people will either be over 65 or under 18. The number of active workers supporting each retiree will decline from four to two. These are only three of the changes that are guaranteed to happen. If we don't take strong and immediate action, several other changes will take place as well. Our entitlement programs will go bankrupt. Debt and deficits will overwhelm our budgets. The number of imbedded poor will increase absolutely from their current 35 million, and relatively from 14 percent of the population. Enclavism will spread epidemically among our several demographic groupings. Our quality of life will sink to irretrievably low levels. Participation in the various aspects of governing will drop below even today's apathetic levels, and democracy will cease to function coherently.

This gloomy prospect is not inevitable. However, our country cannot confront the challenges of the twenty-first century without unity, without understanding or without positivity. These qualities have radiated from our attitudes and values many times throughout United States history. The 55 founders who gathered in Philadelphia during the summer of 1787 were full of positive creative energy. The pioneers who headed West, the immigrants who dotted our shores, the workers who built our great industries were all optimistic about the future of their descendants. Those pursuing civil rights, equality for women, and fair treatment for laborers persevered with conviction and hope. These are only a few of the many positivists we have harbored over the years.

It is also true that at numerous important junctures the people of our country have deeply questioned themselves. Our current uneasiness is not unique. The serious depressions of 1819-1828 and 1930-1939 were periods of doubt. The Civil War made us uncertain about our future. At the end of the last century we were critical and nervous. Muckrakers wrote scathing denunciations about the squalor of inner cities, the power of special interests and the corruption of politicians. A powerful populist third party sprung up advocating political equality through economic equality. It is important for us to remember that these pessimistic eras were conquered. All were followed by a restoration of our national confidence and successively higher levels of achievement.

My belief is that we can start on the road to a positive atmosphere by once again stressing participatory government. During the course of our national existence the locus of governmental power has moved back and forth along an arc that has centralization at the federal level on one end and local autonomy on the other. The precise distribution of power among federal, state, and local entities has varied. In some instances there was a requirement for a more effective center. The year the Constitution was written was one of those. Franklin Roosevelt's assumption of the presidency at the depth of the Great Depression was another.

It is my opinion that we presently live in a period that cries out for greater local political autonomy bolstered by adequate funding. This autonomy is needed to provide a framework within which people of all socio-economic segments can readily involve themselves in government. Many of us have personally witnessed this taking place in some form of a transformation to localism. If not, we have read about such metamorphoses. I believe it is evident that governing grows more vibrant when citizens come to realize that they can matter and that they can make a difference in the factors affecting their lives. An awakening of this nature is what democracy is all about.

Democracy was never conceived for its ability to reach decisions rapidly and crisply. It was created and developed over the ages to facilitate participation and to foster dialogue. Its strength is its nourishment of individual rights, and their flip side—responsibilities. In those areas when democracy has flourished it has been because its members retained respect for the expressions of others and collectively sought the well-being of their communities. As we approach the next millennium, we can resurrect these qualities in our country by a return to democracy's bedrock — widespread participation with a free interchange of ideas. In my view the route to this destination lies via localism.

Regeneration of our democracy means searching for common ground and compromise. It means that "I was wrong" may be as important as any three words in our language. It means not begrudging any effort expended in pursuit of better and more relevant government.

Our democracy once again must hold dear the ability to listen, and the ability to show compassion. In our democracy conscience and perspective should be vital to the interpretation of self-interest. Our democracy can be open and relevant if it provides all of its youth with a comparably first-rate education as the cornerstone for a solid future. It can increase its tensile strength if it gives everyone an equal reason to live by being inclusive. Speaking as a white male who has experienced the lifelong benefits of opportunity, I feel that we cannot justify or sustain our national prominence without extending these prerogatives, and their attendant obligations, to all of our citizens.

Is this being idealistic? I hope so, for we badly need ideals as our very lifeblood. Is this impossible? I hope not, for the lives of our children and grandchildren are at risk. It is my firm belief that properly oriented we can embark upon a new national journey in the twenty-first century. I am convinced that we can restore our confidence. The very diversity of our populace and the richness of its heritage can augment the flexibility of our system to produce an exciting society. Positivity can shine in thousands of localities, reflected by more organizations building on the foundation of the good work already being done. I believe that together these elements can propel us from this troubled decade as a united and caring people, responsible through interaction for the governance of our own lives, with a prospect as bright as any we have ever had. Perhaps then Langston Hughes' dream will be realized and "America will be America again." Perhaps Hartman Turnbow's dream will be realized as well.

> You know what kind of dream I'd like to see? The way I'd love to see America? I'd jus' love to see it that all folks could shake hands an' be brothers and forget they're different. Me and you jus' shake hands and be brothers. I live happy, treat you nice, and you treat me nice, and you forget I'm black and I forget you white, And just live.

> Hartman Turnbow
> interviewed in Stud's Terkel's,
> *American Dreams: Lost and Found*

The last sentence of Turnbow's dream is: "But it won't be." Positive policies can prove that fear unfounded.

---

1 *Cape Cod Times*, 16 September 1995.
2 Christopher Hitchins, "The Baby Boomer Wasteland," *Vanity Fair*, January 1996, 35.
3 Ibid.
4 Studs Terkel, *American Dreams Lost and Found* (New York: Pantheon Books, 1980), 274.
5 James Madison, *Notes of Debates in the Federal Convention of 1787* (New York: W. W. Norton & Company, 1987).
6 Twelve states appointed 55 delegates (Rhode Island declined to send any). Not all of these delegates attended at one time. In the end 39 signed the Constitution.
7 John Adams, *The Work of John Adams*, ed. Charles Francis Adams (Boston 1850-56), 10:283.

Bibliography

Adams, John. *The Works of John Adams.* 10 vols. Edited by Charles Francis Adams. Boston, 1850-56.

Ardrey, Robert. *The Social Contract.* New York: Atheneum Press, 1970.

Arendt, Hannah. *On Revolution.* New York: Penguin Books, 1963.

Bailyn, Bernard. *Voyagers to the West: A Passage in the Peopling of America on the Eve of Revolution.* New York: Alfred A. Knopf, 1986.

— *Personalities and Themes in the Struggle for American Independence.* New York: Alfred A. Knopf, 1990.

Bailyn, Bernard, editor. *The Debate on the Constitution: Federalist and Antifederalist Speeches, Articles and Letters During the Struggle over Ratification.* 2 vols. New York: The Library of America, 1993.

Banfield, Edward C. *Here the People Rule: Selected Essays.* New York: Plenum Press, 1985.

Beer, Samuel H. *To Make A Nation: The Rediscovery of American Federalism.* Cambridge: The Belknap Press of Harvard University Press, 1993.

Berliner, Daniel, and Bruce Biddle. *The Manufactured Crisis.* Bedford: Addison-Wesley, 1965.

Boorstin, Daniel J. *The Americans.* New York: Ayer, 1976.

Brinkley, David. *David Brinkley: A Memoir.* New York: Alfred A. Knopf, 1995.

Bruckey, Stuart. *Enterprise: The Dynamic Economy of a Free People.* Cambridge: Harvard University Press, 1990.

Bryce, James. *The American Commonwealth.* New York: MacMillan, 1937.

Brzezinski, Zbigniew. *Out of Control—Global Turmoil on the Eve of the 21st Century.* New York: Charles Scribner's & Sons, 1993.

Burgess, John Wm. *The Foundations of American Political Science.* New York: Transaction Publishers, 1993.

Carles, Emile. *A Life of Her Own.* New Brunswick: Rutgers University Press, 1991.

Carpenter, William S. *The Development of American Political Thought.* Princeton: Princeton University Press, 1930.

Carrithers, David W. "Montesquieu, Jefferson and the Fundamentals of 18th Century Republican Theory." *French-American Review.* vol. 6 (Fall 1982): 179-182.

Cassidy, John. "Who Killed the Middle Class?" The *New Yorker*, 16 October 1995.

Corbett, Nancy. *Inner Cleansing: Living Clean in A Polluted World.* Bridgeport: Prism, 1993.

Croly, Herbert. *The Promise of American Life.* Reprint of 1909 edition. Boston: Northeastern University Press, 1989.

Csikszentmichaliya, Mihaly. *Flow: The Psychology of Happiness.* London: Rider, 1992.

Delpit Lisa D. "The Silenced Dialogue: Power and Pedagogy in Educating Other People's Children." *Harvard Educational Review*, vol. 58, no. 3 (August 1988).

Dionne, E.J. Jr. *Why Americans Hate Politics.* New York: Simon & Schuster, 1996.

Drucker, Peter. *Post-Capitalist Society.* Oxford: Butterworth Heinemann, 1993.

Dudley, Donald R. *The Civilization of Rome.* New York: Penguin Books, 1960.

Dychtwald, Ken. *Age Wave.* Los Angeles: Tarcher, 1988.

Elkins, Stanley, and Eric McKitrick. *The Age of Federalism: The Early American Republic, 1788-1800.* New York: Oxford University Press, 1993.

Elliot, Jonathan, ed. *The Debates in the Several State Conventions on the Adoption of the Federal Constitution.* Philadelphia: 1863.

Ellis, Richard E. *The Union at Risk—Jacksonian Democracy, States' Rights and the Nullification Crisis.* New York: Oxford University Press, 1987.

Etzioni, Amitai. *The Spirit of Community.* New York: Crown Publishers, 1993.

Fallows, James. *Breaking the News: How the Media Undermines American Democracy.* New York: Pantheon, 1995.

Flexner, James Thomas. *Washington: The Indispensable Man.* New York: Penguin Books, 1984.

Frank, Robert H. and Philip J. Cook. *The Winner Take All Society.* New York: Free Press, 1995.

Gardner, Howard. *Frames of Mind.* New York: Basic Books, 1985.

Giddens, Anthony. *Beyond Left and Right: The Future of Radical Politics.* Stanford: Stanford University Press, 1994.

Glendon, Mary Ann. *Rights Talk: The Impoverishment of Political Discourse.* New York: Free Press, 1991.

— *A Nation Under Lawyers*, New York: Farrar, Strauss & Giroux, 1994.

Goldwin, Robert A. "From Parchment to Power—How to Ratify a Constitution." The Bradley Lecture Series, American Enterprise Institute, Washington DC, 1994.

Gray, John. *Beyond the New Right.* London: Routledge, 1993.

Gwynn, William B. *The Meaning of the Separation of Powers.* New Orleans: Tulane University Press, 1965.

Handy, Charles. *The Age of Paradox.* Boston: Harvard University Press, 1994.

Hatcher, William B. *Edward Livingston's View of the Nature Union.* Louisiana Historical Quarterly, 24 July 1941, 698-728.

Havel, Vacláv. *Open Letters.* Translated by Eazin Kohák and Roger Scranton. New York: Vintage Books, 1991

— *Disturbing the Peace.* Translated by Peter Wilson. New York: Vintage Books, 1991.

Hegel, George W.F. *Essential Writings*. Edited by Frederick G. Weiss. New York: Torch Books Harper Collins, 1977.

Held, David. "Prospects For Democracy." *Political Studies*. Special issue, vol. 40, 1992.

Higgs, Robert. *Crisis and Leviathan: Critical Episodes In the Growth of American Government*. New York: Oxford University Press, 1987.

Hofstadter, Richard. *American Political Tradition*. New York: Vintage Press, 1948.

Holmes, Stephen. *Passions and Constraints: On the Theory of Liberal Democracy*. Chicago: University of Chicago Press, 1995.

Hopkins, Thomas. *Costs of Regulation: Filling the Gaps*. Washington: Regulatory Information Service Center, 1992.

Hyneman, Charles S. and Donald S. Lutz. *American Political Writing During the Founding Era 1760-1805*. Indianapolis: Liberty Press, 1983.

Jarrett, Vernon. *American Dreams: Lost and Found*. New York: Pantheon Books, 1980.

Kammen, Michael, ed. *The Origins of the American Constitution: A Documentary History*. New York: Penguin Books, 1986.

Katz, Michael B. *In the Shadow of the Poorhouse: A Social History of Welfare in America*. New York: Basic Books, 1986.

Kenyon, Cecelia. *Men of Little Faith: The Anti-Federalists on the Nature of Representative Government*. William and Mary Quarterly, 3rd series, vol. 12.

Keohane, Nannerl O. "Virtuous Republics and Glorious Monarchies: Two Models in Montesquieu's Political Thought." *Political Studies*, vol. 20 (1972): 383-396.

Ladd, Carl Everett. *The American Ideology: An Exploration of the Origins, Meaning and Role of American Political Ideas*. Stoors, Connecticut: The Roper Center for Public Opinion Research, 1994.

Lasch, Christopher. *The True and Only Heaven*. New York: W.W. Norton & Company, 1991
—*The Culture of Narcissism*. New York: W.W. Norton & Company, 1979
—*The Revolt of the Elites*. New York: W.W. Norton & Company, 1995

Lind, Michael. *The Next American Nation: The New Naturalism and the Fourth American Revolution*. New York: The Free Press, 1995.

Lowenberg Jacques, ed. *Hegel: Selections*. New York: Random House, 1963.

Machiavelli, Niccolo. *The Prince and the Discourses*. New York: Carlton House, 1946.

Madrick, Jeffrey. *The End of Affluence: The Causes and Consequences of America's Economic Dilemma*. New York: Random House, 1995.

Malkin, John, and Norman Ornstein. *Debt and Taxes*. New York: Times Books, 1994.

Marone, James A. *The Democratic Wish*. New York: Basic Books, 1990.

May, Henry F. *The Enlightenment In America*. New York: Oxford University Press, 1976.

McCoy, Drew R. *The Last of the Fathers: James Madison and the Republican Legacy*. Cambridge: Cambridge University Press, 1989.

Melnick, R. Shep. *Between the Lines: Interpreting Welfare Rights*. Washington: Brookings Institute, 1994.

Montesquieu. *The Spirit of the Laws*. Edited and translated by Anne Cohler; Basisa Miller; and Harold Stone. Cambridge: Cambridge University Press, 1989.

Morris, Richard B. *Forging of the Union 1781-1789*. New York: Harper & Row Publishers, 1987.

Murphy, Emmet C. with Michael Snell. *The Genius of Sitting Bull: 13 Heroic Strategies for Business Leadership*. New York: Prentice Hall, 1992.

Newman, Katherine S. *Declining Fortunes: The Withering of the American Dream*. New York: Basic Books, 1993.

Nozick, Robert. *Examined Life: Philosophical Meditations*. New York: Touchstone Books, 1990.

Olasky, Marvin. *The Tragedy of American Compassion*. Washington: Regnery Publishing, 1992.

Osborne, David, and David Gaebler. *Reinventing Government*. Reading, Massachusetts: Addison-Wesley Publishing, 1992.

Pangle, Thomas. The Federalists and the Idea of Virtue." *This Constitution*, no. 5 (Winter 1984): 19-25.

Perret, Geoffrey. *Days of Sadness, Years of Triumph: The American People 1939-1945*. New York: Penguin Books, 1973.

Randall, William Sterne. *Thomas Jefferson*. New York: Henry Holt and Company, 1993.

Samuelson, Robert. *The Good Life and Its Discontents: The American Dream in the Age of Entitlement, 1945-1995*. New York: Times Books, 1995.

Sandel, Michael J. "America's Search For a New Public Philosophy." *The Atlantic Monthly*, March 1996.

Savage, James D. *Balanced Budgets and American Politics*. Ithaca: Cornell University Press, 1986.

Scraton, Roger. *The Meaning of Conservatism*. London: MacMillan, 1980.

Selznik, Philip. *The Moral Commonwealth*. Berkeley: University of California Press, 1992.

Sewell, Thomas. *The Vision of the Anointed*. New York: Basic Books, 1995.

Shklar, Judith N. *Montesquieu*. Oxford: Oxford University Press, 1987.

Slemrod, Joel, ed. *Do Taxes Matter*. Boston: MIT Press, 1991.

Smith, Charles Page. *James Wilson: Founding Father*. Chapel Hill: University of North Carolina Press, 1956.
—*The Shaping of America: A People's History of the Young Republic*. vol. 3. New York: Penguin Books, 1989

Sparlin, Paul. *Montesquieu in America 1760-1801*. Baton Rouge: Louisiana State University, 1940.

Starobin, Paul. "The Politics of Anxiety." *National Journal* (September 30, 1995).

Storing, Herbert J. *The Complete Anti-Federalist*. 7 vols. Chicago: University of Chicago Press, 1981.
—*What the Antifederalists Were For: Political Thought of the Opponents of the Constitution*. Chicago: University of Chicago Press, 1981.

Sykes, Charles,. *Dumbing Down Our Kids*. New York: St. Martins, 1995.
—*Modern Philosophy*. New York: Allen Lane the Penguin Press, 1994.

Terkel, Studs. *Race*. New York: The New Press, 1992.
—*Coming of Age*. New York: The New Press, 1995.
—*The Great Divide*. New York: Pantheon Books, 1988.
—*American Dreams Lost and Found*. New York: Pantheon Books, 1980.

Tocqueville, Alexis de. *Democracy in America*. 2 vols. New York: Vintage Press, 1945.

Tyack, David, and Larry Cuban. *Tinkering Towards Utopia.* Cambridge: Harvard University Press, 1995.

Wallis, Jim. *The Soul of Politics: Beyond 'Religious Right' and Secular Left.'* New York: Harcourt Brace & Company, 1994.

Wiebe, Robert H. *Self Rule: A Cultural History of American Democracy.* Chicago: University of Chicago Press, 1995.

Wills, Gary. *Lincoln at Gettysburg.* New York: Simon & Schuster, 1992.

Wilson, William Julius. *The Truly Disadvantaged.* Chicago: University of Chicago Press, 1987.

Wolfe, Alan. *Whose Keeper?* Berkeley: University of California Press, 1989.

Wood, Gordon S. *Creation of the American Republic.* New York: W.W. Norton & Company. 1972.
  —*The Radicalism of the American Revolution.* New York: Vintage Books division of Random House, 1991.

Wurtzel, Elizabeth. *The Prozac Nation.* Boston: Houghton Mifflin, 1994.

Index